THE SONG OF ROLAND

II. Oxford Text and English Translation

Published in 1978

in commemoration of the

twelfth centenary

of the Battle of Roncevaux

THE
SONG
OF
ROLAND

AN ANALYTICAL EDITION

II. Oxford Text and English Translation

Gerard J. Brault

THE PENNSYLVANIA STATE UNIVERSITY PRESS

UNIVERSITY PARK AND LONDON

Library of Congress Cataloging in Publication Data

Chanson de Roland. English & Old French.
  The Song of Roland.

  Bibliography: v. 1.
  Contents: v. 1. Introduction and commentary.—
  v. 2. Oxford text and English translation.
  Includes index.
  1. Roland—Romances. I. Brault, Gerard J.
PQ1521.E5B7 1978   841'.1   77-22946
ISBN 0-271-00516-5

Designed by Glenn Ruby

Printed in the United States of America

Second printing, 1981

A Note on the Text and Translation

The Oxford text of the *Song of Roland*, which is the basis for the present edition and translation, offers a version of the poem in 3998 lines. For over a century editors have been adhering to a numbering scheme involving 4002 verses: vv. 580–581 and 3832–3833, which are conflated in this copy, are counted as separate lines, and vv. 1389, 1615 [1666], 3146, 3390, and 3494 are shown as blanks or conjectures.[1] However, the numbering and ordering of laisses varies somewhat from edition to edition.

The copyist made a number of obvious errors, which have been emended here. Each erroneous form is discussed in the NOTES TO THE MANUSCRIPT, which also provide other essential information. Whether forms such as v. 1157 *su* (= sum) and v. 1301 *trechant* (= trenchant) result from denasalization or scribal error (omission of the titulus) is a matter of opinion.[2] In general, no emendation is proposed here whenever a genuine dialectal feature may be involved. The need to be consistent occasionally creates awkward situations for the editor, e.g., v. 16 *epereres* (= empereres). However, all such cases are duly annotated.

Some time after the Oxford manuscript was copied, another scribe (the "revisor") endeavored to correct it, either by erasing letters and words or by adding others.[3] Many of these changes show that the revisor lacked a firm grasp of his predecessor's language, but other substituted forms ring true. Editors generally agree on the treatment of these alterations.

Over the years the methodical comparison of each word in the Oxford copy with the corresponding term found in the other versions has yielded many plausible emendations, especially in the three-hundred-odd instances where a verse does not scan or assonate properly. Very few changes of this sort are made here, although several are listed in the NOTES TO THE OXFORD TEXT, ENGLISH TRANSLATION.

[1] Additionally, v. 2242 has been moved from its original place following v. 1823. Segre, pp. xxviii–xxix.

[2] Cf. Bédier, *Commentaires*, p. 255; Whitehead, pp. xiii–xiv; Moignet, p. 282.

[3] These passages are conveniently listed by Samaran, pp. 20–22 ("Retouches dues au reviseur"). See INTRODUCTION, note 29.

Modern editors distinguish between consonantal and vocalic *i* and *j*, *u* and *v*, and employ the acute accent to indicate a stressed final *e* and the cedilla to show that a *c* is pronounced like an *s*. However, they vary in the manner in which they expand abbreviations and use the diaeresis and other marks as an aid in scansion. The system adopted here is intended to give reasonable assistance to readers who would probably find additional diacritical signs burdensome.

The prose translation avoids any attempt to capture the flavor of the original. However, every effort has been made to render each word and phrase accurately. A number of alternate interpretations are provided in the notes. Translators generally change tenses from time to time to conform to modern practice. At the risk of jarring some readers' feelings, the original tense has been maintained in nearly every case, the idea being to impart some of the narrative pace. At times the punctuation varies slightly between the French and English texts.

The aim here is to focus attention on literary matters. Consequently, paleographical and philological discussions have been kept to a minimum. Readers should consult Bédier, Jenkins, Whitehead, and Segre— to name but the most accessible editions—for additional information of this kind.

THE SONG OF ROLAND

1

Carles li reis, nostre emperere magnes,
Set anz tuz pleins ad estet en Espaigne.
Tresqu'en la mer cunquist la tere altaigne,
N'i ad castel ki devant lui remaigne.
5 Mur ne citet n'i est remés a fraindre,
Fors Sarraguce, ki est en une muntaigne.
Li reis Marsilie la tient, ki Deu nen aimet,
Mahumet sert e Apollin recleimet:
Nes poet guarder que mals ne l'i ateignet.   AOI.

2

10 Li reis Marsilie esteit en Sarraguce,
Alez en est en un verger suz l'umbre.
Sur un perrun de marbre bloi se culched,
Envirun lui plus de vint milie humes.
Il en apelet e ses dux e ses cuntes:
15 "Oëz, seignurs, quel pecchet nus encumbret:
Li epereres Carles de France dulce
En cest païs nos est venuz cunfundre.
Jo nen ai ost qui bataille li dunne,
Ne n'ai tel gent ki la sue derumpet.
20 Cunseilez mei cume mi saive hume,
Si me guarisez e de mort e de hunte!"
N'i ad paien ki un sul mot respundet,
Fors Blancandrins de Castel de Valfunde.

1

King Charles, our great Emperor,
Has been in Spain for seven long years.
He has conquered that haughty land right to the sea,
No fortress can resist him.
5   No wall, no city, remains to be smashed,
Except Saragossa, which is on a mountaintop.
King Marsile, who does not love God, defends it,
He serves Mohammed and prays to Apollo:
He cannot prevent misfortune from befalling him there.   AOI.

2

10   King Marsile was in Saragossa,
He went into a garden, into the shade.
He lies down on a blue marble slab
With more than twenty thousand men around him.
He calls his dukes and his counts:
15   "Now hear, my lords, what misfortune befalls us:
Emperor Charles of fair France
Has come to our land to destroy us.
I have no army capable of giving him battle,
I have no force that can break his.
20   Give me the counsel you owe me as my cunning vassals
And save me from death and shame!"
No pagan utters a single word,
Except Blancandrin of Castel de Valfonde.

3

3

Blancandrins fut des plus saives paiens,
25 De vasselage fut asez chevaler:
Prozdom i out pur sun seignur aider
E dist al rei: "Ore ne vus esmaiez!
Mandez Carlun, a l'orguillus e al fier,
Fedeilz servises e mult granz amistez.
30 Vos li durrez urs e leons e chens,
Set cenz camelz e mil hosturs muërs,
D'or e d'argent .IIII.C. muls cargez,
Cinquante carre qu'en ferat carïer:
Ben en purrat luër ses soldeiers.
35 En ceste tere ad asez osteiet,
En France, ad Ais, s'en deit ben repairer.
Vos le sivrez a la feste seint Michel,
Si recevrez la lei de chrestïens,
Serez ses hom par honur e par ben.
40 S'en volt ostages, e vos l'en enveiez,
U dis u vint pur lui afiancer.
Enveius i les filz de noz muillers:
Par num d'ocire i enveierai le men.
Asez est melz qu'il i perdent le chefs
45 Que nus perduns l'onur ne la deintet,
Ne nus seiuns cunduiz a mendeier." AOI.

4

Dist Blancandrins: "Pa ceste meie destre
E par la barbe ki al piz me ventelet,
L'ost des Franceis verrez sempres desfere.
50 Francs s'en irunt en France, la lur tere.
Quant cascuns ert a sun meillor repaire,
Carles serat ad Ais, a sa capele.
A seint Michel tendrat mult halte feste.
Vendrat li jurz, si passerat li termes,
55 N' orrat de nos paroles ne nuveles.
Li reis est fiers e sis curages pesmes,
De noz ostages ferat trecher les testes.
Asez est mielz qu'il i perdent les testes,
Que nus perduns clere Espaigne, la bele,

4

3

Blancandrin was one of the most cunning pagans,
25 By his courage he was very much a knight:
He had all the required qualities to help his lord.
And he said to the King: "Don't be alarmed!
Offer wicked and fierce Charles
Loyal service and great friendship.
30 Send him bears, lions, dogs,
Seven hundred camels, a thousand moulted hawks,
Four hundred mules laden with gold and silver,
And fifty carts for a wagon train:
With this he will be able to pay his soldiers well.
35 Say that he has campaigned long enough in this country,
That he ought to go back home to France, to Aix.
Tell him you will follow him there at Michaelmas,
Become a convert to Christianity,
And be his vassal in good faith and without deception.
40 If he wants hostages, send him some,
Ten or twenty, to gain his confidence.
Let us send him the sons our wives have given us:
I will send him my own son, even though it means certain death for
    him.
Far better that they should lose their heads
45 Than that we should lose our lands and offices,
And be reduced to begging." AOI.

4

Blancandrin said: "By this right hand of mine
And by the beard upon my chest that blows in the breeze,
You'll see the French army disband at once.
50 The Franks will return to France, their land.
When each man has returned to his favorite abode,
Charles will be in his chapel at Aix.
He will celebrate Saint Michael's Day with great ceremony.
The day will come and the term will expire,
55 But he will not hear a word from us.
The King is fierce and his heart is cruel,
He will have our hostages decapitated.
Far better that they should lose their heads
Than that we should lose fair Spain, the beautiful,

60 Ne nus aiuns les mals ne les suffraites."
    Dient paien: "Issi poet il ben estre!"

5

    Li reis Marsilie out sun cunseill finet.
    Sin apelat Clarin de Balaguet,
    Estamarin e Eudropin, sun per,
65 E Priamun e Guarlan le barbet,
    E Machiner e sun uncle, Maheu,
    E Joüner e Malbien d'Ultremer,
    E Blancandrins, por la raisun cunter.
    Des plus feluns dis en ad apelez:
70 "Seignurs baruns, a Carlemagnes irez,
    Il est al siege a Cordres la citet.
    Branches d'olives en voz mains porterez:
    Ço senefiet pais e humilitet.
    Par voz saveirs sem puëz acorder,
75 Jo vos durrai or e argent asez,
    Teres e fiez tant cum vos en vuldrez."
    Dient paien: "De ço avum nus asez!"   AOI.

6

    Li reis Marsilie out finet sun cunseill.
    Dist a ses humes: "Seignurs, vos en ireiz,
80 Branches d'olive en voz mains portereiz,
    Si me direz a Carlemagne le rei,
    Pur le soen Deu qu'il ait mercit de mei.
    Ja einz ne verrat passer cest premer meis
    Que jel sivrai od mil de mes fedeilz,
85 Si recevrai la chrestïene lei,
    Serai ses hom par amur e par feid.
    S'il voelt ostages, il en avrat par veir."
    Dist Blancandrins: "Mult bon plait en avreiz."   AOI.

7

    Dis blanches mules fist amener Marsilies,
90 Que li tramist li reis de Suatilie.

60 Or that we should suffer disasters and privations."
   The pagans say: "This may work!"

5

King Marsile's council is over.
He called Clarin of Balaguer,
Estamarin and Eudropin, his peer,
65 Priamon and Guarlan the bearded one,
Machiner and his uncle Maheu,
Joüner and Malbien of Outremer,
And Blancandrin, to relate his message.
He summoned ten of his most wicked men:
70 "My lord barons, you will go to Charlemagne,
Who is besieging the city of Cordres.
You will carry olive branches in your hands:
This signifies peace and humility.
If, by your guile, you can reach an accord on my behalf,
75 I shall give you much gold and silver,
And as many lands and fiefs as you may desire."
   The pagans say: "That will suit us fine!"   AOI.

6

King Marsile's council is over.
He said to his men: "My lords, you will go,
80 Carrying olive branches in your hands,
And on my behalf you will ask King Charlemagne
To show me mercy in his God's name.
Tell him that before the end of next month
I shall follow him with a thousand of my trusted men,
85 That I shall become a convert to Christianity,
And that I shall become his vassal in friendship and in good faith.
If he wants hostages, then most assuredly he shall have some."
   Blancandrin said: "With this you will have a very fine pact."   AOI.

7

Marsile had ten white mules brought forward,
90 Which the King of Suatille had sent him.

Li frein sunt d'or, les seles d'argent mises.
Cil sunt muntez ki le message firent,
Enz en lur mains portent branches d'olive.
Vindrent a Charles, ki France ad en baillie:
95 Nes poet guarder que alques ne l'engignent. AOI.

8

Li empereres se fait e balz e liez:
Cordres ad prise e les murs peceiez,
Od ses cadables les turs en abatied.
Mult grant eschech en unt si chevaler,
100 D'or e d'argent e de guarnemenz chers.
En la citet nen ad remés paien
Ne seit ocis u devient chrestïen.
Li empereres est en un grant verger.
Ensembl'od lui Rollant e Oliver,
105 Sansun li dux e Anseïs li fiers,
Gefreid d'Anjou, le rei gunfanuner,
E si i furent e Gerin e Gerers.
La u cist furent, des altres i out bien,
De dulce France i ad quinze milliers.
110 Sur palies blancs siedent cil cevaler,
As tables juent pur els esbaneier,
E as eschecs li plus saive e li veill,
E escremissent cil bacheler leger.
Desuz un pin, delez un eglenter,
115 Un faldestoed i unt, fait tut d'or mer:
La siet li reis ki dulce France tient.
Blanche ad la barbe e tut flurit le chef,
Gent ad le cors e le cuntenant fier:
S'est kil demandet, ne l'estoet enseigner.
120 E li message descendirent a pied,
Sil saluerent par amur e par bien.

9

Blancandrins ad tut premereins parled
E dist al rei: "Salvet seiez de Deu,
Le Glorius, que devuns aürer!

The bridles are all trimmed with gold, the saddles with silver.
The ambassadors mounted,
In their hands they carry olive branches.
They came to Charles, who rules over France:
95   He cannot help being deceived by them in some way.   AOI.

8

The Emperor is jubilant:
He has captured Cordres and smashed its walls,
He has demolished its towers with his catapults.
His knights have taken a huge amount of booty in the process,
100   Gold, silver, and expensive equipment.
Not a single pagan remains in the city
Who has not been slain or become a Christian.
The Emperor is in a great garden.
With him are Roland and Oliver,
105   Duke Samson and fierce Anseïs,
Geoffrey of Anjou, the King's standard-bearer;
Gerin and Gerier were also there.
There were many others, too, where these men were gathered,
There are fifteen thousand men from fair France.
110   The knights are sitting on white silk cloths,
Playing backgammon to while away the time,
The older and wiser among them playing chess;
The agile youths are fencing.
Beneath a pine tree, next to an eglantine,
115   A throne of pure gold has been placed:
There sits the King, who rules fair France.
His beard is white and his head is hoary,
His body is well proportioned and his look is fierce:
Anyone seeking him needs no one to point him out.
120   So the messengers dismounted
And greeted him with words of friendship and good will.

9

Blancandrin was the first to speak,
And he said to the King: "May God save you,
And glory be to Him we should all adore!

125 Iço vus mandet reis Marsilies li bers:
    Enquis ad mult la lei de salvetet;
    De sun aveir vos voelt asez duner,
    Urs e leuns e veltres enchaignez,
    Set cenz cameilz e mil hosturs muëz,
130 D'or e d'argent .IIII. cenz muls trussez,
    Cinquante care que carïer en ferez;
    Tant i avrat de besanz esmerez
    Dunt bien purrez voz soldeiers luër.
    En cest païs avez estet asez,
135 En France, ad Ais, devez bien repairer;
    La vos sivrat, ço dit, mis avoëz."
    Li empereres tent ses mains vers Deu,
    Baisset sun chef, si cumencet a penser.   AOI.

10

    Li empereres en tint sun chef enclin.
140 De sa parole ne fut mie hastifs,
    Sa custume est qu'il parolet a leisir.
    Quant se redrecet, mult par out fier lu vis,
    Dist as messages: "Vus avez mult ben dit:
    Li reis Marsilies est mult mis enemis.
145 De cez paroles que vos avez ci dit,
    En quel mesure en purrai estre fiz?"
    "Voet par hostages," ço dist li Sarrazins,
    "Dunt vos avrez u dis, u quinze, u vint.
    Pa num de ocire i metrai un mien filz,
150 E sin avrez, ço quid, de plus gentilz.
    Quant vus serez el palais seignurill
    A la grant feste seint Michel del Peril,
    Mis avoëz la vos sivrat, ço dit.
    Enz en voz bainz que Deus pur vos i fist,
155 La vuldrat il chrestïens devenir."
    Charles respunt: "Uncore purrat guarir."   AOI.

11

    Bels fut li vespres e li soleilz fut cler,
    Les dis mulez fait Charles establer.

125   Here is what noble King Marsile wishes you to know:
      He has long sought the way to salvation;
      He wants to share his wealth with you,
      Bears, lions, greyhounds on the leash,
      Seven hundred camels, a thousand mewed hawks,
130   Four hundred mules laden with gold and silver,
      Fifty carts for a wagon train;
      There will be a mass of gold bezants,
      Which you can use to pay your soldiers.
      You have been in this country long enough,
135   You should go back home to Aix, in France;
      My lord gives his word that he will follow you there."
      The Emperor lifts up his hands to God,
      He lowers his head and begins to reflect.   AOI.

10

      The Emperor kept his head bowed down.
140   He was not one to speak hastily,
      He customarily replies after deliberation.
      When he raised his head, his look was terrifying to behold.
      He said to the messengers: "What you said was very true:
      King Marsile is my great enemy.
145   These promises that you've conveyed here,
      How can I be sure they'll be kept?"
      "He wishes to reassure you by hostages," said the Saracen,
      "You'll have ten, fifteen, or even twenty of them.
      I'll include one of my own sons, although it means risking his life,
150   And you'll find, among them, even nobler persons, I believe.
      When you are in your royal palace,
      Attending the great feast of Saint Michael of the Peril,
      My lord will join you there, he gives you his word.
      In your baths, which God made for you there,
155   He will wish to be baptized."
      Charles answers: "He may yet be saved."   AOI.

11

      The afternoon was fair and the sun was bright,
      Charles has the ten mules stabled.

El grant verger fait li reis tendre un tref,
160 Les dis messages ad fait enz hosteler;
.XII. serjanz les unt ben cunreez.
La noit demurent tresque vint al jur cler.
Li empereres est par matin levet,
Messe e matines ad li reis escultet.
165 Desuz un pin en est li reis alez,
Ses baruns mandet pur sun cunseill finer:
Par cels de France voelt il del tut errer.   AOI.

12

Li empereres s'en vait desuz un pin,
Ses baruns mandet pur sun cunseill fenir:
170 Le duc Oger e l'arcevesque Turpin,
Richard li Velz e sun neüld Henri
E de Gascuigne li proz quens Acelin,
Tedbald de Reins e Milun, sun cusin,
E si i furent e Gerers e Gerin.
175 Ensembl'od els li quens Rollant i vint
E Oliver, li proz e li gentilz.
Des Francs de France en i ad plus de mil.
Guenes i vint, ki la traïsun fist.
Des ore cumencet le cunseill que mal prist.   AOI.

13

180 "Seignurs barons," dist li empere Carles,
"Li reis Marsilie m'ad tramis ses messages.
De sun aveir me voelt duner grant masse,
Urs e leuns e veltres caeignables,
Set cenz cameilz e mil hosturs muables,
185 Quatre cenz muls cargez de l'or d'Arabe,
Avoec iço plus de cinquante care.
Mais il me mandet que en France m'en alge,
Il me sivrat ad Ais, a mun estage,
Si recevrat la nostre lei plus salve;
190 Chrestïens ert, de mei tendrat ses marches.
Mais jo ne sai quels en est sis curages."
Dient Franceis: "Il nus i cuvent guarde!"   AOI.

The King has a tent pitched in the great garden
160 And has the ten messengers lodged inside;
Twelve sergeants have attended to all their needs.
They remain there through the night until daybreak.
The Emperor rose early in the morning,
The King heard mass and matins.
165 The King went beneath a pine tree
And summoned his barons to conclude his council:
He wishes to be guided by the men of France in this entire matter.
    AOI.

12

The Emperor goes beneath a pine tree,
He summons his barons to conclude his council:
170 Duke Ogier and Archbishop Turpin,
Old Richard and his nephew Henri,
Wise Count Acelin of Gascony,
Tedbald of Reims and his cousin Milon;
Gerier and Gerin were also there.
175 With them came Count Roland
And wise and noble Oliver.
There are more than a thousand Franks from France.
Ganelon, who committed the act of treachery, came too.
Now begins the council that went wrong.   AOI.

13

180 "My lord barons," said Emperor Charles,
"King Marsile has sent me his envoys.
He wants to give me a huge portion of his wealth,
Bears, lions, greyhounds on the leash,
Seven hundred camels, a thousand mewed hawks,
185 Four hundred mules laden with Arabian gold,
And with that more than fifty carts.
But he asks me to return to France,
He will follow me to my residence at Aix
And become a convert to our most holy faith;
190 He will become a Christian and hold his marches as fiefs from me.
However, I do not know this man's mind."
The French say: "We'd better be on our guard!"   AOI.

13

14

    Li empereres out sa raisun fenie.
    Li quens Rollant, ki ne l'otrïet mie,
195 En piez se drecet, si li vint cuntredire.
    Il dist al rei: "Ja mar crerez Marsilie!
    Set anz ad pleins que en Espaigne venimes.
    Jo vos cunquis e Noples e Commibles,
    Pris ai Valterne e la tere de Pine
200 E Balasgued e Tuele e Sezilie.
    Li reis Marsilie i fist mult que traïtre:
    De ses paiens enveiat quinze,
    Chascuns portout une branche d'olive;
    Nuncerent vos cez paroles meïsme.
205 A voz Franceis un cunseill en presistes,
    Loërent vos alques de legerie.
    Dous de voz cuntes al paien tramesistes,
    L'un fut Basan e li altres Basilies;
    Les chef en prist es puis desuz Haltilie.
210 Faites la guer cum vos l'avez enprise:
    En Sarraguce menez vostre ost banie,
    Metez le sege a tute vostre vie,
    Si vengez cels que li fels fist ocire!"   AOI.

15

    Li emperere en tint sun chef enbrunc,
215 Si duist sa barbe, afaitad sun gernun,
    Ne ben ne mal ne respunt sun nevuld.
    Franceis se taisent, ne mais que Guenelun,
    En piez se drecet, si vint devant Carlun.
    Mult fierement cumencet sa raisun
220 E dist al rei: "Ja mar crerez bricun,
    Ne mei ne altre, se de vostre prod nun!
    Quant ço vos mandet li reis Marsiliun
    Qu'il devendrat jointes ses mains tis hom
    E tute Espaigne tendrat par vostre dun,
225 Puis recevrat la lei que nus tenum,
    Ki ço vos lodet que cest plait degetuns,
    Ne li chalt, sire, de quel mort nus murjuns.

14

The Emperor had finished speaking.
Count Roland, who is dead set against the idea,
195   Rises to his feet and comes forward to voice his opposition.
He said to the King: "Believe Marsile and you shall rue the day!
We have been in Spain full seven years.
I conquered Noples and Commibles for you,
I took Valterne and the land of Pine,
200   Balaguer, Tudela, and Sezille.
King Marsile behaved most treacherously:
He sent fifteen of his pagans,
Each was carrying an olive branch;
They spoke to you in these very same terms.
205   You consulted your French barons about this,
They gave you some bad advice.
You sent two of your counts to the pagan,
One was Basan and the other Basile;
He cut off their heads in the hills below Haltille.
210   Wage war the way you set out to do:
Lead the army you have summoned to Saragossa,
Lay siege to the city, put all your heart into it,
And avenge those the villain had killed!"   AOI.

15

The Emperor kept his head lowered,
215   He stroked his beard, smoothed his moustache,
He does not tell his nephew he agrees or disagrees.
The French remain silent, except for Ganelon,
Who rises to his feet and comes before Charles.
He begins his speech in very hostile fashion,
220   And he said to the King: "Believe a fool and you shall rue the day!
Don't listen to me, I mean, or to anyone else unless it's to your
    advantage.
When King Marsile lets you know
That he will place his hands between yours and become your vassal,
And that he will hold all Spain as a fief from you,
225   And, moreover, that he will become a convert to the faith we profess,
Then anyone who advises you to reject such an offer
Doesn't care, sire, how we die.

Cunseill d'orguill n'est dreiz que a plus munt,
Laissun les fols, as sages nus tenuns." AOI.

16

230 Aprés iço i est Neimes venud.
Meillor vassal n'aveit en la curt nul
E dist al rei: "Ben l'avez entendud,
Guenes li quens ço vus ad respondud;
Saveir i ad, mais qu'il seit entendud.
235 Li reis Marsilie est de guere vencud:
Vos li avez tuz ses castels toluz,
Od voz caables avez fruiset ses murs,
Ses citez arses e ses humes vencuz.
Quant il vos mandet qu'aiez mercit de lui,
240 Pecchet fereit ki dunc li fesist plus.
U par ostage vos en voelt faire soürs,
Ceste grant guerre ne deit munter a plus."
Dient Franceis: "Ben ad parlet li dux." AOI.

17

"Seignurs baruns, qui i enveieruns
245 En Sarraguce, al rei Marsiliuns?"
Respunt dux Neimes: "Jo irai, par vostre dun.
Livrez m'en ore le guant e le bastun."
Respunt li reis: "Vos estes saives hom;
Par ceste barbe e par cest men gernun,
250 Vos n'irez pas uan de mei si luign.
Alez sedeir, quant nuls ne vos sumunt!"

18

"Seignurs baruns, qui i purruns enveier
Al Sarrazin ki Sarraguce tient?"
Respunt Rollant: "Jo i puis aler mult ben."
255 "Nu ferez certes!" dist li quens Oliver,
"Vostre curages est mult pesmes e fiers:
Jo me crendreie que vos vos meslisez.
Se li reis voelt, jo i puis aler ben."

Wrongheaded counsel must prevail no longer.
Let us have done with fools and hold with wise men."   AOI.

16

230 After that Naimes came forward.
There was no better knight at court,
And he said to the King: "You heard everything he said,
Count Ganelon has given you his opinion;
There is something in what he says, providing we put it another way.
235 King Marsile no longer poses a military threat:
You have taken all his fortresses away from him,
You have smashed his walls with your catapults,
Burned his cities and vanquished his men.
He begs you to have mercy on him,
240 So anyone pursuing him further would be committing a sin.
Since he wishes to reassure you by hostages,
This great war must no longer continue."
The French say: "The Duke has spoken well."   AOI.

17

"My lord barons, whom shall we send
245 To Saragossa, to King Marsile?"
Duke Naimes replies: "With your permission, I'll go.
Now let me have the gauntlet and the staff."
The King replies: "You're a valuable man;
By this beard and by this moustache of mine,
250 You'll never go so far from me.
Go sit down, no one has called upon you!"

18

"My lord barons, whom can we send
To the Saracen who rules Saragossa?"
Roland replies: "I can accomplish this mission very well."
255 "No you won't!" said Count Oliver,
"You have a very bad temper:
I'd be afraid that you would pick a quarrel.
If the King is willing, I can do the job properly."

17

Respunt li reis: "Ambdui vos en taisez!
260 Ne vos ne il n'i porterez les piez.
Par ceste barbe que veez blancher,
Li duze per mar i serunt jugez!"
Franceis se taisent, as les vus aquisez.

19

Turpins de Reins en est levet del renc
265 E dist al rei: "Laisez ester voz Francs.
En cest païs avez estet set anz,
Mult unt oüd e peines e ahans.
Dunez m'en, sire, le bastun e le guant
E jo irai al Sarazin espan,
270 Sin vois vedeir alques de sun semblant."
Li empereres respunt par maltalant:
"Alez sedeir desur cel palie blanc!
N'en parlez mais, se jo nel vos cumant!"   AOI.

20

"Francs chevalers," dist li emperere Carles,
275 "Car m'eslisez un barun de ma marche,
Qu'a Marsiliun me portast mun message."
Ço dist Rollant: "Ço ert Guenes, mis parastre."
Dient Franceis: "Car il le poet ben faire!
Se lui lessez, n'i trametrez plus saive."
280 E li quens Guenes en fut mult anguisables.
De sun col getet ses grandes pels de martre
E est remés en sun blialt de palie.
Vairs out les oilz e mult fier lu visage,
Gent out le cors e les costez out larges;
285 Tant par fut bels tuit si per l'en esguardent.
Dist a Rollant: "Tut fol, pur quei t'esrages?
Ço set hom ben que jo sui tis parastres,
Si as juget qu'a Marsiliun en alge!
Se Deus ço dunet que jo de la repaire,
290 Jo t'en muvra un si grant contraire
Ki durerat a trestut tun edage."
Respunt Rollant: "Orgoill oi e folage,

The King replies: "Be still the both of you!
260 Neither one of you will ever set foot there.
By this white beard that you see before you,
The Twelve will not be nominated or else!"
The French are silent, see how still they are.

19

Turpin of Reims rose and stood in the middle of the circle,
265 And he said to the King: "Keep your Franks here.
You have been in this land for seven years,
They have suffered many cares and woes.
Give me the gauntlet and the staff, sire,
And I'll go to the Spanish Saracen,
270 So that I can judge him by his looks."
The Emperor replies with irritation:
"Go sit down on that white silk cloth!
Don't say another word unless I order you to!"   AOI.

20

"Worthy knights," said Emperor Charles,
275 "I want you to nominate a baron from my march
Able to deliver my message to Marsile."
Roland said: "I propose my stepfather, Ganelon."
The French say: "He'd be good at it!
If you pass him up, you won't find a worthier individual to send."
280 But Ganelon feels strangled.
He tears his great marten furs away from his throat,
He stood there in his silk tunic.
His eyes flashed and his expression was very fierce,
His body befitted a nobleman and his chest was broad;
285 He was so handsome all his peers stared at him with wonder.
He said to Roland: "You fool, what prompts such wrath?
Everyone knows very well that I am your stepfather,
Yet you have named me to go to Marsile!
If God wills that I should return from there,
290 I'll take such great vengeance on you
That it will last you all your life."
Roland replies: "You're talking drivel,

Ço set hom ben, n'ai cure de manace.
Mai saives hom, il deit faire message:
295 Si li reis voelt, prez sui por vus le face."

21

Guenes respunt: "Pur mei n'iras tu mie! AOI.
Tu n'ies mes hom ne jo ne sui tis sire.
Carles comandet que face sun servise,
En Sarraguce en irai a Marsilie.
300 Einz i frai un poi de legerie,
Que jo n'esclair ceste meie grant ire."
Quant l'ot Rollant, si cumençat a rire. AOI.

22

Quant ço veit Guenes que ore s'en rit Rollant,
Dunc ad tel doel pur poi d'ire ne fent,
305 A ben petit que il ne pert le sens;
E dit al cunte: "Jo ne vus aim nïent,
Sur mei avez turnet fals jugement.
Dreiz emperere, veiz me ci en present,
Ademplir voeill vostre comandement."

23

310 "En Sarraguce sai ben qu'aler m'estoet, AOI.
Hom ki la vait repairer ne s'en poet.
Ensurquetut si ai jo vostre soer,
Sin ai un filz, ja plus bels n'en estoet,
Ço est Baldewin," ço dit, "ki ert prozdoem.
315 A lui lais jo mes honurs e mes fieus.
Guadez le ben, ja nel verrai des oilz."
Carles respunt: "Tro avez tendre coer.
Puis quel comant, aler vus en estoet."

24

Ço dist li reis: "Guenes, venez avant, AOI.
320 Si recevez le bastun e lu guant.

Everyone knows very well that threats don't intimidate me.
But we need a good man to deliver the message:
295 If the King is willing, I'll be happy to go for you."

21

Ganelon replies: "You will not go in my place!   AOI.
You're not my vassal and I'm not your lord.
Charles orders me to render him a service,
So I'll go to Saragossa, to Marsile.
300 But I'll do something a bit ill-advised
Before I purge this great anger of mine."
When Roland heard him he began to laugh.   AOI.

22

When Ganelon sees that Roland is laughing at him now,
He has such a fit of anger that he is ready to burst,
305 He very nearly goes out of his mind;
And he says to the Count: "I don't care what happens to you now.
You arranged to have this rotten nomination fall on me.
Rightful Emperor, I stand here before you,
I wish to carry out your orders."

23

310 "I am well aware that I must go to Saragossa,   AOI.
Any man who goes there cannot return.
Above all, don't forget that I am married to your sister,
And that she gave me a son, the fairest that ever was,
Baldwin," he said, "who will be a man of honor.
315 To him I leave my lands and my fiefs.
Take good care of him, I'll not set eyes on him again."
Charles replies: "You are too soft-hearted.
Since I command it, you must go now."

24

The King said: "Ganelon, come forward   AOI.
320 And receive the staff and the gauntlet.

Oït l'avez, sur vos le jugent Franc."
"Sire," dist Guenes, "ço ad tut fait Rollant!
Ne l'amerai a trestut mun vivant,
Ne Oliver, por ço qu'il est si cumpainz,
325 Li duze per, por qu'il l'aiment tant.
Desfi les ci, sire, vostre veiant."
Ço dist li reis: "Trop avez maltalant.
Or irez vos certes, quant jol cumant."
"Jo i puis aler, mais n'i avrai guarant: AOI.
330 Nu l'out Basilies ne sis freres Basant."

25

Li empereres li tent sun guant, le destre,
Mais li quens Guenes iloec ne volsist estre,
Quant le dut prendre, si li caït a tere.
Dient Franceis: "Deus! que purrat ço estre?
335 De cest message nos avendrat grant perte."
"Seignurs," dist Guenes, "vos en orrez noveles!"

26

"Sire," dist Guenes, "dunez mei le cungied,
Quant aler dei, n'i ai plus que targer."
Ço dist li reis: "Al Jhesu e al mien!"
340 De sa main destre l'ad asols e seignet,
Puis li livrat le bastun e le bref.

27

Guenes li quens s'en vait a sun ostel,
De guarnemenz se prent a cunreer,
De ses meillors que il pout recuvrer.
345 Esperuns d'or ad en ses piez fermez,
Ceint Murglies, s'espee, a sun costed.
En Tachebrun, sun destrer, est munted,
L'estreu li tint sun uncle Guinemer.
La veïsez tant chevaler plorer,
350 Ki tuit li dient: "Tant mare fustes, ber!
En la cort al rei mult i avez ested.

You have heard it, the Franks have nominated you."
"Sire," said Ganelon, "Roland is responsible for all this!
For the rest of my life I shall not care what happens to him,
Nor to Oliver, because he is his companion,
325 Nor to the Twelve Peers, because they love him so.
I hereby defy them, sire, in your presence."
The King said: "You are too bad-tempered.
Now you must certainly go, since I command it."
"I can go there, but I shall have no safe-conduct: AOI.
330 Basile and his brother Basan had none either."

25

The Emperor extends his right gauntlet to him,
But Count Ganelon had no desire to be there,
When he should have taken the glove, it fell to the ground.
The French say: "God! what does this mean?
335 We will suffer a great loss because of this message."
"My lords," said Ganelon, "you shall hear more about this!"

26

"Sire," said Ganelon, "give me permission to leave,
Since I must go, I am only wasting time."
The King said: "Go in Jesus's name and in mine!"
340 With his right hand he gave him absolution and blessed him,
Then he delivered over to him the staff and the letter.

27

Count Ganelon goes to his tent,
He begins to put on his equipment,
The best he can find.
345 He attaches his golden spurs to his feet,
He girds his sword Murgleis at his side.
He has mounted his war-horse Tachebrun,
His uncle Guinemer held the stirrup for him.
There you would have seen many knights weeping,
350 All of them saying to him: "You are to be pitied, worthy knight!
You have served the King at court for a long time,

Noble vassal vos i solt hom clamer.
Ki ço jugat que doüsez aler
Par Charlemagne n'ert guariz ne tensez.
355 Li quens Rollant nel se doüst penser,
Que estrait estes de mult grant parented."
Enprés li dient: "Sire, car nos menez!"
Ço respunt Guenes: "Ne placet Damnedeu!
Mielz est que sul moerge que tant bon chevaler.
360 En dulce France, seignurs, vos en irez:
De meie part ma muiller saluëz
E Pinabel, mun ami e mun per,
E Baldewin, mun filz que vos savez,
E lui aidez e pur seignur le tenez."
365 Entret en sa veie, si s'est achiminez.   AOI.

28

Guenes chevalchet suz une olive halte.
Asemblet s'est as sarrazins messages,
Mais Blancandrins ki envers lu s'atarget;
Par grant saveir parolet li uns a l'altre.
370 Dist Blancandrins: "Merveilus hom est Charles,
Ki cunquist Puille e trestute Calabre.
Vers Engletere passat il la mer salse,
Ad oes seint Perre en cunquist le chevage.
Que nus requert ça en la nostre marche?"
375 Guenes respunt: "Itels est sis curages.
Jamais n'ert hume ki encuntre lui vaille."   AOI.

29

Dist Blancandrins: "Francs sunt mult gentilz home.
Mult grant mal funt e cil duc e cil cunte
A lur seignur, ki tel cunseill li dunent:
380 Lui e altrui travaillent e cunfundent."
Guenes respunt: "Jo ne sai, veirs, nul hume
Ne mes Rollant, ki uncore en avrat hunte.
Er matin sedeit li emperere suz l'umbre.
Vint i ses niés, out vestue sa brunie,
385 E out predet dejuste Carcasonie.

You are hailed by all as a noble knight.
The one who proposed that you should go
Will not be protected or saved by Charlemagne.
355 Count Roland ought not to have thought of that,
For you were born of very high parentage."
Afterward they say to him: "Take us along, my lord!"
Ganelon replies: "God forbid!
Far better that I should die alone than so many good knights.
360 You will return to fair France, my lords:
Greet my wife for me
And Pinabel, my friend and my peer,
And Baldwin, my son whom you all know:
Help him and be his vassals."
365 He started on his way, setting forth along the road.   AOI.

28

Ganelon is riding under a tall olive tree.
He has joined up with the Saracen messengers,
But now Blancandrin lags behind to be alone with him;
They speak to each other with great cunning.
370 Blancandrin said: "Charles is an extraordinary man
Who conquered Apulia and all Calabria.
He crossed the salt sea to reach England
And imposed an annual tax to be paid to Saint Peter.
What does he seek from us here in our land?"
375 Ganelon replies: "Whatever he wills.
There will never be anyone to measure up to him."   AOI.

29

Blancandrin said: "The Franks are most worthy men.
Those dukes and counts do very great harm
To their lord when they counsel him thus:
380 They torment and ruin him, and others too."
Ganelon replies: "In truth, I know this to be so of no man
Except Roland, who will suffer for it some day.
Yesterday morning the Emperor was sitting in the shade.
His nephew came to him wearing his byrnie,
385 For he had been plundering near Carcasoine.

En sa main tint une vermeille pume:
'Tenez, bel sire,' dist Rollant a sun uncle,
'De trestuz reis vos present les curunes.'
Li soens orgoilz le devreit ben cunfundre,
390 Kar chascun jur de mort s'abandunet.
Seit ki l'ociet, tute pais puis avriumes."   AOI.

30

Dist Blancandrins: "Mult est pesmes Rollant,
Ki tute gent voelt faire recreant
E tutes teres met en chalengement!
395 Par quele gent quïet il espleiter tant?"
Guenes respunt: "Par la franceise gent.
Il l'aiment tant ne li faldrunt nïent.
Or e argent lur met tant en present,
Muls e destrers, e palies e guarnemenz.
400 L'emperere meïsmes ad tut a sun talent.
Cunquerrat li les teres d'ici qu'en Orïent."   AOI.

31

Tant chevalcherent Guenes e Blancandrins
Que l'un a l'altre la sue feit plevit
Que il querreient que Rollant fust ocis.
405 Tant chevalcherent e veies e chemins
Que en Sarraguce descendent suz un if.
Un faldestoet out suz l'umbre d'un pin,
Envolupet fut d'un palie alexandrin.
La fut li reis ki tute Espaigne tint,
410 Tut entur lui vint milie Sarrazins.
N'i ad celoi ki mot sunt ne mot tint,
Pur les nuveles qu'il vuldreient oïr.
Atant as vos Guenes e Blanchandrins.

32

Blancandrins vint devant Marsiliun,
415 Par le puig tint le cunte Guenelun
E dist al rei: "Salvez seiez de Mahum

He held a red apple in his hand:
'Here, dear lord,' said Roland to his uncle.
'I present you with the crowns of all the kings.'
His madness will surely bring him to ruin,
390 For he risks his life each day.
If someone were to kill him, then we would have real peace."   AOI.

30

Blancandrin said: "Roland is a maniac
To want to subdue all peoples
And assert a claim to all lands!
395 What people does he count on to accomplish such exploits?"
Ganelon replies: "French people.
They love him so much they will never fail him.
He gives them so many gifts of gold and silver,
Mules and war-horses, silk cloth and battle gear.
400 He holds sway over the Emperor himself.
He will conquer for him all the lands from here to the Orient."
   AOI.

31

Ganelon and Blancandrin rode on,
Eventually they gave each other their word
That they would find a way to have Roland killed.
405 They rode along through highways and byways,
Eventually they dismount in Saragossa under a yew.
There was a throne in the shade of a pine tree,
Covered with a silk cloth made in Alexandria.
The King who ruled all of Spain was there,
410 Twenty thousand Saracens came all around him.
Not a single one of them utters a word or makes a sound,
Because all would like to hear the news.
Here now are Ganelon and Blancandrin.

32

Blancandrin came before Marsile,
415 Holding Count Ganelon by the hand,
And he said to the King: "May Mohammed save you

E d'Apollin, qui seintes leis tenuns!
Vostre message fesime a Charlun.
Ambes ses mains en levat cuntremunt,
420 Loat sun Deu, ne fist altre respuns.
Ci vos enveiet un sun noble barun,
Ki est de France, si est mult riches hom:
Par lui orrez si avrez pais u nun."
Respunt Marsilie: "Or diet, nus l'orrum!"   AOI.

33

425 Mais li quens Guenes se fut ben purpenset.
Par grant saver cumencet a parler
Cume celui ki ben faire le set
E dist al rei: "Salvez seiez de Deu,
Li Glorius, qui devum aürer!
430 Iço vus mandet Carlemagnes li ber
Que recevez seinte chrestïentet,
Demi Espaigne vos voelt en fiu duner.
Se cest acorde ne vulez otrïer,
Pris e liez serez par poësted;
435 Al siege ad Ais en serez amenet,
Par jugement serez iloec finet,
La murrez vus a hunte e a viltet."
Li reis Marsilies en fut mult esfreed.
Un algier tint, ki d'or fut enpenet,
440 Ferir l'en volt, se n'en fust desturnet.   AOI.

34

Li reis Marsilies ad la culur muee,
De sun algier ad la hanste crollee.
Quant le vit Guenes, mist la main a l'espee,
Cuntre dous deie l'ad del furrer getee,
445 Si li ad dit: "Mult estes bele e clere!
Tant vus avrai en curt a rei portee!
Ja nel dirat de France li emperere
Que suls i moerge en l'estrange cuntree,
Einz vos avrunt li meillor cumperee."
450 Dient paien: "Desfaimes la mellee!"

And Apollo, whose holy faith we profess!
We delivered your message to Charles.
He raised both his hands upward,
420 Praised his God, but made no other reply.
He sends you one of his noble barons here,
Who comes from France and is a very powerful man:
From him you will hear whether or not you will have peace."
Marsile replies: "Let him speak, we'll listen!"   AOI.

33

425 Now Count Ganelon had thought everything out carefully.
With great guile he begins to speak
As one well accustomed to such dealings,
And he said to the King: "May God save you,
And glory be to Him we should all adore!
430 Here is what noble Charlemagne wishes you to know:
Become a convert to holy Christianity,
And he will consent to give you half of Spain as a fief.
If you do not submit to this pact,
You will be seized and bound by force;
435 You will be brought to the judgment seat at Aix,
There you will be tried and executed,
There you will die shamefully and in vile fashion."
King Marsile was panic-stricken by this.
He was holding a spear feathered with gold.
440 He tried to strike him with it but was prevented from doing so.
     AOI.

34

King Marsile's color rose and faded,
He brandished his spear, holding it by the shaft.
When Ganelon saw him do this, he put his hand to his sword,
Pulled it out of the sheath about the width of two fingers,
445 And said to it: "How beautiful and bright you are!
I served the King at court for a long time with you!
The Emperor of France will never say
That I died alone in a foreign land
Before the best of them paid dearly for you."
450 The pagans say: "Let's break it up!"

35

    Tuit li preierent li meillor Sarrazin
    Qu'el faldestoed s'es Marsilies asis.
    Dist l'algalifes: "Mal nos avez baillit
    Que li Franceis asmastes a ferir;
455 Vos doüssez esculter e oïr."
    "Sire," dist Guenes, "mei l'avent a suffrir.
    Jo ne lerreie, por tut l'or que Deus fist
    Ne por tut l'aveir ki seit en cest païs,
    Que jo ne li die, se tant ai de leisir,
460 Que Charles li mandet, li reis poësteïfs,
    Par mei li mandet, sun mortel enemi."
    Afublez est d'un mantel sabelin,
    Ki fut cuvert d'un palie alexandrin.
    Getet le a tere, sil receit Blancandrin,
465 Mais de s'espee ne volt mie guerpir,
    En sun puign destre par l'orie punt la tint.
    Dient paien: "Noble baron ad ci!"   AOI.

36

    Envers le rei s'est Guenes aproismet,
    Si li ad dit: "A tort vos curuciez
470 Quar ço vos mandet Carles, ki France tient,
    Que recevez la lei de chrestïens;
    Demi Espaigne vus durat il en fiet.
    L'altre meitet avrat Rollant, sis niés:
    Mult orguillos parçuner i avrez!
475 Si ceste acorde ne volez otrïer,
    En Sarraguce vus vendrat aseger,
    Par poëstet serez pris e liez,
    Menet serez dreit ad Ais le siet.
    Vus n'i avrez palefreid ne destrer,
480 Ne mul ne mule que puissez chevalcher;
    Getet serez sur un malvais sumer.
    Par jugement iloec perdrez le chef.
    Nostre emperere vus enveiet cest bref."
    El destre poign al paien l'ad livret.

35

The shrewdest Saracens all pleaded with Marsile,
With the result that he returned to his seat on the throne.
The Caliph said: "You served us badly
When you tried to strike the Frenchman;
455 You ought to have listened to what he has to say."
"My lord," said Ganelon, "I'll consent to suffer that affront.
I would not fail, for all the gold that God has made,
Nor for all the wealth in this land,
To tell him, if I have an opportunity to do so,
460 What mighty King Charles wishes him to know,
What he wishes his mortal enemy to know through me."
He is wearing a sable cloak
Covered with silk cloth made in Alexandria.
He throws it to the ground, Blancandrin picks it up,
465 But he does not wish to part with his sword,
He kept his right hand on its golden hilt.
The pagans say: "There's a worthy knight for you!"   AOI.

36

Ganelon moved close to the King,
And he said to him: "It is wrong of you to be angry,
470 For here is what Charles, who rules France, wishes you to know:
Become a convert to the Christian faith;
He will give you half of Spain as a fief.
His nephew Roland will have the other half:
What a madman you'll have for a partner!
475 If you do not submit to this pact,
He will come to besiege you in Saragossa,
You will be seized and bound by force,
You will be led directly to the capital at Aix.
You will have neither a palfrey nor a war-horse,
480 Neither a mule nor a jenny as a mount;
You will be thrown on a lowly packhorse.
There you will be tried and will lose your head.
Our Emperor sends you this letter."
He gave it to the pagan, who took it in his right hand.

37

485 Marsilies fut esculurez de l'ire,
Freint le seel, getet en ad la cire.
Guardet al bref, vit la raisun escrite:
"Carle me mandet, ki France ad en baillie,
Que me remembre de la dolur e de l'ire,
490 Ço est de Basan e de sun frere Basilie
Dunt pris les chefs as puis de Haltoïe.
Se de mun cors voeil aquiter la vie,
Dunc li envei mun uncle, l'algalife,
Altrement ne m'amerat il mie."
495 Aprés parlat ses filz envers Marsilies
E dist al rei: "Guenes ad dit folie,
Tant ad erret nen est dreiz que plus vivet.
Livrez le mei, jo en ferai la justise."
Quant l'oït Guenes, l'espee en ad branlie,
500 Vait s'apuier suz le pin a la tige.

38

Enz el verger s'en est alez li reis,
Ses meillors humes en meinet ensembl'od sei:
E Blancandrins i vint, al canud peil,
E Jurfaret, ki est ses filz e ses heirs,
505 E l'algalifes, sun uncle e sis fedeilz.
Dist Blancandrins: "Apelez le Franceis,
De nostre prod m'ad plevie sa feid."
Ço dist li reis: "E vos l'i ameneiz."
E Guenes l'ad pris par la main destre ad deiz,
510 Enz el verger l'en meinet josqu'al rei.
La purparolent la traïsun seinz dreit. AOI.

39

"Bel sire Guenes," ço li ad dit Marsilie,
"Jo vos ai fait alques de legerie
Quant por ferir vus demustrai grant ire.
515 Guaz vos en dreit par cez pels sabelines.
Melz en valt l'or que ne funt cinc cenz livres.
Einz demain noit en iert bele l'amendise."

37

485   Marsile was in a white rage,
He breaks the seal, he threw away the wax.
He looks at the letter, sees the written offer:
"Charles, who rules over France, wishes me to know
That I should bear in mind the chagrin and the anger
490   Occasioned by Basan and his brother Basile,
Whose heads I took in the mountains of Haltille.
If I wish to escape with life and limb,
I must send him my uncle, the Caliph,
Otherwise he will not care what happens to me."
495   Then Marsile's son spoke up
And said to the King: "Ganelon talked nonsense,
He went so far he doesn't deserve to live any longer.
Let me have him and I'll dispense justice to him."
When Ganelon heard him, he brandished his sword,
500   He goes under the pine tree and backs up against the trunk.

38

The King went into the garden,
He takes his best advisers along with him:
White-haired Blancandrin came,
And Jurfaret, who is his son and heir,
505   And the Caliph, his uncle and his loyal companion.
Blancandrin said: "Call the Frenchman,
He has given me his word he'll act in our interest."
The King said: "Go and fetch him personally."
But Ganelon took him by the fingers of his right hand,
510   He leads him into the garden up to the King.
There they negotiate the wrongful act of treachery.   AOI.

39

"Dear Sir Ganelon," said Marsile to him,
"I did something a bit ill-advised to you
When I gave vent to my great anger and made as if to strike you.
515   I pledge to make things straight between us with these sable furs
Worth more than five hundred pounds in gold.
Before tomorrow night I shall make a handsome reparation to you."

Guenes respunt: "Jo nel desotrei mie.
Deus, se lui plaist, a bien le vos mercie!"   AOI.

40

520 Ço dist Marsilies: "Guenes, par veir sacez,
En talant ai que mult vos voeill amer.
De Carlemagne vos voeill oïr parler.
Il est mult vielz, si ad sun tens uset,
Men escïent, dous cenz anz ad passet.
525 Par tantes teres ad sun cors demened,
Tanz colps ad pris sur sun escut bucler,
Tanz riches reis cunduit a mendisted:
Quant ert il mais recreanz d'osteier?"
Guenes respunt: "Carles n'est mie tels.
530 N'est hom kil veit e conuistre le set
Que ço ne diet que l'emperere est ber.
Tant nel vos sai ne preiser ne loër
Que plus n'i ad d'onur e de bontet.
Sa grant valor, kil purreit acunter?
535 De tel barnage l'ad Deus enluminet,
Meilz voelt murir que guerpir sun barnet."

41

Dist li paiens: "Mult me puis merveiller
De Carlemagne, ki est canuz e vielz.
Men escïentre, dous cenz anz ad e mielz.
540 Par tantes teres ad sun cors traveillet,
Tanz cols ad pris de lances e d'espiet,
Tanz riches reis cunduiz a mendistiet:
Quant ert il mais recreanz d'osteier?"
"Ço n'iert," dist Guenes, "tant cum vivet sis niés.
545 N'at tel vassal suz la cape del ciel.
Mult par est proz sis cumpainz Oliver.
Les .XII. pers, que Carles ad tant chers,
Funt les enguardes a .XX. milie chevalers.
Soürs est Carles, que nuls home ne crent."   AOI.

34

Ganelon replies: "I shall not turn it down.
May it please God to make it up to you!"   AOI.

40

520 Marsile said: "Ganelon, believe me when I say
That I intend to take care of you handsomely.
I want you to tell me about Charlemagne.
He is very old and his time is running out,
I understand he is over two hundred years old.
525 He has knocked about so many lands,
He has taken so many blows on his shield,
He has reduced so many powerful kings to beggary:
When will he ever forsake waging war?"
Ganelon replies: "Charles is not like that.
530 There is not a man who sees him and knows him well
Who won't agree that the Emperor is a man's man.
No matter how much I praise and extoll him to you,
He has more honor and nobility in him still.
Who can relate his great worth?
535 God has cast such rays of manly virtue on him
That he would rather die than abandon his barons."

41

The pagan said: "I marvel greatly
At Charlemagne who is old and gray.
I understand he is better than two hundred years old.
540 He has punished his body in so many lands,
He has taken so many blows from lances and spears,
He has reduced so many powerful kings to beggary:
When will he ever forsake waging war?
"Not," said Ganelon, "so long as his nephew lives.
545 There's no knight like him under the canopy of heaven.
His companion Oliver also has great worth.
The Twelve Peers, whom Charles cherishes so,
Are in the van with twenty thousand knights.
Charles is secure and fears no man."   AOI.

42

550 Dist li Sarrazins: "Merveille en ai grant
De Carlemagne, ki est canuz e blancs.
Mien escïentre, plus ad de .II.C. anz.
Par tantes teres est alet cunquerant,
Tanz colps ad pris de bons espiez trenchanz,
555 Tanz riches reis morz e vencuz en champ:
Quant ier il mais d'osteier recreant?"
"Ço n'iert," dist Guenes, "tant cum vivet Rollant.
N'ad tel vassal d'ici qu'en Orïent.
Mult par est proz Oliver, sis cumpainz.
560 Li .XII. per, que Carles aimet tant,
Funt les enguardes a .XX. milie de Francs.
Soürs est Carlles, ne crent hume vivant."   AOI.

43

"Bel sire Guenes," dist Marsilies li reis,
"Jo ai tel gent, plus bele ne verreiz,
565 Quatre cenz milie chevalers puis aveir.
Puis m'en cumbatre a Carlle e a Franceis?"
Guenes respunt: "Ne vus a ceste feiz!
De voz paiens mult grant perte i avreiz.
Lessez la folie, tenez vos al saveir.
570 L'empereür tant li dunez aveir,
N'i ait Franceis ki tot ne s'en merveilt.
Par .XX. hostages que li enveiereiz
En dulce France s'en repairerat li reis.
Sa rereguarde lerrat derere sei:
575 Iert i sis niés, li quens Rollant, ço crei,
E Oliver, li proz e li curteis.
Mort sunt li cunte, se est ki mei en creit!
Carlles verrat sun grant orguill cadeir,
N'avrat talent, que jamais vus guerreit."   AOI.

44

580 "Bel sire Guenes, . . .
Cumfaitement purrai Rollant ocire?"
Guenes respont: "Ço vos sai jo ben dire.

42

550 The Saracen said: "I marvel greatly
At Charlemagne, who is hoary and white-haired.
I understand he is more than two hundred years old.
He has conquered his way across so many lands,
He has taken so many blows from good sharp spears,
555 He has slain and vanquished in battle so many powerful kings:
When will he ever forsake waging war?"
"Not," said Ganelon, "so long as Roland lives.
There's no knight like him from here to the Orient.
His companion Oliver also has great worth.
560 The Twelve Peers, whom Charles loves so well,
Are in the van with twenty thousand Franks.
Charles is secure and fears no man alive."   AOI.

43

"Dear Sir Ganelon," said King Marsile,
"You'll never see a finer army than mine,
565 I may have as many as four hundred thousand knights.
With them can I give battle to Charles and to the French?"
Ganelon replies: "Don't do it right away!
You will suffer a great loss of your pagans if you do.
Don't act foolishly, keep your wits about you.
570 Give the Emperor such riches
That every Frenchman's head will turn.
Send him twenty hostages,
And the King will return home to fair France.
He will position his rearguard behind him:
575 His nephew Count Roland will be there, I know,
And worthy and reliable Oliver.
The counts are already dead, believe me!
Charles will see his great pride fall,
He won't have the will to war against you ever again."   AOI.

44

580 "Dear Sir Ganelon, ...
How can I kill Roland?"
Ganelon replies: "I can tell you exactly how.

Li reis serat as meillors porz de Sizer,
Sa rereguarde avrat detrés sei mise;
585   Iert i sis niés, li quens Rollant, li riches,
E Oliver, en qui il tant se fiet;
.XX. milie Francs unt en lur cumpaignie.
De voz paiens lur enveiez .C. milie,
Une bataille lur i rendent cil primes.
590   La gent de France iert blecee e blesmie;
Nel di por ço, des voz iert la martirie.
Altre bataille lur livrez de meïsme:
De quel que seit Rollant n'estoertrat mie.
Dunc avrez faite gente chevalerie,
595   N'avrez mais guere en tute vostre vie."   AOI.

45

"Chi purreit faire que Rollant i fust mort,
Dunc perdreit Carles le destre braz del cors,
Si remeindreient les merveilluses oz.
N'asemblereit jamais Carles si grant esforz,
600   Tere Major remeindreit en repos."
Quan l'ot Marsilie, si l'ad baiset el col,
Puis si cumencet a venir ses tresors.   AOI.

46

Ço dist Marsilies: "Qu'en parlereient . . .
Cunseill n'est proz dunt hume . . .
605   La traïsun me jurrez de Rollant."
Ço respunt Guenes: "Issi seit cum vos plaist!"
Sur les reliques de s'espee Murgleis
La traïsun jurat, e si s'en est forsfait.   AOI.

47

Un faldestoed i out d'un olifant.
610   Marsilies fait porter un livre avant,
La lei i fut Mahum e Tervagan.
Ço ad juret li Sarrazins espans:
Se en rereguarde troevet le cors Rollant,

The King will be at the main pass of Cize,
He will have positioned his rearguard behind him;
585 His nephew, mighty Count Roland, will be there,
And Oliver, on whom he relies so much;
They are accompanied by twenty thousand Franks.
Send a hundred thousand of your pagans against them,
Let these men join battle with them first.
590 The men from France will be battered and bruised;
Not that your men won't be massacred too.
Offer them battle a second time in similar fashion:
Roland will not escape from both engagements.
Then you will have achieved a noble feat of arms,
595 You will never have war for the rest of your life."   AOI.

45

"If one could cause Roland to die,
Then Charles would lose his right arm from his body,
His formidable armies would cease to exist.
Charles would never again muster such great forces,
600 The Fatherland would remain in peace."
Hearing this, Marsile kissed him on the neck,
Then he begins to bring out his treasures.   AOI.

46

Marsile said: "Why discuss it . . . ?
Advice is worthless when one . . .
605 You must swear to me to betray Roland."
Ganelon replies: "Just as you please!"
On the relics of his sword Murgleis
He swore the oath of treason, thus he committed a felony.   AOI.

47

There was a throne there made of ivory.
610 Marsile has a book brought forward,
It contained the scriptures of Mohammed and Tervagant.
The Spanish Saracen swore this:
If he finds Roland in the rearguard,

Cumbatrat sei a trestute sa gent
615 E, se il poet, murrat i veirement.
Guenes respunt: "Ben seit vostre comant!" AOI.

48

Atant i vint uns paiens, Valdabruns,
Icil en vait al rei Marsiliun.
Cler en riant l'ad dit a Guenelun:
620 "Tenez m'espee, meillur n'en at nuls hom,
Entre les helz ad plus de mil manguns.
Par amistiez, bel sire, la vos duins,
Que nos aidez de Rollant le barun,
Qu'en rereguarde trover le poüsum."
625 "Ben serat fait," li quens Guenes respunt.
Puis se baiserent es vis e es mentuns.

49

Aprés i vint un paien, Climorins.
Cler en riant a Guenelun l'ad dit:
"Tenez mun helme, unches meillor ne vi.
630 Si nos aidez de Rollant li marchis,
Par quel mesure le poüssum hunir."
"Ben serat fait," Guenes respundit.
Puis se baiserent es buches e es vis. AOI.

50

Atant i vint la reïne Bramimunde:
635 "Jo vos aim mult, sire," dist ele al cunte,
"Car mult vos priset mi sire e tuit si hume.
A vostre femme enveierai dous nusches;
Bien i ad or, matices e jacunces,
Eles valent mielz que tut l'aveir de Rume.
640 Vostre emperere si bones n'en out unches."
Il les ad prises, en sa hoese les butet. AOI.

He will give battle with all his army
615 And, if it be in his power, Roland will surely die there.
Ganelon replies: "May your wish come true!"   AOI.

48

At that moment, a pagan, Valdabron, came forward,
He went before King Marsile.
With peals of laughter he said to Ganelon:
620 "Take my sword, no man has a better one,
There are more than a thousand mangons in its hilt.
I give it to you, dear sir, as a token of friendship,
So that you may help us in the matter of the knight Roland,
So that we may find him in the rearguard."
625 "That will be taken care of," Count Ganelon replies.
Then they kissed each other on the face and chin.

49

Then a pagan, Climborin, came forward.
With peals of laughter he said to Ganelon:
"Take my helmet, I've never seen a better one.
630 Help us concerning the marquis Roland,
Show us how we may shame him."
"That will be taken care of," Ganelon replied.
Then they kissed each other on the mouth and face.   AOI.

50

At that moment, Queen Bramimonde came forward:
635 "I care very much for you, sir," she said to the Count,
"Because my lord and all his men hold you in high esteem.
I will send two brooches to your wife;
They are wrought with much gold, amethysts, and jacinths,
They are worth more than all the riches of Rome.
640 Your Emperor never had such fine ones."
He took them, he sticks them in his boot.   AOI.

51

Li reis apelet Malduit, sun tresorer:
"L'aveir Carlun est il apareilliez?"
E cil respunt: "Oïl, sire, asez bien:
645 .VII.C. cameilz, d'or e argent cargiez,
E .XX. hostages, des plus gentilz desuz cel." AOI.

52

Marsilies tint Guenelun par l'espalle,
Si li ad dit: "Mult par ies ber e sage.
Par cele lei que vos tenez plus salve,
650 Guardez de nos ne turnez le curage.
De mun aveir vos voeill dunner grant masse:
.X. muls cargez del plus fin or d'Arabe,
Jamais n'iert an altretel ne vos face.
Tenez les clefs de ceste citet large,
655 Le grant aveir en presentez al rei Carles,
Pois me jugez Rollant a rereguarde.
Sel pois trover a port ne a passage,
Liverrai lui une mortel bataille."
Guenes respunt: "Mei est vis que trop targe!"
660 Pois est munted, entret en sun veiage. AOI.

53

Li empereres aproismet sun repaire,
Venuz en est a la citet de Galne.
Li quens Rollant, il l'ad e prise e fraite,
Puis icel jur en fut cent anz deserte.
665 De Guenelun atent li reis nuveles
E le treüd d'Espaigne, la grant tere.
Par main en l'albe, si cum li jurz esclairet,
Guenes li quens est venuz as herberges. AOI.

54

Li empereres est par matin levet.
670 Messe e matines ad li reis escultet,
Sur l'erbe verte estut devant sun tref.

51

The King summons his treasurer, Malduit:
"Is Charles's tribute ready?"
And he replies: "Yes indeed, sire, in full:
645   Seven hundred camels laden with gold and silver
And twenty of the noblest hostages on the face of the earth."   AOI.

52

Marsile placed a hand on Ganelon's shoulder,
And he said to him: "You are extremely worthy and wise.
By that faith which you hold most holy,
650   See to it you don't have a change of heart concerning us.
I wish to give you a huge portion of my wealth:
Ten mules laden with the finest gold of Arabia;
I shall make you an identical gift every year.
Take the keys of this vast city,
655   Present its great riches to King Charles,
Then volunteer Roland to the rearguard for me.
If I manage to find him in a mountain pass or defile,
I'll engage him in mortal combat."
Ganelon replies: "I think I'm wasting time!"
660   Then he mounted up, he begins his return voyage.   AOI.

53

The Emperor is approaching his homeland,
He came to the city of Galne.
Count Roland captured and destroyed it.
From that day forward, it remained deserted for a hundred years.
665   The King is awaiting news of Ganelon
And the tribute of the great land of Spain.
In the morning, at dawn, as the day is breaking,
Count Ganelon arrived at the camp.   AOI.

54

The Emperor rose early in the morning.
670   The King hears mass and matins,
He stood before his tent on the green grass.

Rollant i fut e Oliver li ber,
Neimes li dux e des altres asez.
Guenes i vint, li fels, li parjurez,
675 Par grant veisdie cumencet a parler
E dist al rei : "Salvez seiez de Deu!
De Sarraguce ci vos aport les clefs ;
Mult grant aveir vos en faz amener
E .XX. hostages, faites les ben guarder!
680 E si vos mandet reis Marsilies li ber,
De l'algalifes nel devez pas blasmer,
Kar a mes oilz vi .IIII.C. milie armez,
Halbers vestuz, alquanz healmes fermez,
Ceintes espees as punz d'or neielez,
685 Ki l'en cunduistrent tresqu'en la mer.
De Marcilie s'en fuient por la chrestïentet
Que il ne voelent ne tenir ne guarder.
Einz qu'il oüssent .IIII. liues siglet,
Sis aquillit e tempeste e ored.
690 La sunt neiez, jamais nes en verrez ;
Se il fust vif, jo l'oüsse amenet.
Del rei paien, sire, par veir creez,
Ja ne verrez cest premer meis passet
Qu'il vos sivrat en France le regnet,
695 Si recevrat la lei que vos tenez ;
Jointes ses mains iert vostre comandet,
De vos tendrat Espaigne le regnet."
Ço dist li reis : "Graciet en seit Deus!
Ben l'avez fait, mult grant prod i avrez."
700 Par mi cel ost funt mil grailles suner.
Franc desherbergent, funt lur sumers trosser,
Vers dulce France tuit sunt achiminez.   AOI.

55

Carles li magnes ad Espaigne guastede,
Les castels pris, les citez violees.
705 Ço dit li reis que sa guere out finee,
Vers dulce France chevalchet l'emperere.
Li quens Rollant ad l'enseigne fermee,
En sum un tertre cuntre le ciel levee.

44

Roland was there and worthy Oliver,
Duke Naimes and many other knights.
Ganelon, the felon, the perjurer, arrived,
675 He begins to speak with great deceit
And he said to the King: "May God save you!
I bring you the keys of Saragossa;
I bring very great riches for you from there
And twenty hostages, have them carefully guarded!
680 But worthy King Marsile wishes you to know
That you shouldn't blame him on account of the Caliph,
For with my own eyes I saw four hundred thousand armed men,
Wearing hauberks, some with helmets laced,
Swords with gold enameled hilts at their sides,
685 Who accompanied him to the sea.
They flee from Marsile because of Christianity,
Which they neither wish to accept nor uphold.
Before they had sailed four leagues,
A tempest and a storm overtook them.
690 They drowned there, you will never see them again;
Had he survived, I would have brought him.
As for the pagan king, believe me, sire,
Before the end of next month,
He will follow you to the kingdom of France
695 And become a convert to your religion;
His hands placed between yours, he will become your vassal,
He will hold the kingdom of Spain as a fief from you."
The King said: "Thank God!
You rendered good service, you shall have a very great reward."
700 A thousand bugles are sounded throughout the army.
The Franks break camp, they have their beasts of burden packed up,
All have taken the road for fair France.   AOI.

55

Charlemagne has laid waste to Spain,
Captured its fortresses, penetrated its citadels.
705 The King says that his war is over,
The Emperor is riding toward fair France.
Count Roland has mounted the standard,
Raised it against the sky at the top of a hill.

Franc se herbergent par tute la cuntree.
710 Paien chevalchent par cez greignurs valees,
Halbercs vestuz e . . .
Healmes lacez e ceintes lur espees,
Escuz as cols e lances adubees.
En un bruill par sum les puis remestrent.
715 .IIII.C. milie atendent l'ajurnee.
Deus! quel dulur que li Franceis nel sevent! AOI.

56

Tresvait le jur, la noit est aserie,
Carles se dort, li empereres riches.
Sunjat qu'il eret as greignurs porz de Sizer,
720 Entre ses poinz teneit sa hanste fraisnine.
Guenes li quens l'ad sur lui saisie,
Par tel aïr l'at estrussee e brandie
Qu'envers le cel en volent les escicles.
Carles se dort, qu'il ne s'esveillet mie.

57

725 Aprés iceste altre avisiun sunjat
Qu'il ert en France, a sa capele, ad Ais.
El destre braz li morst uns uers si mals.
Devers Ardene vit venir uns leuparz,
Sun cors demenie mult fierement asalt.
730 D'enz de sale uns veltres avalat,
Que vint a Carles le galops e les salz.
La destre oreille al premer uer trenchat,
Ireement se cumbat al lepart.
Dient Franceis que grant bataille i ad,
735 Il ne sevent liquels d'els la veintrat.
Carles se dort, mie ne s'esveillat. AOI.

58

Tresvait la noit e apert la clere albe.
Par mi cel host . . .
Li empereres mult fierement chevalchet.

The Franks bivouac throughout the countryside.
710 The pagans are riding through deep valleys,
Wearing hauberks and . . .
Helmets laced and swords at their sides,
Shields slung from their necks and lances with gonfanons attached.
They remain in a woods on top of the mountains.
715 Four hundred thousand await daybreak.
God! what a pity the Franks do not know it! AOI.

56

The day passes, the night is still,
Charles, the mighty emperor, sleeps.
He dreamed he was at the main pass of Cize,
720 He was holding his ashen lance in his hands.
Count Ganelon seized it from him,
He twisted and brandished it so violently
That its splinters fly toward heaven.
Charles sleeps, he does not wake up.

57

725 After this vision he dreamed anew,
This time that he was in France, in his chapel, at Aix.
A fierce bear bit him on the right arm.
He saw a leopard coming from the direction of the Ardennes,
It attacks his body with great ferocity.
730 A hunting dog came down the steps from inside the hall,
Running toward Charles by leaps and bounds.
It slices off the bear's right ear,
It fights madly against the leopard.
The French say that there is a great battle,
735 They do not know which one of them will win it.
Charles sleeps, he did not wake up. AOI.

58

The night passes and the bright dawn appears.
Throughout the army . . .
The Emperor rides very fiercely.

740   "Seignurs barons," dist li emperere Carles,
      "Veez les porz e les destreiz passages:
      Kar me jugez ki ert en la rereguarde."
      Guenes respunt: "Rollant, cist miens fillastre,
      N'avez baron de si grant vasselage."
745   Quant l'ot li reis, fierement le reguardet,
      Si li ad dit: "Vos estes vifs diables,
      El cors vos est entree mortel rage!
      E ki serat devant mei en l'ansguarde?"
      Guenes respunt: "Oger de Denemarche,
750   N'avez barun ki mielz de lui la facet."

59

      Li quens Rollant, quant il s'oït juger,   AOI.
      Dunc ad parled a lei de chevaler:
      "Sire parastre, mult vos dei aveir cher,
      La rereguarde avez sur mei jugiet.
755   N'i perdrat Carles, li reis ki France tient,
      Men escïentre, palefreid ne destrer,
      Ne mul ne mule que deiet chevalcher,
      Ne n'i perdrat ne runcin ne sumer
      Que as espees ne seit einz eslegiet."
760   Guenes respunt: "Veir dites, jol sai bien."   AOI.

60

      Quant ot Rollant qu'il ert en la rereguarde,
      Ireement parlat a sun parastre:
      "Ahi! culvert, malvais hom de put aire,
      Quias le guant me caïst en la place,
765   Cume fist a tei le bastun devant Carle?"   AOI.

61

      "Dreiz emperere," dist Rollant le barun,
      "Dunez mei l'arc que vos tenez el poign.
      Men escïentre, nel me reproverunt
      Que il me chedet cum fist a Guenelun
770   De sa main destre, quant reçut le bastun."

740 "My lord barons," said Emperor Charles,
    "See the passes and the narrow defiles:
    "Help me decide who will be in the rearguard."
    Ganelon replies: "Roland, this stepson of mine,
    You have no other knight with such great courage."
745 When the King hears this, he looks at him fiercely,
    He said to him: "You're a living devil,
    A deadly frenzy has entered your body!
    And who will be before me in the vanguard?"
    Ganelon replies: "Ogier of Denmark,
750 You have no knight who can lead it better than he."

59

When Count Roland heard himself nominated,   AOI.
He spoke as a true knight:
"Sir stepfather, I am much indebted to you,
You have nominated me for the rearguard.
755 Charles, the king who rules France, shall not lose,
So long as I'm aware of it, a single palfrey or war-horse,
A single mule or jenny that must be ridden,
Nor shall he lose a single packhorse or sumpter
That shall not first have been disputed with swords."
760 Ganelon replies: "You speak the truth, I'm sure."   AOI.

60

Hearing that he will be in the rearguard,
Roland spoke angrily to his stepfather:
"Oh! you dirty son of a bitch,
Did you expect me to drop the gauntlet to the ground
765 The way you let the staff fall before Charles?"   AOI.

61

"Rightful Emperor," said the knight Roland,
"Give me the bow you hold in your hand.
So help me, they'll never have cause to reproach me
That I dropped it the way Ganelon did,
770 From his right hand, when he received the staff."

Li empereres en tint sun chef enbrunc,
Si duist sa barbe e detoerst sun gernun.
Ne poet muër que des oilz ne plurt.

62

Anprés iço i est Neimes venud.
775 Meillor vassal n'out en la curt de lui
E dist al rei: "Ben l'avez entendut,
Li quens Rollant, il est mult irascut.
La rereguarde est jugee sur lui,
N'avez baron ki jamais la remut.
780 Dunez li l'arc que vos avez tendut,
Si li truvez ki tres bien li aiut!"
Li reis li dunet, e Rollant l'a reçut.

63

Li empereres apelet ses niés Rollant:
"Bel sire niés, or savez veirement,
785 Demi mun host vos lerrai en present.
Retenez les, ço est vostre salvement."
Ço dit li quens: "Jo n'en ferai nïent,
Deus me cunfunde, se la geste en desment!
.XX. milie Francs retendrai ben vaillanz.
790 Passez les porz trestut soürement:
Ja mar crendrez nul hume a mun vivant!"

64

Li quens Rollant est muntet el destrer.   AOI.
Cuntre lui vient sis cumpainz Oliver,
Vint i Gerins e li proz quens Gerers
795 E vint i Otes, si i vint Berengers
E vint i Astors e Anseïs li veillz,
Vint i Gerart de Rossillon li fiers,
Venuz i est li riches dux Gaifiers.
Dist l'arcevesque: "Jo irai, par mun chef!"
800 "E jo od vos," ço dist li quens Gualters,

The Emperor kept his head bowed down,
He stroked his beard and twisted his moustache.
He cannot prevent the tears welling from his eyes.

62

After that Naimes came forward.
775 There was not a better knight at court than he,
And he said to the King: "You heard everything he said,
Count Roland is very angry.
He has been nominated for the rearguard,
No knight in your service can ever change that.
780 Give him the bow that you have strung,
But arrange for him to have very reliable companions!"
The King gives him the bow, Roland has received it.

63

The Emperor calls his nephew Roland:
"Dear nephew, sir, believe me when I say
785 That I will give half of my army over to you.
Keep these men, it will be your salvation."
The Count said: "I'll do no such thing,
I'll be damned if I'll act unworthily of my family!
I shall keep twenty thousand very brave Franks.
790 Cross the mountain passes with complete peace of mind:
You need fear no man while I'm alive!"

64

Count Roland has mounted his war-horse.   AOI.
His companion Oliver comes toward him,
Gerin and worthy Count Gerier came,
795 Oton came and Berengier also came,
Astor and old Anseïs came,
Fierce Gerard of Roussillon came,
Mighty Duke Gaifier came.
The Archbishop said: "I'll go, by my head!"
800 "I'm with you too," said Count Gautier,

51

"Hom sui Rollant, jo ne li dei faillir."
Entr'els eslisent .XX. milie chevalers.   AOI.

65

Li quens Rollant Gualter de l'Hum apelet:
"Pernez mil Francs de France, nostre tere,
805   Si purpernez les deserz e les tertres,
Que l'emperere nisun des soens n'i perdet."   AOI.
Respunt Gualter: "Pur vos le dei ben faire."
Od mil Franceis de France, la lur tere,
Gualter desrenget les destreiz e les tertres.
810   N'en descendrat pur malvaises nuveles
Enceis qu'en seient .VII.C. espees traites.
Reis Almaris del regne de Belferne
Une bataille lur livrat le jur pesme.

66

Halt sunt li pui e li val tenebrus,
815   Les roches bises, les destreiz merveillus.
Le jur passerent Franceis a grant dulur,
De .XV. lius en ot hom la rimur.
Puis que il venent a la Tere Majur,
Virent Guascuigne, la tere lur seignur.
820   Dunc le remembret des fius e des honurs
E des pulcele e des gentilz oixurs:
Cel nen i ad ki de pitet ne plurt.
Sur tuz le altres est Carles anguissus,
As porz d'Espaigne ad lesset sun nevold.
825   Pitet l'en prent, ne poet muër n'en plurt.   AOI.

67

Li .XII. per sunt remés en Espaigne.
.XX. milie Frrancs unt en lur cumpaigne,
N'en unt poür ne de murir dutance.
Li emperere s'en repairet en France,
830   Suz sun mantel en fait la cuntenance.
Dejuste lui li dux Neimes chevalchet

"I'm Roland's vassal, I must not fail him."
Between them they select twenty thousand knights.   AOI.

65

Count Roland calls Gautier de l'Hum:
"Take a thousand Franks from France, our land,
805 Patrol the deserts and the heights
So the Emperor will not lose a single one of his men."   AOI.
Gautier replies: "I'll do my utmost for you."
With a thousand Frenchmen from France, their land,
Gautier leads a detachment through the mountain passes and
elevations.
810 He will not descend when the news is bad
Before seven hundred swords have been drawn.
King Almaris of the kingdom of Belferne
Gave them a fierce battle that day.

66

The mountains are high and the valleys are shadowy,
815 The rocks dark, the defiles frightening.
That day, the French passed through, enduring great pain,
The groaning can be heard for fifteen leagues around.
Reaching the Fatherland,
They saw Gascony, their sovereign's land.
820 Then they are reminded of their fiefs and of their domains,
And of maidens and of noble spouses:
All eyes are brimming with tears of yearning.
Charles suffers anguish more than anyone else,
He has left his nephew in the Spanish pass.
825 He is suddenly distressed, he cannot help weeping.   AOI.

67

The Twelve Peers have remained in Spain.
Twenty thousand Franks accompany them,
They have no fear and are not afraid to die.
The Emperor is returning home to France.
830 Beneath his cloak, his face betrays his anguish.
Duke Naimes is riding beside him,

E dit al rei: "De quei avez pesance?"
Carles respunt: "Tort fait kil me demandet!
Si grant doel ai ne puis muër nel pleigne.
835 Par Guenelun serat destruite France.
Enoit m'avint un avisiun d'angele
Que entre mes puinz me depeçout ma hanste,
Chi ad juget mis nes a rereguarde.
Jo l'ai lesset en une estrange marche,
840 Deus! se jol pert, ja n'en avrai escange!" AOI.

68

Carles li magnes ne poet muër n'en plurt.
.C. milie Francs pur lui unt grant tendrur
E de Rollant merveilluse poür.
Guenes li fels en ad fait traïsun,
845 Del rei paien en ad oüd granz duns,
Or e argent, palies e ciclatuns,
Muls e chevals e cameilz e leuns.
Marsilies mandet d'Espaigne les baruns,
Cuntes, vezcuntes e dux e almaçurs,
850 Les amirafles e les filz as cunturs:
.IIII.C. milie en ajustet en .III. jurz.
En Sarraguce fait suner ses taburs.
Mahumet levent en la plus halte tur,
N'i ad paien nel prit e ne l'aort.
855 Puis si chevalchent, par mult grant cuntençun,
La Tere Certeine e les vals e les munz.
De cels de France virent les gunfanuns.
La rereguarde des .XII. cumpaignuns
Ne lesserat bataille ne lur dunt.

69

860 Li niés Marsilie, il est venuz avant
Sur un mulet od un bastun tuchant.
Dist a sun uncle belement en riant:
"Bel sire reis, jo vos ai servit tant,
Sin ai oüt e peines e ahans,
865 Faites batailles e vencues en champ:

And he says to the King: "What weighs upon your mind?"
Charles replies: "I wish you hadn't asked me!
I am suffering such anguish that I can't help showing it.
835 France will be destroyed by Ganelon.
Last night an angel appeared to me,
I dreamed that Ganelon was shattering the lance in my hands,
Now he has nominated my nephew for the rearguard.
I have left him exposed in dangerous country.
840 God! if I lose him, I'll not find anyone capable of replacing him!"
AOI.

68

Charlemagne cannot help weeping.
A hundred thousand Franks sympathize with him deeply
And feel terrifying fear for Roland.
The villain Ganelon has betrayed him,
845 He received huge bribes from the pagan king,
Gold and silver, silk cloths and brocades,
Mules and horses, camels and lions.
Marsile summons the barons of Spain,
The counts, viscounts, dukes, and almaçors,
850 The amirafles and the sons of the contors:
He assembles four hundred thousand in three days.
He orders his drummers to sound the alarm in Saragossa.
They hoist Mohammed up to the highest tower,
Every single pagan prays to him and adores him.
855 Then they ride, exerting themselves to the utmost,
Across Tere Certeine, through valleys, and over mountains.
They saw the ensigns of the men from France.
The rearguard of the twelve companions
Will not fail to give them battle.

69

860 Marsile's nephew came forward
On a mule, which he prodded with a stick.
Laughing heartily, he said to his uncle:
"Dear King, sire, I have served you such a long time,
And I have had so many cares and woes,
865 Fought and won so many battles in the field:

Dunez m'un feu, ço est le colp de Rollant!
Jo l'ocirai a mun espiet trenchant.
Se Mahumet me voelt estre guarant,
De tute Espaigne aquiterai les pans
870 Des porz d'Espaigne entresqu'a Durestant.
Las serat Carles, si recrerrunt si Franc,
Ja n'avrez mais guere en tut vostre vivant."
Li reis Marsilie l'en ad dunet le guant.   AOI.

70

Li niés Marsilies tient le guant en sun poign,
875 Sun uncle apelet de mult fiere raisun:
"Bel sire reis, fait m'avez un grant dun.
Eslisez mei .XII. de voz baruns,
Sim cumbatrai as .XII. cumpaignuns."
Tut premerein l'en respunt Falsaron,
880 Icil ert frere al rei Marsiliun:
"Bel sires niés, e jo e vos irum,
Ceste bataille veirement la ferum.
La rereguarde de la grant host Carlun,
Il est juget que nus les ocirum."   AOI.

71

885 Reis Corsalis, il est de l'altre part,
Barbarins est e mult de males arz.
Cil ad parlet a lei de bon vassal,
Pur tut l'or Deu ne volt estre cuard.
As vos poignant Malprimis de Brigant,
890 Plus curt a piet que ne fait un cheval.
Devant Marsilie cil s'escriet mult halt:
"Jo cunduirai mun cors en Rencesvals,
Se truis Rollant, ne lerrai que nel mat!"

72

Uns amurafles i ad de Balaguez,
895 Cors ad mult gent e le vis fier e cler.
Puis que il est sur sun cheval muntet,

Grant me a boon, the first blow against Roland!
I'll kill him with my sharp spear.
If Mohammed will protect me,
I shall recover every portion of Spanish territory
870   From the Spanish passes to Durestant.
Charles will be worn out and his Franks will forsake combat,
You will never have war for the rest of your life."
King Marsile gave the gauntlet to him.   AOI.

70

Marsile's nephew holds the gauntlet in his hand,
875   He makes a very fierce speech to his uncle:
"Dear King, sire, you have bestowed a great favor on me.
Select twelve of your barons for me
And I'll fight the twelve companions."
The first to reply to him was Falsaron,
880   Brother of King Marsile:
"Dear nephew, sir, you and I will go together,
We'll fight this battle properly.
The rearguard of Charles's great army,
We shall kill them all, the matter is settled."   AOI.

71

885   King Corsalis came forward from another direction,
He is a Berber and steeped in the black arts.
He spoke as a good knight,
He would not be a coward for all God's gold.
Here now is Malprimes of Brigant spurring forward,
890   He runs faster on foot than any horse.
He cries out in a loud voice before Marsile:
"I'll betake myself to Roncevaux,
If I find Roland, I shall not fail to bring him low!"

72

There is an amurafle there from Balaguer,
895   He has a well-proportioned body and his face is fierce and open.
When he is mounted on his horse,

Mult se fait fiers de ses armes porter.
De vasselage est il ben alosez,
Fust chrestïens, asez oüst barnet.
900 Devant Marsilie cil en est escriet:
"En Rencesvals irai mun cors juër;
Se truis Rollant, de mort serat finet
E Oliver e tuz les .XII. pers.
Franceis murrunt a doel e a viltiet.
905 Carles li magnes velz est e redotez,
Recreanz ert de sa guerre mener,
Si nus remeindrat Espaigne en quitedet."
Li reis Marsilie mult l'en ad mercïet.   AOI.

73

Uns almaçurs i ad de Moriane,
910 N'ad plus felun en la tere d'Espaigne.
Devant Marsilie ad faite sa vantance:
"En Rencesvals guierai ma cumpaigne,
.XX. milie ad escuz e a lances.
Se trois Rollant, de mort li duins fiance,
915 Jamais n'ert jor que Carles ne se pleignet."   AOI.

74

D'altre part est Turgis de Turteluse,
Cil est uns quens, si est la citet sue.
De chrestïens voelt faire male vode.
Devant Marsilie as altres si s'ajustet.
920 Ço dist al rei: "Ne vos esmaiez unches!
Plus valt Mahum que seint Perre de Rume,
Se lui servez, l'onur del camp ert nostre.
En Rencesvals a Rollant irai juindre,
De mort n'avrat guarantisun pur hume.
925 Veez m'espee, ki est e bone e lunge:
A Durendal jo la metrai encuntre,
Asez orrez laquele irat desure.
Franceis murrunt, si a nus s'abandunent.
Carles li velz avrat e deol e hunte,
930 Jamais en tere ne porterat curone."

He bears his arms very fiercely.
He is renowned for his bravery,
If he were a Christian, he would be a very worthy knight.
900 He cried out in front of Marsile:
"I'll go risk my life at Roncevaux;
If I find Roland, he shall be put to death
With Oliver and every last one of the Twelve Peers.
The French shall suffer an agonizing and shameful death.
905 Charlemagne is old and decrepit,
He will forsake the war he is waging,
He will abandon Spain to us and leave us in peace."
King Marsile thanked him very much.   AOI.

73

There is an almaçor from Moriane,
910 There is no greater villain in the land of Spain.
He made his boast in front of Marsile:
"I shall lead my company to Roncevaux,
Twenty thousand with shields and lances.
If I find Roland, I give my oath that he shall die,
915 A day shall not go by that Charles will not lament".   AOI.

74

From another direction comes Turgis of Turtelose,
He is a count and the city is his.
He seeks the destruction of the Christians.
He joins the others in front of Marsile.
920 He said to the King: "Do not be dismayed!
Mohammed is superior to Saint Peter of Rome,
If you serve him, we shall be left in possession of the field.
I shall seek out Roland at Roncevaux,
No man shall preserve him from death.
925 See my sword, which is good and long:
I shall test it against Durendal,
You shall hear to your satisfaction which one will triumph.
The French shall die if they risk battle with us.
Old Charles shall be in pain and disgrace,
930 He shall never wear a crown on this earth."

75

De l'altre part est Escremiz de Valterne,
Sarrazins est, si est sue la tere.
Devant Marsilie s'escriet en la presse:
"En Rencesvals irai l'orgoill desfaire.
935   Se trois Rollant, n'en porterat la teste,
Ne Oliver, ki les altres cadelet.
Li .XII. per tuit sunt jugez a perdre.
Franceis murrunt e France en ert deserte,
De bons vassals avrat Carles suffraite."   AOI.

76

940   D'altre part est uns paiens, Esturganz,
Estramariz i est, un soens cumpainz,
Cil sunt felun, traïtur suduiant.
Ço dist Marsilie: "Seignurs, venez avant!
En Rencesvals irez as porz passant,
945   Si aiderez a cunduire ma gent."
E cil respundent: "A vostre comandement!
Nus asaldrum Oliver e Rollant,
Li .XII. per n'avrunt de mort guarant.
Noz espees sunt bones e trenchant,
950   Nus les feruns vermeilles de chald sanc.
Franceis murrunt, Carles en ert dolent,
Tere Majur vos metrum en present.
Venez i, reis, sil verrez veirement:
L'empereor vos metrum en present."

77

955   Curant i vint Margariz de Sibilie,
Cil tient la tere entrequ'as Cazmarine.
Pur sa beltet dames li sunt amies,
Cele nel veit vers lui ne s'esclargisset,
Quant ele le veit, ne poet muër ne riet.
960   N'i ad paien de tel chevalerie.
Vint en la presse, sur les altres s'escriet
E dist al rei: "Ne vos esmaiez mie!
En Rencesvals irai Rollant ocire,

75

From another direction comes Escremis of Valterne,
He is a Saracen and the land is his.
He cried out in the crowd pressing in front of Marsile:
"I shall go to Roncevaux to destroy this evil.
935 If I find Roland, he shall not escape with his head,
Oliver, too, who commands the others.
The Twelve Peers are all condemned to death.
The French shall die and France shall be deserted,
Charles will be at a loss for good knights."   AOI.

76

940 From another direction comes a pagan, Esturgant,
One of his companions, Estramaris, is there too,
They are villains, perfidious traitors.
Marsile said: "My lords, come forward!
You shall go to the pass at Roncevaux,
945 And you shall help guide my army."
And they replied: "At your command!
We shall attack Oliver and Roland,
The Twelve Peers shall have no safeguard against death.
Our swords are good and sharp,
950 We'll make them red with hot blood.
The French shall die, Charles shall be plunged into sorrow,
We'll deliver the Fatherland over to you.
Come along, King, and you'll see it for yourself:
We'll deliver the Emperor over to you."

77

955 Margariz of Seville came rushing up,
He rules the land up to the Cazmarines.
The women love him for his beauty,
Not one of them sees him without becoming all aglow,
When she sees him she cannot help becoming all smiles.
960 No other pagan has such knightly qualities.
He joined the crowd and, his voice booming over the others,
He said to the King: "Do not be dismayed!
I shall go slay Roland at Roncevaux,

Ne Oliver n'en porterat la vie;
965   Li .XII. per sunt remés en martirie.
Veez m'espee, ki d'or est enheldie,
Si la tramist li amiralz de Primes.
Jo vos plevis qu'en vermeill sanc ert mise.
Franceis murrunt e France en ert hunie.
970   Carles li velz a la barbe flurie,
Jamais n'ert jurn qu'il n'en ait doel e ire.
Jusqu'a un an avrum France saisie,
Gesir porrum el burc de seint Denise."
Li reis paiens parfundement l'enclinet.   AOI.

78

975   De l'altre part est Chernubles de Munigre,
Josqu'a la tere si chevoel li balient.
Greignor fais portet, par giu, quant il s'enveiset,
Que .IIII. mulez ne funt, quant il sumeient.
Icele tere, ço dit, dun il esteit,
980   Soleill n'i luist ne blet n'i poet pas creistre,
Pluie n'i chet, rusee n'i adeiset,
Piere n'i ad que tute ne seit neire:
Dient alquanz que diables i meignent.
Ce dist Chernubles: "Ma bone espee ai ceinte,
985   En Rencesvals jo la teindrai vermeille.
Se trois Rollant li proz enmi ma veie,
Se ne l'asaill, dunc ne faz jo que creire.
Si cunquerrai Durendal od la meie.
Franceis murrunt e France en ert deserte."
990   A icez moz li .XII. per s'alient.
Itels .C. milie Sarrazins od els meinent
Ki de bataille s'arguënt e hasteient,
Vunt s'aduber desuz une sapide.

79

Paien s'adubent des osbercs sarazineis,
995   Tuit li plusur en sunt dublez en treis.
Lacent lor elmes mult bons sarraguzeis,
Ceignent espees de l'acer vianeis.

And Oliver shall not escape with his life either;
965 The Twelve Peers stay but for their own martyrdom.
See my sword, whose hilt is made of gold,
The Emir of Primes sent it.
I swear to you that it will be plunged into red blood.
The French shall die and France shall be disgraced.
970 Old Charles with his white beard
Will never be without sorrow and anger.
In a year's time we shall be masters of France,
We shall be able to rest at Saint-Denis-en-France."
The pagan king bows deeply to him.   AOI.

78

975 From another direction comes Chernuble of Munigre,
His hair sweeps down to the ground.
For amusement and sport, he carries a greater weight
Than do four mules when they bear a load.
The land from whence he came, they say,
980 No sun shines there nor can wheat grow,
Rain does not fall, nor dew touch the ground,
All the stones are completely black:
Some say that devils reside there.
Chernuble said: "I am wearing my good sword,
985 I shall stain it red at Roncevaux.
If I find worthy Roland on my way
And do not attack him, then consider me to be a worthless braggart.
But I shall conquer Durendal with my sword.
The French shall die and France will be deserted."
990 As soon as he has spoken, the Twelve Peers assemble.
They take a hundred thousand Saracens along with them,
Who jostle and prod one another in their eagerness to start the battle,
They go arm themselves in a pine grove.

79

The pagans arm themselves with Saracen hauberks,
995 Nearly all have three layers of mail.
They lace their very strong helmets made in Saragossa,
Put on their steel swords made in Vienna.

Escuz unt genz, espiez valentineis,
E gunfanuns blancs e blois e vermeilz.
1000 Laissent les muls e tuz les palefreiz,
Es destrers muntent, si chevalchent estreiz.
Clers fut li jurz e bels fut li soleilz,
N'unt guarnement que tut ne reflambeit.
Sunent mil grailles por ço que plus bel seit,
1005 Granz est la noise, si l'oïrent Franceis.
Dist Oliver: "Sire cumpainz, ce crei,
De Sarrazins purum bataille aveir."
Respont Rollant: "E Deus la nus otreit!
Ben devuns ci estre pur nostre rei:
1010 Pur sun seignor deit hom susfrir destreiz
E endurer e granz chalz e granz freiz,
Sin deit hom perdre e del quir e del peil.
Or guart chascuns que granz colps i empleit
Que malvaise cançun de nus chantet ne seit!
1015 Paien unt tort e chrestïens unt dreit.
Malvaise essample n'en serat ja de mei." AOI.

80

Oliver est desur un pui . . .
Guardet su destre par mi un val herbus,
Si veit venir cele gent paienur,
1020 Sin apelat Rollant, sun cumpaignun:
"Devers Espaigne vei venir tel bruur,
Tanz blancs osbercs, tanz elmes flambius!
Icist ferunt nos Franceis grant irur.
Guenes le sout, li fel, li traïtur,
1025 Ki nus jugat devant l'empereür."
"Tais, Oliver," li quens Rollant respunt,
"Mis parrastre est, ne voeill que mot en suns."

81

Oliver est desur un pui muntet.
Or veit il ben d'Espaigne le regnet
1030 E Sarrazins, ki tant sunt asemblez.
Luisent cil elme, ki ad or sunt gemmez,

64

They have sturdy shields, spears made in Valence,
And white, blue, and red ensigns.
1000 They set aside the mules and all the palfreys,
They mount their war-horses and ride in close order.
The day was clear and the sun was shining,
Every bit of their equipment is glittering bright.
They sound a thousand bugles to make a fine impression,
1005 The noise is great and the French heard it.
Oliver said: "Companion, sir, I believe
We may have a battle with the Saracens on our hands."
Roland replies: "May God grant it to us!
We must make a stand here for our king:
1010 One must suffer hardships for one's lord
And endure great heat and great cold,
One must also lose hide and hair.
Now let each see to it that he employ great blows,
So that bad songs not be sung about us!
1015 Pagans are in the wrong and Christians are in the right.
I shall never be cited as a bad example." AOI.

80

Oliver is on a hilltop . . .
He looks to his right down a grassy valley,
He sees the pagan army coming,
1020 So he calls to his companion, Roland:
"I see such a dazzling reflection moving toward us from Spain,
So many gleaming hauberks, so many blazing helmets!
Our French will become enraged by this.
Ganelon, the villain, the traitor, knew this,
1025 He nominated us before the Emperor."
"Be still, Oliver," Count Roland replies,
"He's my stepfather, I don't want you to breathe another word
     about him."

81

Oliver has climbed up a hill.
Now he can see the kingdom of Spain very well
1030 And the Saracens, who are assembled in such great numbers.
The helmets, whose gold is wrought with gems, are all shiny,

E cil escuz e cil osbercs safrez
E cil espiez, cil gunfanun fermez.
Sul les escheles ne poet il acunter,
1035 Tant en i ad que mesure n'en set.
E lui meïsme en est mult esguaret.
Cum il einz pout, del pui est avalet,
Vint as Franceis, tut lur ad acuntet.

82

Dist Oliver: "Jo ai paiens veüz,
1040 Unc mais nuls hom en tere n'en vit plus.
Cil devant sunt .C. milie ad escuz,
Helmes laciez e blancs osbercs vestuz;
Dreites cez hanstes, luisent cil espiet brun.
Bataille avrez, unches mais tel ne fut.
1045 Seignurs Franceis, de Deu aiez vertut!
El camp estez, que ne seium vencuz!"
Dient Franceis: "Dehet ait ki s'en fuit!
Ja pur murir ne vus en faldrat uns."   AOI.

83

Dist Oliver: "Paien unt grant esforz,
1050 De noz Franceis m'i semblet aveir mult poi!
Cumpaign Rollant, kar sunez vostre corn,
Si l'orrat Carles, si returnerat l'ost."
Respunt Rollant: "Jo fereie que fols!
En dulce France en perdreie mun los.
1055 Sempres ferrai de Durendal granz colps,
Sanglant en ert li branz entresqu'a l'or.
Felun paien mar i vindrent as porz,
Jo vos plevis, tuz sunt jugez a mort."   AOI.

84

"Cumpainz Rollant, l'olifan car sunez,
1060 Si l'orrat Carles, ferat l'ost returner,
Succurrat nos li reis od sun barnet."
Respont Rollant: "Ne placet Damnedeu

As are the shields and saffron hauberks,
The spears and mounted standards.
He cannot even count the divisions,
1035 There are so many he cannot estimate their number.
Within himself he is very bewildered by this.
He descended the hill as quickly as he could,
He came to the French and told them everything.

82

Oliver said: "I have seen pagans,
1040 No man on earth has ever seen more of them.
In the forefront there are a hundred thousand men with shields,
Helmets laced on and wearing shiny hauberks;
The shafts are straight, the burnished spears are shiny.
You'll have a battle, there will never have been one like it.
1045 French lords, may you have strength from God!
Make a stand in the field, let us not be vanquished!"
The French say: "Damn anyone who flees!
Not a single one of us will fail you even if it means death."   AOI.

83

Oliver said: "The pagans have a huge army,
1050 Our French, it seems to me, are in mighty small number!
Comrade Roland, do sound your horn,
Charles will hear it and the army will turn back."
Roland replies: "I would be behaving like a fool!
I would lose my good name in fair France.
1055 I shall immediately strike great blows with Durendal,
Its blade will be bloody up to the golden hilt.
The vile pagans shall rue the day they came to the pass,
I swear to you, all are condemned to death."   AOI.

84

"Comrade Roland, do sound the oliphant,
1060 Charles will hear it and he will make the army turn back,
The King with all his knights will come to our assistance."
Roland replies: "May it not please the Lord God

Que mi parent pur mei seient blasmet
Ne France dulce ja cheet en viltet!
1065 Einz i ferrai de Durendal asez,
Ma bone espee que ai ceint al costet,
Tut en verrez le brant ensanglentet.
Felun paien mar i sunt asemblez,
Jo vos plevis, tuz sunt a mort livrez."   AOI.

85

1070 Cumpainz Rollant, sunez vostre olifan,
Si l'orrat Carles, ki est as porz passant.
Je vos plevis, ja returnerunt Franc."
"Ne placet Deu," ço li respunt Rollant,
"Que ço seit dit de nul hume vivant,
1075 Ne pur paien, que ja seie cornant!
Ja n'en avrunt reproece mi parent.
Quant jo serai en la bataille grant
E jo ferrai e mil colps e .VII. cenz,
De Durendal verrez l'acer sanglent.
1080 Franceis sunt bon, si ferrunt vassalment,
Ja cil d'Espaigne n'avrunt de mort guarant."

86

Dist Oliver: "D'iço ne sai jo blasme.
Jo ai veüt les Sarrazins d'Espaigne,
Cuverz en sunt li val e les muntaignes
1085 E li lariz e trestutes les plaignes.
Granz sunt les oz de cele gent estrange,
Nus i avum mult petite cumpaigne."
Respunt Rollant: "Mis talenz en est graigne.
Ne placet Damnedeu ne ses angles
1090 Que ja pur mei perdet sa valur France!
Melz voeill murir que huntage me venget.
Pur ben ferir l'emperere plus nos aimet."

87

Rollant est proz e Oliver est sage:
Ambedui unt meveillus vasselage,

That my kinsmen incur reproaches on my account,
Or that fair France should ever fall into disgrace!
1065 First I'll strike hard with Durendal,
My good sword, which I am wearing at my side,
You'll see its blade all bloody.
The vile pagans shall rue the day they assembled,
I swear to you, all are doomed to die." AOI.

85

1070 "Comrade Roland, sound your oliphant,
Charles, who is going through the pass, will hear it.
Then, I promise you, the Franks will return."
"May it not please God," Roland replies to him,
"That it be said by any man alive,
1075 Nor by any pagan, that I ever sound the horn!
My kinsmen shall never incur reproaches.
When I shall be in the great battle,
Striking a thousand and seven hundred blows,
You'll see Durendal's steel all blood-stained.
1080 The French are reliable and they will strike courageously,
Those from Spain shall have no safeguard against death."

86

Oliver said: "I can't believe there'd be any blame in what I propose.
I have seen the Saracens from Spain,
The valleys and mountains are covered with them,
1085 The hillsides, too, and all the plains.
The armies of that foreign people are huge,
We have a mighty small company."
Roland replies: "My determination is greater because of it.
May it not please the Lord God nor his angels
1090 That France lose its worth on my account!
I'd rather die than be disgraced.
The Emperor loves us more when we strike well."

87

Roland is worthy and Oliver is wise:
Both have amazing courage,

1095 Puis que il sunt as chevals e as armes,
　　 Ja pur murir n'eschiverunt bataille;
　　 Bon sunt li cunte e lur paroles haltes.
　　 Felun paien par grant irur chevalchent.
　　 Dist Oliver: "Rollant, veez en alques!
1100 Cist nus sunt pres, mais trop nus est loinz Carles.
　　 Vostre olifan, suner vos nel deignastes,
　　 Fust i li reis, n'i oüssum damage.
　　 Guardez amunt devers les porz d'Espaigne:
　　 Veeir poëz, dolente est la rereguarde,
1105 Ki ceste fait, jamais n'en ferat altre."
　　 Respunt Rollant: "Ne dites tel ultrage!
　　 Mal seit del coer ki el piz se cuardet!
　　 Nus remeindrum en estal en la place,
　　 Par nos i ert e li colps e li caples."　　 AOI.

88

1110 Quant Rollant veit que la bataille serat,
　　 Plus se fait fiers que leon ne leupart.
　　 Franceis escriet, Oliver apelat:
　　 "Sire cumpainz, amis, nel dire ja!
　　 Li emperere, ki Franceis nos laisat,
1115 Itels .XX. milie en mist a une part,
　　 Sun escïentre, n'en i out un cuard.
　　 Pur sun seignur deit hom susfrir granz mals
　　 E endurer e forz freiz e granz chalz,
　　 Sin deit hom perdre del sanc e de la char.
1120 Fier de la lance e jo de Durendal,
　　 Ma bone espee, que li reis me dunat.
　　 Se jo i moerc, dire poet ki l'avrat
　　 . . . que ele fut a noble vassal."

89

　　 D'altre part est li arcevesques Turpin,
1125 Sun cheval broche e muntet un lariz.
　　 Franceis apelet, un sermun lur ad dit:
　　 "Seignurs baruns, Carles nus laissat ci,
　　 Pur nostre rei devum nus ben murir:

1095 When they are on horseback and armed,
They shall not avoid battle even if it means death;
Both counts are worthy and their words noble.
The vile pagans ride on like fury.
Oliver said: "Roland, see the first of them coming!
1100 They're close to us and Charles is very far away.
You did not deign to sound your oliphant,
Were the King here, we would have suffered no harm.
Look up toward the Spanish pass:
You can see, the rearguard is to be pitied,
1105 The ones who form it can never form another."
Roland replies: "Don't say such an outrageous thing!
Damn the heart that turns coward in the breast!
We shall make a stand in this place,
The first blow and the first cut will be ours."   AOI.

88

1110 When Roland sees the battle about to begin,
He becomes fiercer than a lion or leopard.
He cries out to the French, he called to Oliver:
"Comrade, sir, friend, don't ever say that!
The Emperor, who left the French in our care,
1115 Set apart twenty thousand men of such a sort
That, in his judgment, there was no coward among them.
One must suffer great hardships for one's lord
And endure severe cold and great heat,
And one must also lose blood and flesh.
1120 Strike with your lance and I with Durendal,
My good sword given to me by the King.
If I die, he who will have it next can say
... that it belonged to a noble knight."

89

From another direction comes Archbishop Turpin,
1125 He spurs his horse and climbs a hill.
He calls the French, he preached a sermon to them:
"My lord barons, Charles left us here,
We must die well for our King:

71

Chrestïentet aidez a sustenir!
1130 Bataille avrez, vos en estes tuz fiz,
Kar a voz oilz veez les Sarrazins.
Clamez voz culpes, si preiez Deu mercit!
Asoldrai vos pur voz anmes guarir.
Se vos murez, esterez seinz martirs,
1135 Sieges avrez el greignor pareïs."
Franceis decendent, a tere se sunt mis,
E l'arcevesque de Deu les beneïst:
Par penitence les cumandet a ferir.

90

Franceis se drecent, si se metent sur piez.
1140 Ben sunt asols e quites de lur pecchez,
E l'arcevesque de Deu les ad seignez,
Puis sunt muntez sur lur curanz destrers.
Adobez sunt a lei de chevalers
E de bataille sunt tuit apareillez.
1145 Li quens Rollant apelet Oliver:
"Sire cumpainz, mult ben le savïez
Que Guenelun nos ad tuz espïez;
Pris en ad or e aveir e deners.
Li emperere nos devreit ben venger.
1150 Li reis Marsilie de nos ad fait marchet,
Mais as espees l'estuvrat esleger."   AOI.

91

As porz d'Espaigne en est passet Rollant
Sur Veillantif, sun bon cheval curant.
Portet ses armes, mult li sunt avenanz.
1155 Mais sun espiet vait li bers palmeiant,
Cuntre le ciel vait la mure turnant,
Laciet en su un gunfanun tut blanc,
Les renges li batent josqu'as mains.
Cors ad mult gent, le vis cler e riant.
1160 Sun cumpaignun aprés le vait sivant
E cil de France le cleiment a guarant.
Vers Sarrazins reguardet fierement

Help sustain Christianity!
1130 You are to fight a battle, you are all certain of that,
For you see the Saracens before your eyes.
Say your confessions and pray for God's mercy!
I will absolve you to save your souls.
If you die, you'll be holy martyrs,
1135 You'll have seats in highest Paradise."
The French dismount, they knelt to the ground,
And the Archbishop blessed them in God's name.
For a penance, he commands them to strike.

90

The French stand up, they rise to their feet.
1140 They are completely absolved and free from their sins,
And the Archbishop signed them in God's name,
Then they mounted their swift war-horses.
They are armed like knights
And are fully equipped for battle.
1145 Count Roland calls to Oliver:
"Comrade, sir, you surmised quite correctly
That Ganelon betrayed us all;
He took gold and riches and pieces of silver.
The Emperor will surely avenge us well.
1150 King Marsile made a deal for our lives,
But he shall have to dispute them with swords."   AOI.

91

Roland has gone into the Spanish pass
On Veillantif, his good swift horse.
He bears his arms, they are very becoming to him.
1155 As for his spear, the knight brandishes it,
He twirls the tip against the sky,
A pure white ensign is lashed to its point,
The fringes flap against his hands.
He has a well-proportioned body, his face is open and smiling.
1160 His companion follows right behind him,
And the men of France call him their protector.
He looks fiercely toward the Saracens

73

E vers Franceis humeles e dulcement,
Si lur ad dit un mot curteisement:
1165 "Seignurs barons, suëf pas alez tenant!
Cist paien vont grant martirie querant.
Encoi avrum un eschec bel e gent,
Nuls reis de France n'out unkes si vaillant."
A cez paroles vunt les oz ajustant.   AOI.

92

1170 Dist Oliver: "N'ai cure de parler.
Vostre olifan ne deignastes suner,
Ne de Carlun mie vos n'en avez.
Il n'en set mot, n'i ad culpes li bers,
Cil ki la sunt ne funt mie a blasmer.
1175 Kar chevalchez a quanque vos puëz!
Seignors baruns, el camp vos retenez!
Pur Deu vos pri, ben seiez purpensez
De colps ferir, de receivre e de duner!
L'enseigne Carle n'i devum ublïer."
1180 A icest mot sunt Franceis escriet.
Ki dunc oïst Munjoie demander,
De vasselage li poüst remembrer.
Puis si chevalchent, Deus! par si grant fiertet!
Brochent ad ait pur le plus tost aler,
1185 Si vunt ferir, que fereient il el?
E Sarrazins nes unt mie dutez;
Francs e paiens, as les vus ajustez.

93

Li niés Marsilie, il ad a num Aelroth,
Tut premereins chevalchet devant l'ost.
1190 De noz Franceis vait disant si mals moz:
"Feluns Franceis, hoi justerez as noz.
Traït vos ad ki a guarder vos out:
Fols est li reis ki vos laissat as porz.
Enquoi perdrat France dulce sun los,
1195 Charles li magnes le destre braz del cors."
Quant l'ot Rollant, Deus! si grant doel en out!

74

And amicably and gently toward the French,
And he spoke to them in comradely fashion:
1165 "My lord barons, move forward at a slow trot!
These pagans are heading for a great massacre.
Today we shall have a fine and noble battle,
No king of France ever had such a worthy challenge."
As he speaks, the armies close in.   AOI.

92

1170 Oliver said: "I don't feel like talking.
You did not deign to sound your oliphant,
So you see no sign of Charles.
He knows nothing about it, the worthy man is not at fault,
Those who are with him over there are not to be blamed.
1175 Now ride with all your might!
My lord barons, keep the field!
I beseech you in God's name, be completely absorbed
In striking blows, in giving and taking!
We must not forget Charles's battle cry."
1180 As soon as he has spoken, the French cry out.
Anyone having heard "Monjoie!" shouted on that occasion
Would remember true courage.
Then they ride, God! at such a furious pace!
They dig their spurs in vigorously to go as fast as they can,
1185 They go to strike, what else could they do?
And the Saracens were not afraid of them;
See now Franks and pagans joining battle.

93

Marsile's nephew, whose name is Aelroth,
Rides out in front of the army.
1190 He says very insulting words about our French:
"Vile Frenchmen, today you are going to close with our men.
The one who was supposed to protect you has betrayed you:
The king who left you in the pass is contemptible.
Today fair France shall lose its good name
1195 And Charlemagne, the right arm from his body."
When Roland hears him, God! how it hurts him!

Sun cheval brochet, laiset curre a esforz,
Vait le ferir li quens quanque il pout.
L'escut li freint e l'osberc li desclot,
1200 Trenchet le piz, si li briset les os,
Tute l'eschine li desevret del dos,
Od sun espiet l'anme li getet fors,
Enpeint le ben, fait li brandir le cors,
Pleine sa hanste del cheval l'abat mort,
1205 En dous meitiez li ad briset le col.
Ne leserat, ço dit, que n'i parolt:
"Ultre, culvert! Carles n'est mie fol,
Ne traïsun unkes amer ne volt:
Il fist que proz qu'il nus laisad as porz,
1210 Oi n'en perdrat France dulce sun los.
Ferez i, Francs, nostre est li premers colps!
Nos avum dreit, mais cist glutun unt tort." AOI.

94

Un duc i est, si ad num Falsaron,
Icil er frere al rei Marsiliun,
1215 Il tint la tere Dathan e Habirun.
Suz cel nen at plus encrisme felun.
Entre les dous oilz mult out large le front,
Grant demi pied mesurer i pout hom.
Asez ad doel quant vit mort sun nevold,
1220 Ist de la prese, si se met en bandun
E se s'escriet l'enseigne paienor.
Envers Franceis est mult cuntrarius:
"Enquoi perdrat France dulce s'onur!"
Ot le Oliver, sin ad mult grant irur.
1225 Le cheval brochet des oriez esperuns,
Vait le ferir en guise de baron.
L'escut li freint e l'osberc li derumpt,
El cors li met les pans del gunfanun,
Pleine sa hanste l'abat mort des arçuns.
1230 Guardet a tere, veit gesir le glutun,
Si li ad dit par mult fiere raison:
"De voz manaces, culvert, jo n'ai essoign.
Ferez i, Francs, kar tres ben les veintrum!"
Munjoie escriet, ço est l'enseigne Carlun. AOI.

He spurs his horse, he lets him run full speed,
The Count goes to strike him with all his might.
He smashes his shield and tears open his hauberk,
1200 Cuts into his breast and shatters his bones,
He severs his spine from his back,
He thrusts out his soul with his spear,
He sticks it deeply into him, he impales his whole body,
Running him through, he throws him dead from his horse,
1205 He has broken his neck in two halves.
He will not be through, he says, until he speaks to him:
"Away with you, scoundrel! Charles is not contemptible
And does not care for treachery:
He who left us in the pass did a wise thing.
1210 Today fair France shall not lose its good name.
Strike, Franks, the first blow is ours!
We are in the right and these wretches are in the wrong." AOI.

94

There is a duke there named Falsaron,
He was the brother of King Marsile,
1215 He ruled the land of Dathan and Abiram.
There is no more hardened criminal on the face of the earth.
The space between his two eyes was very large,
It measures a full half-foot.
He was very distressed when he saw his nephew killed,
1220 He leaves the melee, takes on all comers,
And shouts the pagan war cry.
He is very insulting toward the French:
"Today fair France will lose its honor!"
Oliver hears him and has a terrible fit of anger.
1225 He urges his horse on with his golden spurs,
He goes to strike him as a true knight.
He smashes his shield and rips open his hauberk,
He forces the tails of his ensign into his body,
Running him through, he throws him dead from his saddle.
1230 He looks on the ground, sees the wretch lying there,
He speaks to him very fiercely:
"I am none the worse off, scoundrel, because of your threats.
Strike, Franks, for we shall vanquish them in stunning fashion!"
He shouts "Monjoie!", Charles's battle cry. AOI.

95

1235 Uns reis i est, si ad num Corsablix,
Barbarins est, d'un estrage païs.
Si apelad le altres Sarrazins:
"Ceste bataille ben la puum tenir,
Kar de Franceis i ad asez petit.
1240 Cels ki ci sunt devum aveir mult vil,
Ja pur Charles n'i ert un sul guarit,
Or est le jur qu'els estuvrat murir."
Ben l'entendit li arcvesques Turpin,
Suz ciel n'at hume que tant voeillet haïr.
1245 Sun cheval brochet des esperuns d'or fin,
Par grant vertut si l'est alet ferir.
L'escut li freinst, l'osberc li descumfist,
Sun grant espiet par mi le cors li mist,
Empeint le ben, que mort le fait brandir,
1250 Pleine sa hanste l'abat mort el chemin.
Guardet arere, veit le glutun gesir,
Ne laisserat que n'i parolt, ço dit:
"Culvert paien, vos i avez mentit!
Carles, mi sire, nus est guarant tuz dis,
1255 Nostre Franceis n'unt talent de fuïr.
Voz cumpaignuns feruns trestuz restifs,
Nuveles vos di: mort vos estoet susfrir.
Ferez, Franceis, nul de vus ne s'ublit!
Cist premer colp est nostre, Deu mercit!"
1260 Munjoie escriet por le camp retenir.

96

E Gerins fiert Malprimis de Brigal.
Sis bons escuz un dener ne li valt,
Tute li freint la bucle de cristal,
L'une meitiet li turnet cuntreval.
1265 L'osberc li rumpt entresque a la charn,
Sun bon espiet enz el cors li enbat.
Li paiens chet cuntreval a un quat,
L'anme de lui en portet Sathanas.   AOI.

95

1235   There is a king there named Corsablix,
       He is a Berber from a foreign land.
       He called to the other Saracens:
       "We can fight this battle well,
       For there are very few Frenchmen.
1240   We must show great contempt for the men before us here,
       Charles shall never be able to save a single one of them,
       Today is the day they must die."
       Archbishop Turpin heard him well,
       There is no one on earth whom he bears greater ill will.
1245   He urges his horse on with his pure gold spurs,
       He went to strike him with great force.
       He smashes his shield and rips apart his hauberk,
       He plunges his great spear through his middle,
       He sticks it deeply into him, impaling him dead,
1250   Running him through, he throws him dead on the road.
       He looks back and sees the wretch lying there,
       He will not be through, he says, until he speaks to him:
       "Dirty pagan, you lied!
       My lord Charles is ever our safeguard,
1255   Our French have no intention of fleeing.
       We shall make your companions rest in peace,
       I have news for you: You must suffer death.
       Strike, Frenchmen, let none of you forget his duty!
       This first blow is ours, thank God!"
1260   He cries "Monjoie!" to hold the field.

96

       And Gerin strikes Malprimes of Brigal.
       His good shield is not worth a penny to him,
       He smashes its crystal boss,
       He lops off half of it, which falls to the ground.
1265   He rips open his hauberk down to the flesh,
       He thrusts his good spear into his body.
       The pagan falls down in a heap,
       Satan carries away his soul.   AOI.

97

E sis cumpainz Gerers fiert l'amurafle,
1270 L'escut li freint e l'osberc li desmailet,
Sun bon espiet li met en la curaille,
Empeint le bien, par mi le cors li passet,
Que mort l'abat el camp, pleine sa hanste.
Dist Oliver: "Gente est nostre bataille!"

98

1275 Sansun li dux, il vait ferir l'almaçur,
L'escut li freinst, ki est a flurs e ad or,
Li bons osbercs ne li est guarant prod,
Trenchet li le coer, le firie e le pulmun,
Que mort l'abat, qui qu'en peist u qui nun.
1280 Dist l'arcevesque: "Cist colp est de baron!"

99

E Anseïs laiset le cheval curre,
Si vait ferir Turgis de Turteluse,
L'escut li freint desuz l'oree bucle,
De sun osberc li derumpit les dubles,
1285 Del bon espiet el cors li met la mure,
Empeinst le ben, tut le fer li mist ultre,
Pleine sa hanste el camp mort le tresturnet.
Ço dist Rollant: "Cist colp est de produme!"

100

Et Engelers, li Guascuinz de Burdele,
1290 Sun cheval brochet, si li laschet la resne,
Si vait ferir Escremiz de Valterne,
L'escut del col li freint e escantelet,
De sun osberc li rumpit la ventaille,
Sil fiert el piz entre les dous furceles,
1295 Pleine sa hanste l'abat mort de la sele.
Aprés li dist: "Turnet estes a perdre!"   AOI.

97

His companion Gerier strikes the amurafle,
1270 He smashes his shield and breaks the metal links of his hauberk,
He drives his good spear into his guts,
He sticks it deeply into him, he forces it through his middle,
Running him through, he throws him dead in the field.
Oliver said: "Our battle is a noble one!"

98

1275 Duke Samson goes to strike the almaçor,
He smashes his shield, ornamented with a flower design and with gold,
His good hauberk offers him scant protection,
He pierces his heart, his liver, and his lung,
Come what may, he throws him down dead.
1280 The Archbishop said: "That's a true knight's blow!"

99

Anceïs gives his horse the reins
And goes to strike Turgis of Tortelose,
He smashes his shield under the golden boss,
He breaks the double links of his hauberk,
1285 He pierces his body with the point of his good spear,
He sticks it deeply into him, he pushes the iron right through him,
Running him through, he tumbles him over on the field dead.
Roland said: "That's a worthy man's blow!"

100

Engelier, the Gascon from Bordeaux,
1290 Spurs his horse and gives him free rein
And goes to strike Escremis of Valterne,
He smashes and breaks in pieces the shield hanging from his neck,
He tears the mail coif from his hauberk,
He strikes him full in the chest, on the sternum,
1295 Running him through, he throws him dead from the saddle.
Afterward he said to him: "You've met your doom!"   AOI.

101

E Otes fiet un paien, Estorgans,
Sur sun escut en la pene devant,
Que tut li trenchet le vermeill e le blanc;
1300 De sun osberc li ad rumput les pans,
El cors li met sun bon espiet trechant,
Que mort l'abat de sun cheval curant.
Aprés li dist: "Ja n'i avrez guarant!"

102

E Berenger, il fiert Astramariz,
1305 L'escut li freinst, l'osberc li descumfist,
Sun fort espiet par mi le cors li mist,
Que mort l'abat entre mil Sarrazins.
Des .XII. pers li .X. en sunt ocis,
Ne mes que dous n'en i ad remés vifs,
1310 Ço est Chernubles e li quens Margariz.

103

Margariz est mult vaillant chevalers,
E bels e forz e isnels e legers.
Le cheval brochet, vait ferir Oliver,
L'escut li freint suz la bucle d'or mer,
1315 Lez le costet li conduist sun espiet.
Deus le guarit, qu'ell cors ne l'ad tuchet.
La hanste fruisset, mie n'en abatiet.
Ultre s'en vait, qu'il n'i ad desturber,
Sunet sun gresle pur les soens ralïer.

104

1320 La bataille est merveilluse e cumune.
Li quens Rollant mie ne s'asoüret,
Fiert de l'espiet tant cume hanste li duret,
A .XV. cols l'ad fraite e perdue.
Trait Durendal, sa bone espee, nue,
1325 Sun cheval brochet, si vait ferir Chernuble.
L'elme li freint u li carbuncle luisent,

101

Oton strikes a pagan, Estorgant,
On the upper edge of his shield,
The red and white paint is all cut away;
1300 He ripped off sections of his hauberk,
He plunges his good sharp spear into his body,
Throwing him down dead from his galloping horse.
Afterward he said to him: "There's no saving you now!"

102

Berengier strikes Astramariz,
1305 He smashed his shield and ripped apart his hauberk,
He plunged his sturdy spear through his middle,
Throwing him down dead amid a thousand Saracens.
Ten of the Twelve Saracen Peers have been killed,
Now only two of them remain alive,
1310 Chernuble and Count Margariz.

103

Margariz is a very worthy knight,
Well proportioned, strong, swift, and agile.
He spurs his horse and goes to strike Oliver,
He smashes his shield under the pure gold boss,
1315 His spear shaves him on one side.
God preserved him so that the pagan did not wound him in his
    body.
The spear shaft shatters, but he is not thrown down.
The Saracen goes away, for there is no one to stop him,
He sounds his bugle to rally his men.

104

1320 The battle is prodigious and involves everyone.
Count Roland has no concern for his own safety,
He strikes with his spear for as long as the shaft lasts him,
With fifteen blows he smashed and destroyed it.
He bares Durendal, his good sword,
1325 He spurs his horse and goes to strike Chernuble.
He smashes his helmet where the carbuncles glow,

Trenchet le cors e la cheveleüre,
Si li trenchat les oilz e la faiture,
·Le blanc osberc, dunt la maile est menue,
1330 E tut le cors tresqu'en la furcheüre,
Enz en la sele, ki est a or batue,
El cheval est l'espee aresteüe;
Trenchet l'eschine, hunc n'i out quis jointure,
Tut abat mort el pred sur l'erbe drue.
1335 Aprés li dist: "Culvert, mar i moüstes!
De Mahumet ja n'i avrez aiude.
Par tel glutun n'ert bataille oi vencue."

105

Li quens Rollant par mi le champ chevalchet,
Tient Durendal, ki ben trenchet e taillet,
1340 Des Sarrazins lur fait mult grant damage.
Ki lui veïst l'un geter mort su l'altre,
Li sanc tuz clers gesir par cele place!
Sanglant en ad e l'osberc e la brace,
Sun bon cheval le col e les espalles.
1345 E Oliver de ferir ne se target,
Li .XII. per n'en deivent aveir blasme,
E li Franceis i fierent e si caplent.
Moerent paien e alquanz en i pasment.
Dist l'arcevesque: "Ben ait nostre barnage!"
1350 Munjoie escriet, ço est l'enseigne Carle.   AOI.

106

E Oliver chevalchet par l'estor,
Sa hanste est frait, n'en ad que un trunçun.
E vait ferir un paien, Malun,
L'escut li freint, ki est ad or e a flur,
1355 Fors de la teste li met les oilz ansdous
E la cervele li chet as piez desuz.
Mort le tresturnet od tut .VII.C. des lur,
Pois ad ocis Turgis e Esturguz.
La hanste briset e esclicet josqu'as poinz.
1360 Ço dist Rollant: "Cumpainz, que faites vos?

He hacks through the body and the scalp,
He hacked through his eyes and his face,
Through the shiny hauberk, whose chain mail is close-meshed,
1330 Through his entire body down to the crotch,
Through the saddle, which is wrought with gold.
The sword has come to rest in the horse;
He hacks through the spine, he never sought out a joint,
He throws him dead in the meadow on the thick grass.
1335 Afterward he said to him: "Scoundrel, your doom was sealed when
    you set out!
You'll never receive any aid from Mohammed.
The battle today shall not be won by a wretch like you."

105

Count Roland rides in the middle of the field,
He holds Durendal, which cuts and hacks well,
1340 He causes great harm to the Saracens.
One could see him dispatching his adversaries, piles of them,
And the bright blood in profusion in that place!
His hauberk and his two arms are bloody as a consequence,
Also the neck and shoulders of his good horse.
1345 Oliver does not hang back from striking,
The Twelve Peers must not incur any blame,
And the French strike and hack away.
The pagans die, others fall down in a faint.
The Archbishop said: "Success to our knights!"
1350 He shouts "Monjoie!", Charles's battle cry.   AOI.

106

Oliver rides in the thick of the battle,
His spear shaft is broken, he has nothing but a stump.
He goes to strike a pagan, Malon,
He smashes his shield, ornamented with gold and a flower design,
1355 He knocks both eyes out of his head
And his brains spill down over his feet.
He tumbles him over dead with seven hundred of their men,
Then he killed Turgis and Esturgos.
The spear shaft breaks and shatters down to his hands.
1360 Roland said: "Comrade, what are you up to?

En tel bataille n'ai cure de bastun,
Fers e acers i deit aveir valor.
U est vostre espee, ki Halteclere ad num?
D'or est li helz e de cristal li punz."
1365 "Ne la poi traire," Oliver li respunt,
"Kar de ferir oi jo si grant bosoign!" AOI.

107

Danz Oliver trait ad sa bone espee
Que ses cumpainz Rollant li ad tant demandee
E il li ad cum chevaler mustree.
1370 Fiert un paien, Justin de Val Ferree,
Tute la teste li ad par mi sevree,
Trenchet le cors e la bronie safree,
La bone sele, ki a or est gemmee,
E al ceval a l'eschine trenchee,
1375 Tut abat mort devant loi en la pree.
Ço dist Rollant: "Vos reconois jo, frere!
Por itels colps nos eimet li emperere."
De tutes parz est Munjoe escriee. AOI.

108

Li quens Gerins set el ceval Sorel
1380 E sis cumpainz Gerers en Passecerf.
Laschent lor reisnes, brochent amdui a ait,
E vunt ferir un paien, Timozel,
L'un en l'escut e li altre en l'osberc.
Lur dous espiez enz el cors li unt frait,
1385 Mort le tresturnent tres enmi un guaret.
Ne l'oï dire ne jo mie nel sai
Liquels d'els dous en fut li plus isnels.
Espuers icil fut filz Burdel

. . . .

1390 E l'arcevesque lor ocist Siglorel,
L'encanteür ki ja fut en enfer,
Par artimal l'i cundoist Jupiter.
Co dist Turpin: "Icist nos ert forsfait!"
Respunt Rollant: "Vencut est le culvert.
1395 Oliver, frere, itels colps me sunt bel!"

I have no use for a stick in a battle like this,
Iron and steel must prevail.
Where is your sword that is called Halteclere?
Its hilt is made of gold and its pommel of crystal."
1365 "I could not draw it," Oliver replies to him,
"For striking blows was taking up all my attention!"   AOI.

107

Sir Oliver has drawn his good sword,
Which his companion Roland beseeched him to do,
He showed it to him like a true knight.
1370 He strikes a pagan, Justin of Val Ferree,
He cut his head right in two,
He hacks his body and his saffron byrnie,
His good saddle, which is wrought in gold and gems,
And slices through the horse's spine,
1375 He throws him down dead before him in the meadow.
Roland said: "Now I recognize you, comrade!
The Emperor loves us for such blows."
Everywhere the shout "Monjoie!" is heard.   AOI.

108

Count Gerin sits astride his horse Sorel
1380 And his companion Gerier on Passecerf.
They loose their reins, they both spur like fury,
And they go to strike a pagan, Timozel,
The one on the shield and the other on the hauberk.
They break their two spears in his body,
1385 They tumble him over dead in a fallow field.
I have not heard nor do I really know
Which one of the two was the swifter.
Espuers was the son of Burdel

. . . .

1390 And the Archbishop killed Siglorel,
The sorcerer who was once in Hell,
Jupiter led him there by sorcery.
Turpin said: "This one did us wrong!"
Roland replies: "The scoundrel is vanquished.
1395 Oliver, comrade, such blows are worthy in my eyes!"

109

La bataille est aduree endementres,
Franc e paien merveilus colps i rendent,
Fierent li un, li altre se defendent.
Tant hanste i ad e fraite e sanglente,
1400 Tant gunfanun rumpu e tant enseigne!
Tant bon Franceis i perdent lor juvente!
Ne reverrunt lor meres ne lor femmes,
Ne cels de France ki as porz les atendent.   AOI.
Karles li magnes en pluret, si se demente.
1405 De ço qui calt? N'en avrunt sucurance.
Malvais servis le jur li rendit Guenes
Qu'en Sarraguce sa maisnee alat vendre.
Puis en perdit e sa vie e ses membres,
El plait ad Ais en fut juget a pendre,
1410 De ses parenz ensembl'od lui tels trente
Ki de murir nen ourent esperance.   AOI.

110

La bataille est merveilluse e pesant.
Mult ben i fiert Oliver e Rollant,
Li arcevesques plus de mil colps i rent,
1415 Li .XII. per ne s'en targent nïent
E li Franceis i fierent cumunement.
Moerent paien a millers e a cent:
Ki ne s'en fuit de mort n'i ad guarent,
Voillet o nun, tut i laisset sun tens.
1420 Franceis i perdent lor meillors guarnemenz,
Ne reverrunt lor peres ne lor parenz,
Ne Carlemagne, ki as porz les atent.
En France en ad mult merveillus turment:
Orez i ad de tuneire e de vent,
1425 Pluies e gresilz desmesureement;
Chiedent i fuildres e menut e suvent,
E terremoete ço i ad veirement.
De Seint Michel del Peril josqu'as Seinz,
Des Besentun tresqu'as porz de Guitsand,
1430 N'en ad recet dunt del mur ne cravent.
Cuntre midi tenebres i ad granz,

88

109

Meanwhile the battle has grown more desperate,
The Franks and pagans deal each other mighty blows,
Some strike, the others defend themselves.
There are so many spear shafts smashed and bloody,
1400 So many standards and so many ensigns torn!
So many good Frenchmen lose their lives there!
They shall not see their mothers again, nor their wives,
Nor the men of France who await them in the mountain
     pass. AOI.
Charlemagne weeps for them and makes an outcry.
1405 But what does it matter? They shall not be rescued anyhow.
Ganelon rendered him ill service on the day
That he went to sell the members of his household at Saragossa.
Later he lost his life and limbs,
In the trial at Aix, he was sentenced to be hanged,
1410 Along with thirty of his relatives,
Who were not expecting to die. AOI.

110

The battle is wild and oppressive.
Oliver and Roland strike very hard,
The Archbishop deals more than a thousand blows,
1415 The Twelve Peers do not hang back in the least,
And the French strike in a joint effort.
Hundreds and thousands of pagans die:
Whoever does not flee has no safeguard from death,
Willy-nilly, he departs from this life.
1420 The French lose their best protectors there,
They shall not see their fathers again nor their relatives,
Nor Charlemagne, who is waiting for them in the mountain pass.
In France there is a very terrifying disturbance:
Thunder and windstorms,
1425 Rain and hail to excess;
Lightning strikes in rapid succession over and over again,
Indeed there is an earthquake.
From Saint-Michel-du-Péril to Sens,
From Besançon to the port of Wissant,
1430 All the fortress walls come tumbling down.
At high noon the heavens cloud over completely,

N'i ad clartet, se li ciels nen i fent.
Hume nel veit ki mult ne s'espoënt.
Dient plusor: "Ço est li definement,
1435 La fin del secle ki nus est en present!"
Il nel sevent, ne dient veir nïent:
Ço est li granz dulors por la mort de Rollant.

111

Franceis i unt ferut de coer e de vigur,
Paien sunt morz a millers e a fuls,
1440 De cent millers n'en poënt guarir dous.
Dist l'arcevesques: "Nostre hume sunt mult proz,
Suz ciel n'ad home plus en ait de meillors.
Il est escrit en la Geste Francor
Que vassals est li nostre empereür."
1445 Vunt par le camp, si requerent les lor,
Plurent des oilz de doel e de tendrur
Por lor parenz par coer e par amor.
Li reis Marsilie od sa grant ost lor surt.   AOI.

112

Marsilie vient par mi une valee
1450 Od sa grant ost que il out asemblee,
.XX. escheles ad li reis anumbrees.
Luisent cil elme as perres d'or gemmees
E cil escuz e cez bronies sasfrees.
.VII. milie graisles i sunent la menee,
1455 Grant est la noise par tute la contree.
Ço dist Rollant: "Oliver, compaign, frere,
Guenes li fels ad nostre mort juree,
La traïsun ne poet estre celee.
Mult grant venjance en prendrat l'emperere.
1460 Bataille avrum e forte e aduree,
Unches mais hom tel ne vit ajustee.
Jo i ferrai de Durendal, m'espee,
E vos, compainz, ferrez de Halteclere.
En tanz lius les avum nos portees!
1465 Tantes batailles en avum afinees!
Male chançun n'en deit estre cantee."   AOI.

There is no light except when the sky is rent by lightning.
No one sees this without becoming very terrified.
Many say: "This is the end of all things,
1435 The end of the world that we are witnessing!"
They do not know, they do not talk sense:
This is the great mourning for the death of Roland.

111

The French have struck courageously and vigorously,
The pagans have died by the thousands and in masses,
1440 Not even two can be saved out of a hundred thousand.
The Archbishop said: "Our men are very courageous,
No one on the face of the earth has better fighters.
It is written in the Annals of the Franks
That our Emperor is brave."
1445 They go through the battlefield searching for their own,
With tears in their eyes from grief and pity
For their relatives, whom they love with all their hearts.
King Marsile with his great army bursts upon their sight.   AOI.

112

Marsile comes through a valley
1450 With the great army that he had assembled,
The King has organized them in twenty divisions.
The helmets, with their gemstones set in gold, glitter,
As do the shields and saffron byrnies.
Seven thousand bugles sound the charge,
1455 The noise is deafening throughout the countryside.
Roland said: "Oliver, companion, friend,
Ganelon the traitor has conspired to have us killed,
But the betrayal cannot be concealed.
The Emperor will take great revenge for this.
1460 We shall have a bitter and hard-fought battle,
Never has anyone seen such an encounter.
I shall strike with my sword, Durendal,
And you, comrade, strike with Halteclere.
We have borne them in so many places!
1465 We have ended so many battles successfully with them!
Bad songs must not be sung about them."   AOI.

113 [*115*]

1467	Franceis veient que paiens i ad tant,	[1510]
	De tutes parz en sunt cuvert li camp.	
	Suvent regretent Oliver e Rollant,	
1470	Les .XII. pers, qu'il lor seient guarant.	
	E l'arcevesque lur dist de sun semblant:	
	"Seignors barons, n'en alez mespensant!	[1515]
	Pur Deu vos pri que ne seiez fuiant,	
	Que nuls prozdom malvaisement n'en chant.	
1475	Asez est mielz que moerjum cumbatant.	
	Pramis nus est, fin prendrum a itant,	
	Ultre cest jurn ne serum plus vivant.	[1520]
	Mais d'une chose vos soi jo ben guarant:	
	Seint pareïs vos est abandunant,	
1480	As Innocenz vos en serez seant."	
	A icest mot si s'esbaldissent Franc,	
	Cel nen i ad Munjoie ne demant. AOI.	[1525]

114 [*116*]

	Un Sarrazin i out de Sarraguce,	
	De la citet l'une meitet est sue,	
1485	Ço est Climborins, ki pas ne fut produme.	
	Fiance prist de Guenelun le cunte,	
	Par amistiet l'en baisat en la buche,	[1530]
	Si l'en dunat sun helme e s'escarbuncle.	
	Tere Major, ço dit, metrat a hunte,	
1490	A l'emperere si toldrat la curone.	
	Siet el ceval qu'il cleimet Barbamusche,	
	Plus est isnels que esprever ne arunde.	[1535]
	Brochet le bien, le frein li abandunet,	
	Si vait ferir Engeler de Guascoigne.	
1495	Nel poet guarir sun escut ne sa bronie:	
	De sun espiet el cors li met la mure,	
	Empeint le ben, tut le fer li mist ultre,	[1540]
	Pleine sa hanste el camp mort le tresturnet.	
	Aprés escriet: "Cist sunt bon a cunfundre!	
1500	Ferez, paien, pur la presse derumpre!"	
	Dient Franceis: "Deus! quel doel de prodome!" AOI.	

113 [*115*]

1467 The French see that there are so many pagans   [1510]
      That the fields are covered with them on all sides.
      Time and again they implore Oliver and Roland
1470 And the Twelve Peers to be their protectors.
      But the Archbishop gave them his view:
      "My lord barons, don't harbor base thoughts!   [1515]
      For God's sake I beg you not to flee,
      So that no worthy individual sing bad songs about it.
1475 It is much better that we should die fighting.
      We shall soon meet our end, we've been promised that,
      After this day we shall no longer be alive.   [1520]
      But I can guarantee you one thing:
      Holy Paradise awaits you,
1480 You will be seated with the Innocents."
      As soon as he has spoken, the Franks rejoice,
      Not a single one of them refrains from shouting "Monjoie!"   AOI.
             [1525]

114 [*116*]

      There was a Saracen there from Saragossa,
      Half of the city is his,
1485 It is Climborin, who was not a man of honor.
      He took Count Ganelon's oath,
      He kissed him on the mouth as a sign of friendship,   [1530]
      He also gave him his helmet and his carbuncle.
      He will, he says, cover the Fatherland with shame
1490 And take the Emperor's crown away from him.
      He sits astride the horse he calls Barbamusche,
      Which is swifter than a sparrow hawk or swallow.   [1535]
      He spurs him hard, he gives him the reins,
      He goes to strike Engelier of Gascony.
1495 The latter's shield and byrnie cannot save him:
      The pagan plunges the point of his spear into his body,
      He sticks it deeply into him, he pushes the iron completely through
         him,   [1540]
      Running him through, he tumbles him over dead in the field.
      Afterward he cries: "These men are worthy of destruction!
1500 Strike, pagans, to break up the close formation!"
      The French say: "God! what a pity to lose such a worthy man!"
      AOI.

115 [*117*]

Li quens Rollant en apelet Oliver: [1545]
"Sire cumpainz, ja est morz Engeler,
Nus n'avium plus vaillant chevaler."
1505 Respont li quens: "Deus le me doinst venger!"
Sun cheval brochet des esperuns d'or mier,
Tient Halteclere, sanglent en est l'acer,   [1550]
Par grant vertut vait ferir le paien.
Brandist sun colp e li Sarrazins chiet,
1510 L'anme de lui en portent aversers.
Puis ad ocis le duc Alphaïen,
Escababi i ad le chef trenchet,   [1555]
.VII. Arrabiz i ad deschevalcet,
Cil ne sunt proz jamais pur guerreier.
1515 Ço dist Rollant: "Mis cumpainz est irez!
Encuntre mei fait asez a preiser.
Pur itels colps nos ad Charles plus cher."   [1560]
A voiz escriet: "Ferez i, chevaler!"   AOI.

116 [*118*]

D'altre part est un paien, Valdabrun,
1520 Celoi levat le rei Marsiliun.
Sire est par mer de .IIII.C. drodmunz,
N'i ad eschipre quis cleimt se par loi nun.   [1565]
Jerusalem prist ja par traïsun,
Si violat le temple Salomon,
1525 Le patriarche ocist devant les funz.
Cil ot fiance del cunte Guenelon,
Il li dunat s'espee e mil mangüns.   [1570]
Siet el cheval qu'il cleimet Gramimund,
Plus est isnels que nen est uns falcuns.
1530 Brochet le bien des aguz esperuns,
Si vait ferir li riche duc Sansun.
L'escut li freint e l'osberc li derumpt,   [1575]
El cors li met les pans del gunfanun,
Pleine sa hanste l'abat mort des arçuns:
1535 "Ferez, paien, car tres ben les veintrum!"
Dient Franceis: "Deus! quel doel de baron!"   AOI.

115 [117]

Count Roland calls to Oliver: [1545]
"Companion, sir, Engelier is now dead,
We had no worthier knight than he."
1505 The Count replies: "God grant that I avenge him!"
He urges his horse on with his pure gold spurs,
He holds Halteclere, whose steel is bloody,   [1550]
He goes to strike the pagan with great force.
He delivered his blow and the Saracen falls,
1510 The devils take away his soul.
Then he killed Duke Alphaïen,
He cut off Escababi's head,   [1555]
He unhorsed seven Arabs,
They are not fit for waging war anymore.
1515 Roland said: "My companion is fighting mad!
He acts so as to deserve as much praise as I.
Charles holds us in greater esteem for such blows."   [1560]
He cries aloud: "Strike, knights!"   AOI.

116 [118]

From another direction comes a pagan, Valdabron,
1520 It was he who knighted King Marsile.
He is master of four hundred galleys at sea,
Every seaman claims protection from him.   [1565]
Earlier he took Jerusalem by treacherous means,
Violated the Temple of Solomon,
1525 And killed the Patriarch before the fonts.
He took Count Ganelon's oath,
He gave him his sword and a thousand mangons.   [1570]
He sits astride the horse he calls Gramimont,
It is swifter than a falcon.
1530 He urges it on hard with his sharp spurs,
He goes to strike mighty Duke Samson.
He smashes his shield and rips open his hauberk,   [1575]
He forces the tails of his ensign into his body,
Running him through, he throws him dead from his saddle:
1535 "Strike, pagans, for we shall vanquish them in stunning fashion!"
The French say: "God! what a pity to lose such a knight!"   AOI.

117 [*119*]

Li quens Rollant, quant il veit Sansun mort,   [1580]
Podez saveir que mult grant doel en out.
Sun ceval brochet, si li curt ad esforz,
1540   Tient Durendal, qui plus valt que fin or.
Vait le ferir li bers quanque il pout
Desur sun elme, ki gemmet fut ad or,   [1585]
Trenchet la teste e la bronie e le cors,
La bone sele, ki est gemmet ad or,
1545   E al cheval parfundement le dos,
Ambure ocit, ki quel blasme ne quil lot.
Dient paient: "Cist colp nus est mult fort!"   [1590]
Respont Rollant: "Ne pois amer les voz,
Devers vos est li orguilz e li torz."   AOI.

118 [*120*]

1550   D'Affrike i ad un Affrican venut,
Ço est Malquiant, le filz al rei Malcud.
Si guarnement sunt tut a or batud,   [1595]
Cuntre le ciel sur tuz les altres luist.
Siet el ceval qu'il cleimet Salt Perdut,
1555   Beste nen est ki poisset curre a lui.
Il vait ferir Anseïs en l'escut,
Tut li trenchat le vermeill e l'azur.   [1600]
De sun osberc li ad les pans rumput,
El cors li met e le fer e le fust.
1560   Morz est li quens, de sun tens n'i ad plus.
Dient Franceis: "Barun, tant mare fus!"

119 [*121*]

Par le camp vait Turpin, li arcevesque.   [1605]
Tel coronet ne chantat unches messe
Ki de sun cors feïst tantes proëcces.
1565   Dist al paien: "Deus tut mal te tramette!
Tel ad ocis dunt al coer me regrette."
Sun bon ceval i ad fait esdemetre,   [1610]
Si l'ad ferut sur l'escut de Tulette
Que mort l'abat desur le herbe verte.

117 [*119*]

When Count Roland sees Samson dead,   [1580]
You may be certain that he was very greatly afflicted by this.
He spurs his horse, it runs full speed,
1540 He holds Durendal, which is worth more than pure gold.
The knight goes to strike the pagan as hard as he can
On his helmet, whose gold is wrought with gems,   [1585]
He slices through head, byrnie, and body,
The good saddle, whose gold is wrought with gems,
1545 And deeply into the horse's back,
He kills both of them, caring not a whit for blame or for praise.
The pagans say: "That's a crushing blow for us!"   [1590]
Roland answers: "I cannot brook you people,
Your side is evil and wrong."   AOI.

118 [*120*]

1550 From Africa there came an African,
It is Malquiant, the son of King Malcud.
His trappings are all of beaten gold,   [1595]
They glitter more than all the others against the sky.
He sits astride the horse he calls Salt Perdu,
1555 No other beast can run like him.
He goes to strike Anseïs on the shield,
He cut away all its red and blue paint,   [1600]
He ripped off sections of his hauberk,
He plunges the iron and the wood into his body.
1560 The Count is dead, his sands have run out.
The French say: "You are to be pitied, worthy knight!"

119 [*121*]

Archbishop Turpin·goes through the battlefield.   [1605]
No tonsured person who ever sang mass
Was personally responsible for so many meritorious deeds.
1565 He said to the pagan: "God rain misfortunes on you!
Your killing this man cuts me to the heart."
He made his good horse lunge forward,   [1610]
He struck the pagan on his shield made in Toledo,
Throwing him dead on the green grass.

120 [*122*]

1570 De l'altre part est un paien, Grandonies,
Filz Capuël, le rei de Capadoce.
Siet el cheval que il cleimet Marmorie,   [1615]
Plus est isnels que n'est oisel ki volet.
Laschet la resne, des esperuns le brochet,
1575 Si vait ferir Gerin par sa grant force.
L'escut vermeill li freint, de col li portet,
Aprof li ad sa bronie desclose,   [1620]
El cors li met tute l'enseingne bloie
Que mort l'abat en une halte roche.
1580 Sun cumpaignun Gerers ocit uncore
E Berenger e Guiun de Seint Antonie.
Puis vait ferir un riche duc, Austorje,   [1625]
Ki tint Valeri e Envers sur le Rosne.
Il l'abat mort, paien en unt grant joie.
1585 Dient Franceis: "Mult decheent li nostre!"

121 [*123*]

Li quens Rollant tint s'espee sanglente.
Ben ad oït que Franceis se dementent,   [1630]
Si grant doel ad que par mi quïet fendre.
Dist al paien: "Deus tut mal te consente!
1590 Tel as ocis que mult cher te quid vendre!"
Sun ceval brochet, ki oït del cuntence.
Ki quel cumpert, venuz en sunt ensemble.   [1635]

122 [*124*]

Grandonie fut e prozdom e vaillant
E vertuus e vassal cumbatant.
1595 Enmi sa veie ad encuntret Rollant.
Enceis nel vit, sil recunut veirement
Al fier visage e al cors qu'il out gent   [1640]
E al reguart e al contenement:
Ne poet muër qu'il ne s'en espoënt.
1600 Fuïr s'en voel, mais ne li valt nïent.
Li quens le fiert tant vertuusement
Tresqu'al nasel tut le elme li fent,   [1645]
Trenchet le nes e la buche e les denz,

98

120 [*122*]

1570 From another direction comes a pagan, Grandoine,
Son of Capuel, the King of Cappadocia.
He sits astride the horse he calls Marmoire,   [1615]
It is swifter than any bird that flies.
He gives him free rein, he urges him on with his spurs,
1575 He goes to strike Gerin with all his might.
He smashes his red shield, he rips it from his neck,
Then he tore open his byrnie,   [1620]
He plunges his whole blue ensign into his body,
Throwing him dead on a high rock.
1580 He also kills his companion Gerier,
And Berengier and Gui of Saint-Antoine.
Then he goes to strike Austorge, a mighty duke   [1625]
Who ruled Valeri and Envers on the Rhone.
He throws him down dead, giving the pagans great joy.
1585 The French say: "Our men are rapidly collapsing!"

121 [*123*]

Count Roland held his bloody sword.
He has heard well the French crying out their distress,   [1630]
His fury is so great that he thinks he will burst in two.
He said to the pagan: "God shower misfortunes on you!
1590 I expect to make you pay very dearly the man you've killed!"
He spurs his horse, who exerts himself to the utmost.
Caring not a whit who will pay for it, they close with each other.
       [1635]

122 [*124*]

Grandoine was reliable and worthy,
Strong and courageous in combat.
1595 He has encountered Roland in his path.
He had never seen him before, yet he recognized him very well
By his fierce look and by the well-proportioned body he had, [1640]
By his gaze and by his countenance:
He cannot help being terrified.
1600 He tries to flee, but it is no use.
The Count deals him such a mighty blow
That he splits his whole helmet down to the nasal,   [1645]
Hacks through nose, mouth, teeth,

Trestut le cors e l'osberc jazerenc,
1605 De l'oree sele le dous alves d'argent
E al ceval le dos parfundement.
Ambure ocist seinz nul recoevrement, [1650]
E cil d'Espaigne s'en cleiment tuit dolent.
Dient Franceis: "Ben fiert nostre guarent!"

123 [126]

1610 La bataille est merveilluse e hastive. [1661]
Franceis i ferent par vigur e par ire,
Trenchent cez poinz, cez costez, cez eschines,
Cez vestemenz entresque as chars vives.
Sur l'erbe verte li cler sancs s'en afilet. [1665]
1615 . . . .
"Tere Major, Mahummet te maldie!
Sur tute gent est la tue hardie."
Cel nen i ad ki ne criet: "Marsilie!
Cevalche, rei, bosuign avum d'aïe!" [1670]

124 [125]

1620 La bataille est e merveillose e grant, [1653]
Franceis i fierent des espiez brunisant.
La veïssez si grant dulor de gent, [1655]
Tant hume mort e nasfret e sanglent!
L'un gist sur l'altre e envers e adenz.
1625 Li Sarrazin nel poënt susfrir tant,
Voelent u nun, si guerpissent le camp.
Par vive force les encacerent Franc. AOI. [1660]

125 [113]

Marsilies veit de sa gent le martirie, [1467]
Si fait suner ses cors e ses buisines,
1630 Puis si chevalchet od sa grant ost banie.
Devant chevalchet un sarrazin, Abisme, [1470]
Plus fel de lui n'out en sa cumpagnie.
Teches ad males e mult granz felonies,
Ne creit en Deu, le filz seinte Marie;

His entire body and the hauberk from Algiers,
1605 The two silver side pieces of the golden saddle,
And deeply into the horse's back.
He killed both of them, no recovery is possible,   [1650]
And, because of this, the men from Spain proclaim their great
  sorrow.
The French say: "Our protector strikes well!"

123 [126]

1610 The battle is wild and desperate.   [1661]
The French strike vigorously and furiously,
They hack through fists, ribs, spines,
Through clothing down to living flesh.
The bright blood streams on the green grass.   [1665]
1615 .   .   .   .
"Mohammed damn you, Fatherland!
Your followers are bolder than all other peoples."
Every single one cries: "Marsile!
Ride, King, we need help!"

124 [125]

1620 The battle is wild and mighty,   [1653]
The French strike with burnished spears.
There you would have seen people in such great anguish,   [1655]
So many men dead, wounded, and bleeding!
One lies on top of the other, faceup, facedown.
1625 The Saracens can bear it no longer,
Willy-nilly, they flee from the battlefield.
The Franks pursue them hotly.   AOI.   [1660]

125 [113]

Marsile sees his men being massacred,   [1467]
He orders his horns and trumpets to be sounded,
1630 Then he rides with the great army he has assembled.
In the forefront rides a Saracen, Abisme,   [1470]
There was no viler man than he in his company.
He has evil vices and has committed many great crimes,
He does not believe in God, the Son of Holy Mary;

1635 Issi est neirs cume peiz ki est demise.
Plus aimet il traïsun e murdrie   [1475]
Que il ne fesist trestut l'or de Galice,
Unches nuls hom nel vit juër ne rire.
Vasselage ad e mult grant estultie,
1640 Por ço est drud al felun rei Marsilie,
Sun dragun portet a qui sa gent s'alïent.   [1480]
Li arcevesque ne l'amerat ja mie,
Cum il le vit, a ferir le desiret.
Mult quiement le dit a sei meïsme:
1645 "Cel Sarrazins me semblet mult herite,
Mielz est mult que jo l'alge ocire.   [1485]
Unches n'amai cuard ne cuardie."   AOI.

126 [114]

Li arcevesque cumencet la bataille.
Siet el cheval qu'il tolit a Grossaille,
1650 Ço ert uns reis qu'il ocist en Denemarche.
Li destrers est e curanz e aates,   [1490]
Piez ad copiez e les gambes ad plates,
Curte la quisse e la crupe bien large,
Lungs les costez e l'eschine ad ben halte,
1655 Blanche la cue e la crignete jalne,
Petites les oreilles, la teste tute falve,   [1495]
Beste nen est nule ki encontre lui alge.
Li arcevesque brochet par tant grant vasselage,
Ne laisserat qu'Abisme nen asaillet.
1660 Vait le ferir en l'escut a miracle:
Pierres i ad, ametistes e topazes,   [1500]
Esterminals e carbuncles ki ardent.
En Val Metas li dunat uns diables,
Si li tramist li amiralz Galafes.
1665 Turpins i fiert, ki nïent ne l'esparignet,
Enprés sun colp ne quid que un dener vaillet. [1505]
Le cors li trenchet tres l'un costet qu'a l'altre
Que mort l'abat en une voide place.
Dient Franceis: "Ci ad grant vasselage!
1670 En l'arcevesque est ben la croce salve."

1635   He is as black as molten pitch.
       He loves treachery and murder more   [1475]
       Than all the gold in Galicia,
       No man ever saw him play or smile.
       He has courage and very great impetuousness,
1640   That is why he is a close friend of vile King Marsile,
       He carries the latter's dragon ensign round which his men
           rally.   [1480]
       The Archbishop will never brook him,
       On seeing him, he wishes to strike him.
       He said very softly to himself:
1645   "That Saracen looks like a great heretic to me,
       It is much better that I should go kill him.   [1485]
       I never cared for cowards or for cowardice."   AOI.

126 [*114*]

       The Archbishop opens the battle.
       He sits astride the horse he took from Grossaille,
1650   A king he killed in Denmark.
       · The war-horse is swift and spirited,
       It has hollowed-out hooves and flat legs,   [1490]
       Short haunch and very broad croup,
       Long flanks and very high back,
1655   White tail and yellow mane,
       Small ears, a completely tawny head,   [1495]
       There is no animal that can outrun it.
       The Archbishop spurs on with such great courage,
       He will not stop until he assails Abisme.
1660   He goes to strike him on his fabulous shield:
       It has precious stones, amethysts, and topazes,   [1500]
       Esterminals and carbuncles that glow.
       A devil gave it to him in Val Metas,
       Emir Galafe transmitted it to him.
1665   Turpin strikes, sparing it in no way,
       After his blow, I do not think it is worth a penny.   [1505]
       He runs him through from one side to the other,
       Throwing him dead in an empty place.
       The French say: "Here is a mighty heroic deed!
1670   The crozier is quite safe in the Archbishop's hands."

127

Li quens Rollant apelet Oliver:
"Sire cumpaign, sel volez otrïer,
Li arcevesque est mult bon chevaler.
Nen ad meillor en tere ne suz cel,
1675 Ben set ferir e de lance e d'espiet."
Respunt li quens: "Kar li aluns aider!"
A icest mot l'unt Francs recumencet.
Dur sunt li colps e li caples est grefs,
Mult grant dulor i ad de chrestïens.
1680 Ki puis veïst Rollant e Oliver
De lur espees e ferir e capler!
Li arcevesque i fiert de sun espiet.
Cels qu'il unt mort, ben les poet hom preiser:
Il est escrit es cartres e es brefs,
1685 Ço dit la Geste, plus de .IIII. milliers.
As quatre turs lor est avenut ben,
Li quint aprés lor est pesant e gref.
Tuz sunt ocis cist franceis chevalers,
Ne mes seisante, que Deus i ad esparniez.
1690 Einz que il moergent, se vendrunt mult cher.   AOI.

128

Li quens Rollant des soens i veit grant perte.
Sun cumpaignun Oliver en apelet:
"Bel sire, chers cumpainz, pur Deu, que vos en haitet?
Tanz bons vassals veez gesir par tere!
1695 Pleindre poüms France dulce, la bele,
De tels barons cum or remeint deserte!
E! reis, amis, que vos ici nen estes!
Oliver, frere, cum le purrum nus faire,
Cumfaitement li manderum nuveles?"
1700 Dist Oliver: "Jo nel sai cument quere.
Mielz voeill murir que hunte nus seit retraite."   AOI.

129

Ço dist Rollant: "Cornerai l'olifant,
Si l'orrat Carles, ki est as porz passant.

127

Count Roland calls to Oliver:
"Comrade, sir, you will grant, I'm sure,
That the Archbishop is a very good knight.
There is no finer one on the face of the earth,
1675 He is formidable with lance and spear."
The Count replies: "Come on, let's go help him!"
When they heard this, the Franks began striking anew.
The blows are hard and the fighting is heavy,
The Christians suffer very heavy losses.
1680 One could see then Roland and Oliver
Striking and slashing with their swords!
The Archbishop strikes with his spear.
We have a good idea of the number they killed:
It is written in the documents and records,
1685 The Chronicle says that there were more than four thousand.
It went well with them during four assaults,
But afterward the fifth brought them to ruin and grief.
The French knights are now all dead,
Except for sixty whom God has spared.
1690 Before they die, they will sell their lives dearly.   AOI.

128

Count Roland sees the great slaughter of his men.
He calls his companion Oliver:
"Dear sir, dear comrade, in God's name, what do you make of this?
You see so many good knights lying on the ground!
1695 Sweet France, the fair, is to be pitied,
How impoverished she is now of such knights!
O dear King, what a shame you're not here!
Dear Oliver, how shall we do it,
How shall we break the news to him?"
1700 Oliver said: "I don't know how to reach him.
I'd rather die than have something to blame ourselves for."   AOI.

129

Roland said: "I shall sound the oliphant.
Charles, who is going through the pass, will hear it.

Jo vos plevis ja returnerunt Franc."

1705 Dist Oliver: "Vergoigne sereit grant
E reprover a trestuz voz parenz,
Iceste hunte dureit al lur vivant!
Quant jel vos dis, n'en feïstes nïent,
Mais nel ferez par le men loëment.

1710 Se vos cornez, n'ert mie hardement.
Ja avez vos ambsdous les braz sanglanz!"
Respont li quens: "Colps i ai fait mult genz!"   AOI.

130

Ço dit Rollant: "Forz est nostre bataille,
Jo cornerai, si l'orrat li reis Karles."

1715 Dist Oliver: "Ne sereit vasselage!
Quant jel vos dis, cumpainz, vos ne deignastes.
S'i fust li reis, n'i oüsum damage.
Cil ki la sunt n'en deivent aveir blasme."
Dist Oliver: "Par ceste meie barbe,

1720 Se puis veeir ma gente sorur Alde,
Ne jerreiez jamais entre sa brace!"   AOI.

131

Ço dist Rollant: "Por quei me portez ire?"
E il respont: "Cumpainz, vos le feïstes,
Kar vasselage par sens nen est folie;

1725 Mielz valt mesure que ne fait estultie.
Franceis sunt morz par vostre legerie.
Jamais Karlon de nus n'avrat servise.
Sem creïsez, venuz i fust mi sire,
Ceste bataille oüsum faite u prise,

1730 U pris u mort i fust li reis Marsilie.
Vostre proëcce, Rollant, mar la veïmes!
Karles li magnes de nos n'avrat aïe.
N'ert mais tel home desqu'a Deu juïse.
Vos i murrez e France en ert hunie.

1735 Oi nus defalt la leial cumpaignie,
Einz le vespre mult ert gref la departie."   AOI.

I give you my word that the Franks will return now."
1705 Oliver said: "That would be dishonorable
And a reproach to all your relatives,
The shame of it would last the rest of their lives!
When I told you to, you did nothing at all,
Don't expect my consent to do it now.
1710 If you sound the horn, it will not be a brave act.
See how bloody both your arms are!"
The Count replies: "I have struck mighty fine blows!"   AOI.

130

Roland says: "Our battle is hard,
I shall sound the horn and Charles will hear it."
1715 Oliver said: "That would not be a heroic deed!
When I told you to, comrade, you did not deign to.
If the King had been here, we would have suffered no harm.
Those who are with him over there are not to be blamed."
Oliver said: "By this beard of mine,
1720 If I manage to see my fair sister Alda again,
You shall never lie in her arms!"   AOI.

131

Roland said: "Why are you angry with me?"
The other replies: "Comrade, you brought it on yourself,
For heroism tempered with common sense is a far cry from madness;
1725 Reasonableness is to be preferred to recklessness.
Frenchmen have died because of your senselessness.
We shall never again be of service to Charles.
If you had believed me, my lord would have come,
We would have fought or won (?) this battle,
1730 King Marsile would be captured or slain.
I have come to rue your prowess, Roland!
Charlemagne will not have any help from us.
There shall never be such a man again until Judgment Day.
You will die here and France will be dishonored.
1735 Today our loyal companionage comes to an end,
Before nightfall, our parting will be very sad."   AOI.

132

Li arcevesques les ot cuntrarïer.
Le cheval brochet des esperuns d'or mer,
Vint tresqu'a els, sis prist a castïer:
1740 "Sire Rollant, e vos, sire Oliver,
Pur Deu vos pri, ne vos cuntralïez!
Ja li corners ne nos avreit mester,
Mais nepurquant si est il asez melz:
Venget li reis, si nus purrat venger,
1745 Ja cil d'Espaigne ne s'en deivent turner liez.
Nostre Franceis i descendrunt a pied,
Truverunt nos e morz e detrenchez.
Leverunt nos en bieres sur sumers,
Si nus plurrunt de doel e de pitet.
1750 Enfuërunt en aitres de musters,
N'en mangerunt ne lu ne porc ne chen."
Respunt Rollant: "Sire, mult dites bien."   AOI.

133

Rollant ad mis l'olifan a sa buche,
Empeint le ben, par grant vertut le sunet.
1755 Halt sunt li pui e la voiz est mult lunge,
Granz .XXX. liwes l'oïrent il respundre.
Karles l'oït e ses cumpaignes tutes.
Ço dit li reis: "Bataille funt nostre hume!"
E Guenelun li respundit encuntre:
1760 "S'altre le desist, ja semblast grant mençunge!"   AOI.

134

Li quens Rollant, par peine e par ahans,
Par grant dulor sunet sun olifan.
Par mi la buche en salt fors li cler sancs,
De sun cervel le temple en est rumpant.
1765 Del corn qu'il tient l'oïe en est mult grant,
Karles l'entent, ki est as porz passant.
Naimes li duc l'oïd, si l'escultent li Franc.
Ce dist li reis: "Jo oi le corn Rollant!
Unc nel sunast se ne fust cumbatant."

132

The Archbishop hears them quarreling.
He urges on his horse with his pure gold spurs,
He comes up to them, he began to reprove them:
1740   "Sir Roland and you, Sir Oliver,
In God's name I beg you, don't argue!
Sounding the horn would be of no use to us now,
Nevertheless it is best:
The King will come, he will be able to avenge us,
1745   The men of Spain must not return home joyful.
Our Frenchmen will dismount,
They will find us dead and cut to pieces.
They will raise us in coffins on sumpters,
They will shed tears of sorrow and pity for us.
1750   They will bury us in hallowed ground within church walls,
Neither wolves, nor pigs, nor dogs will devour us."
Roland replies: "Well said, sir."   AOI.

133

Roland has brought the oliphant up to his mouth,
He grasps it firmly, he sounds it with all his might.
1755   The mountains are high and the sound travels a great distance,
They heard it echo a full thirty leagues away.
Charles heard it, all his men too.
The King said: "Our men are giving battle!"
But Ganelon contradicted him:
1760   "If anyone else said this, it would seem a great lie!"   AOI.

134

Count Roland, with pain and suffering,
With great agony sounds his oliphant.
Bright blood comes gushing from his mouth,
The temple of his brain has burst.
1765   The sound of the horn he is holding carries very far,
Charles, who is going through the pass, hears it.
Duke Naimes heard it, the Franks listen for it.
The King says: "I hear Roland's horn!
He'd never sound it if he weren't fighting."

1770 Guenes respunt: "De bataille est nïent!
Ja estes veilz e fluriz e blancs,
Par tels paroles vus resemblez enfant.
Asez savez le grant orgoill Rollant,
Co est merveille que Deus le soefret tant.
1775 Ja prist il Noples seinz le vostre comant;
Fors s'en eissirent li Sarrazins dedenz,
Sis cumbatirent al bon vassal Rollant.
Puis od les ewes lavat les prez del sanc,
Pur cel le fist ne fust aparissant.
1780 Pur un sul levre vat tute jur cornant.
Devant ses pers vait il ore gabant,
Suz cel n'ad gent ki l'osast querre en champ.
Car chevalcez! Pur qu'alez arestant?
Tere Major mult est loinz ça devant." AOI.

135

1785 Li quens Rollant ad la buche sanglente,
De sun cervel rumput en est li temples.
L'olifan sunet a dulor e a peine,
Karles l'oït e ses Franceis l'entendent.
Ço dist li reis: "Cel corn ad lunge aleine!"
1790 Respont dux Neimes: "Baron i fait la peine!
Bataille i ad, par le men escïentre.
Cil l'at traït ki vos en roevet feindre.
Adubez vos, si criez vostre enseigne,
Si sucurez vostre maisnee gente:
1795 Asez oëz que Rollant se dementet!"

136

Li empereres ad fait suner ses corns.
Franceis descendent, si adubent lor cors
D'osbercs e de helmes e d'espees a or.
Escuz unt genz e espiez granz e forz,
1800 E gunfanuns blancs e vermeilz e blois.
Es destrers muntent tuit li barun de l'ost,

1770   Ganelon replies: "There's no battle!
      You're old now, you're grizzled and white-haired,
      Yet such words make you seem a child.
      You know Roland's great folly perfectly well,
      It's a wonder God suffers him so.
1775   He took Noples without your orders;
      The Saracens inside came rushing out,
      They fought the good knight Roland.
      Then he washed the blood from the meadows with streams of
        water,
      He did this so it wouldn't show.
1780   He sounds his horn all day long for a mere hare.
      He's showing off now before his peers,
      No force on earth would dare challenge him in the field.
      Ride on! Why are you stopping?
      The Fatherland is very far ahead of us."   AOI.

135

1785   Count Roland's mouth is bleeding,
      The temple of his brain has burst.
      He sounds the oliphant in agony and in pain,
      Charles heard it, and his Frenchmen too.
      The King said: "That horn has been blowing a long time!"
1790   Duke Naimes replies: "A worthy knight is pouring out his suffering!
      There is a battle, so help me.
      The one who begs you to pretend you have heard nothing has
        betrayed him.
      To arms, shout your battle cry,
      Save your noble household:
1795   You hear as plain as can be Roland signaling his distress!"

136

      The Emperor has ordered his trumpets to be sounded.
      The French dismount, they arm themselves
      With hauberks, helmets, and gilded swords.
      They have fine shields and long and sturdy spears,
1800   And white, red, and blue ensigns.
      All the knights of the army mount their war-horses,

Brochent ad ait tant cum durent li port.
N'i ad celoi a l'altre ne parolt:
"Se veïssum Rollant einz qu'il fust mort,
1805   Ensembl'od lui i durriums granz colps!"
De ço qui calt? Car demuret i unt trop.

137

Esclargiz est li vespres e li jurz.
Cuntre le soleil reluisent cil adub,
Osbercs e helmes i getent grant flabur,
1810   E cil escuz, ki ben sunt peinz a flurs,
E cil espiezz, cil oret gunfanun.
Li empereres cevalchet par irur
E li Franceis dolenz e curuçus.
N'i ad celoi ki durement ne plurt,
1815   E de Rollant sunt en grant poür.
Li reis fait prendre le cunte Guenelun,
Sil cumandat as cous de sa maisun.
Tut li plus maistre en apelet, Besgun:
"Ben le me guarde, si cume tel felon!
1820   De ma maisnee ad faite traïsun."
Cil le receit, s'i met .C. cumpaignons
De la quisine, des mielz e des pejurs.
Icil li peilent la barbe e les gernuns,
Cascun le fiert .IIII. colps de sun puign;
1825   Ben le batirent a fuz e a bastuns,
E si li metent el col un caeignun,
Si l'encaeinent altresi cum un urs.
Sur un sumer l'unt mis a deshonor.
Tant le guardent quel rendent a Charlun.

138

1830   Halt sunt li pui e tenebrus e grant,   AOI.
Li val parfunt e les ewes curant.
Sunent cil graisle e derere e devant,
E tuit rachatent encuntre l'olifant.
Li empereres chevalchet ireement
1835   E li Franceis curuçus e dolent.

They spur furiously until they are out of the pass.
They say to one another:
"If only we could see Roland before he's killed,
1805   We would strike mighty blows with him!"
But what is the use? They have tarried too long.

137

The afternoon has brightened up, as has the day.
The equipment shines in the sun,
Hauberks and helmets blaze forth great flashes,
1810   The shields, too, which are beautifully painted with flowers,
The spears, and the golden ensigns.
The Emperor rides furiously,
And the French are vexed and angry.
They are all crying bitterly,
1815   And they have great fear for Roland.
The King has Count Ganelon seized,
He turns him over to the kitchen help in his employ.
He calls Besgon, their master:
"Guard him well, as befits the felon that he is!
1820   He has betrayed my household."
The head cook takes charge of him, he assigns this duty to a hundred
        of his fellows
From the kitchen, the most reliable and the toughest.
They pluck out his beard and his moustache,
Each strikes him four blows with his fist;
1825   They thrash him soundly with rods and sticks,
They put an iron collar around his neck,
And they chain him like a bear.
They placed him shamefully on a sumpter.
They guard him until they deliver him back to Charles.

138

1830   The mountains are high, shadowy, and massive,   AOI.
The valleys deep and the waters swift.
The trumpets sound in the rear and in front,
And all respond to the oliphant's call.
The Emperor rides furiously,
1835   And the French are angry and vexed.

N'i ad celoi n'i plurt e se dement,
E prient Deu qu'il guarisset Rollant
Josque il vengent el camp cumunement:
Ensembl'od lui i ferrunt veirement.
1840　De ço qui calt? Car ne lur valt nïent,
Demurent trop, n'i poedent estre a tens.　　AOI.

139

Par grant irur chevalchet li reis Charles,
Desur sa brunie li gist sa blanche barbe.
Puignent ad ait tuit li barun de France,
1845　N'i ad icel ne demeint irance
Que il ne sunt a Rollant le cataigne,
Ki se cumbat as Sarrazins d'Espaigne.
Si est blecet, ne quit que anme i remaigne.
Deus! quels seisante humes i ad en sa cumpaigne!
1850　Unches meillurs n'en out reis ne cataignes.　　AOI.

140

Rollant reguardet es munz e es lariz,
De cels de France i veit tanz morz gesir,
E il les pluret cum chevaler gentill:
"Seignors barons, de vos ait Deus mercit!
1855　Tutes voz anmes otreit il pareïs,
En seintes flurs il les facet gesir!
Meillors vassals de vos unkes ne vi,
Si lungement tuz tens m'avez servit!
A oes Carlon si granz païs cunquis!
1860　Li empereres tant mare vos nurrit!
Tere de France, mult estes dulz païs,
Oi desertet a tant rubostl exill!
Barons franceis, pur mei vos vei murir,
Jo ne vos pois tenser ne guarantir.
1865　Aït vos Deus, ki unkes ne mentit!
Oliver, frere, vos ne dei jo faillir,
De doel murra, se altre ne m'i ocit.
Sire cumpainz, alum i referir!"

They are all weeping and showing distress,
And they pray God to protect Roland
Until they arrive together on the battlefield:
With him they will strike properly.
1840 But what is the use? It is of no avail,
They tarry too long, they cannot be there in time.   AOI.

139

King Charles rides like fury,
His white beard is spread over his hauberk.
The knights from France all spur furiously,
1845 They are all in a state of blind anger
For not being with Roland, the captain,
Who is fighting the Saracens of Spain.
He is so badly hurt I do not think his soul can remain in him.
God! what men, the sixty who are in his company!
1850 No king or captain ever had finer.   AOI.

140

Roland gazes at the mountains and hills.
He sees so many men from France lying dead,
He weeps over them like a noble knight:
"My lord barons, God have mercy on you!
1855 May He grant Paradise to all your souls,
May He cause them to lie among the holy flowers!
I have never seen worthier knights than you,
You have served me constantly and for so long!
You have conquered such great nations for Charles!
1860 The Emperor raised you, but how unfortunate the outcome!
Land of France, you are a very sweet realm,
Today made desolate by such a cruel disaster!
French knights, I see you dying for my sake:
I cannot protect or save you.
1865 May God, who never did lie, help you!
Oliver, my friend, I must not fail you,
I shall die of sorrow if nothing else kills me.
Comrade, sir, let's go strike again!"

141

Li quens Rollant el champ est repairet,
1870 Tient Durendal, cume vassal i fiert.
Faldrun de Pui i ad par mi trenchet
E .XXIIII. de tuz les melz preisez,
Jamais n'iert home plus se voeillet venger.
Si cum li cerfs s'en vait devant les chiens,
1875 Devant Rollant si s'en fuient paiens.
Dist l'arcevesque: "Asez le faites ben!
Itel valor deit aveir chevaler
Ki armes portet e en bon cheval set!
En bataille deit estre forz e fiers,
1880 U altrement ne valt .IIII. deners,
Einz deit monie estre en un de cez mustiers,
Si prierat tuz jurz por noz peccez."
Respunt Rollant: "Ferez, nes esparignez!"
A icest mot l'unt Francs recumencet.
1885 Mult grant damage i out de chrestïens.

142

Home ki ço set que ja n'avrat prisun
En tel bataill fait grant defension:
Pur ço sunt Francs si fiers cume leuns.
As vus Marsilie en guise de barunt.
1890 Siet el cheval qu'il apelet Gaignun,
Brochet le ben, si vait ferir Bevon,
Icil ert sire de Belne e de Digun.
L'escut li freint e l'osberc li derumpt,
Que mort l'abat seinz altre descunfisun.
1895 Puis ad ocis Yvoeries e Ivon,
Ensembl'od els Gerard de Russillun.
Li quens Rollant ne li est guaires loign,
Dist al paien: "Damnesdeus mal te duinst!
A si grant tort m'ociz mes cumpaignuns!
1900 Colp en avras einz que nos departum,
E de m'espee enquoi savras le nom."
Vait le ferir en guise de baron,
Trenchet li ad li quens le destre poign.
Puis prent la teste de Jurfaleu le Blund,

141

Count Roland has returned to the battlefield,
1870 He holds Durendal, he strikes like a worthy knight.
He cuts Faldron of Pui in two
And twenty-four of the most esteemed Saracens.
There shall never be a man more bent on revenge.
As the stag runs before the hounds,
1875 So the pagans flee before Roland.
The Archbishop said: "You are doing very well!
That's the sort of valor any knight must have
Who bears arms and sits astride a good horse!
He must be strong and fierce in battle,
1880 Otherwise he is not worth four pennies,
Instead he should be in one of those monasteries
Praying all the time for our sins."
Roland replies: "Strike, do not spare them!"
When they heard this, the Franks attacked again.
1885 There were very heavy losses among the Christians.

142

Anyone who knows no prisoners will ever be taken
Puts up a stout resistance in such a battle:
That is why the Franks are as fierce as lions.
Here now is Marsile looking like a true knight.
1890 He sits astride the horse he calls Gaignon,
He spurs him hard and goes to strike Bevon,
Who was lord of Beaune and of Dijon.
He smashes his shield and rips open his hauberk,
Throwing him down dead without a single other blow.
1895 Then he killed Yvoire and Yvon,
And with them Gerard of Roussillon.
Count Roland is not very far away from him,
He said to the pagan: "The Lord God rain misfortune on you!
You were absolutely unjustified in killing my companions!
1900 You'll get a blow for that before we part,
And today you'll learn my sword's name."
He goes to strike him like a true knight,
The Count cut off his right hand.
Then he takes Jurfaleu le Blond's head off,

1905   Icil ert filz al rei Marsiliun.

Paien escrient: "Aïe nos, Mahum!

Li nostre deu, vengez nos de Carlun!

En ceste tere nus ad mis tels feluns,

Ja pur murir le camp ne guerpirunt."

1910   Dist l'un a l'altre: "E car nos en fuiums!"

A icest mot tels .C. milie s'en vunt,

Ki ques rapelt, ja n'en returnerunt.   AOI.

143

De ço qui calt? Se fuit s'en est Marsilies,

Remés i est sis uncles, Marganices,

1915   Ki tint Kartagene, Alfrere, Garmalie

E Ethiope, une tere maldite.

La neire gent en ad en sa baillie,

Granz unt les nes e lees les oreilles,

E sunt ensemble plus de cinquante milie.

1920   Icil chevalchent fierement e a ire,

Puis escrient l'enseigne paënime.

Ço dist Rollant: "Ci recevrums matyrie,

E or sai ben n'avons guaires a vivre,

Mais tut seit fel cher ne se vende primes!

1925   Ferez, seignurs, des espees furbies,

Si calengez e vos cors e voz vies,

Que dulce France par nus ne seit hunie!

Quant en cest camp vendrat Carles, mi sire,

De Sarrazins verrat tel discipline,

1930   Cuntre un des noz en truverat morz .XV.:

Ne lesserat que nos ne beneïsse."   AOI.

144

Quan Rollant veit la contredite gent

Ki plus sunt neirs que nen est arrement,

Ne n'unt de blanc ne mais que sul les denz,

1935   Ço dist li quens: "Or sai jo veirement

Que hoi murrum, par le mien escïent.

Ferez, Franceis, car jol vos recumenz!"

Dist Oliver: "Dehet ait li plus lenz!"

A icest mot Franceis se fierent enz.

118

1905 He was King Marsile's son.
The pagans shout: "Help us, Mohammed!
Our gods, avenge us on Charles!
He has sent such scoundrels to this land,
They won't leave the field even if it means death."
1910 One said to the other: "Let's flee from here!"
When they heard this, a hundred thousand left,
No matter who calls them back, they will never return.   AOI.

143

What is the use? Although Marsile has fled,
His uncle Marganice remains,
1915 He who rules Carthage, Alfrere, Garmalie,
And Ethiopia, an accursed land.
He has the black people under his command,
Their noses are big and their ears broad,
And together they number more than fifty thousand.
1920 They ride fiercely and furiously,
Then they shout the pagan battle cry.
Roland said: "We are to receive martyrdom here,
And I know very well now that we have not long to live,
But damn whoever doesn't sell his life dearly first!
1925 Strike, my lords, with your furbished swords,
Sell your lives dearly,
So that fair France not incur reproach on our account!
When my lord Charles comes to this battlefield,
He'll see such a slaughter of the Saracens
1930 That he'll find fifteen of them dead for every one of ours:
He shall not fail to bless us."   AOI.

144

When Roland sees the accursed people,
Who are blacker than ink
And whose teeth alone are white,
1935 The Count said: "Now I know for certain
That today we shall surely die.
Strike, Frenchmen, for I am attacking again!"
Oliver said: "The devil take the hindmost!"
When they hear this, the French throw themselves into the fray.

145

1940 Quant paien virent que Franceis i out poi,
Entr'els en unt e orgoil e cunfort.
Dist l'un a l'altre: "L'empereor ad tort."
Li Marganices sist sur un ceval sor,
Brochet le ben des esperuns a or,
1945 Fiert Oliver derere enmi le dos.
Le blanc osberc li ad descust el cors,
Par mi le piz sun espiet li mist fors,
E dit aprés: "Un col avez pris fort!
Carles li Magnes mar vos laissat as porz!
1950 Tort nos ad fait, nen est dreiz qu'il s'en lot,
Kar de vos sul ai ben venget les noz."

146

Oliver sent que a mort est ferut.
Tient Halteclere, dunt li acer fut bruns,
Fiert Marganices sur l'elme a or agut,
1955 E flurs e cristaus en acraventet jus,
Trenchet la teste d'ici qu'as denz menuz,
Brandist sun colp, si l'ad mort abatut,
E dit aprés: "Paien, mal aies tu!
Iço ne di que Karles n'i ait perdut;
1960 Ne a muiler ne a dame qu'aies veüd
N'en vanteras el regne dunt tu fus
Vaillant a un dener que m'i aies tolut,
Ne fait damage ne de mei ne d'altrui."
Aprés escriet Rollant qu'il li aiut.   AOI.

147

1965 Oliver sent qu'il est a mort nasfret,
De lui venger jamais ne li ert sez.
En la grant presse or i fiert cume ber,
Trenchet cez hanstes e cez escuz buclers,
E piez e poinz e seles e costez.
1970 Ki lui veïst Sarrazins desmembrer,
Un mort sur altre geter,
De bon vassal li poüst remembrer.

145

1940 The pagans, seeing that there were few Frenchmen left,
Become overconfident and are much relieved.
One said to the other: "The Emperor is in the wrong."
Marganice sat astride a sorrel horse,
He urges him on with his golden spurs,
1945 He strikes Oliver from behind full in the back.
He broke the white hauberk away from his body,
He pushed his spear through his chest, until it came out in front.
Afterward he said: "You've taken quite a blow!
Charlemagne left you in the pass, that's his misfortune!
1950 He did us wrong, it's not right that he should boast about it,
For on you alone I have taken ample revenge for all our losses."

146

Oliver feels that he has received a mortal blow.
He holds Halteclere, whose steel was shiny,
He strikes Marganice on his pointed golden helmet,
1955 He knocks its flower and crystal ornaments to the ground,
He cuts his head down to the front teeth,
He delivered his blow and threw him down dead.
Afterward he said: "Damn you, pagan!
I don't say that Charles hasn't suffered any losses;
1960 But before any woman or lady you may have seen
You shall not boast, in the realm you came from,
That you have taken anything worth a penny from me,
Nor inflicted any harm on me or anyone else."
Then he cries out to Roland for help.   AOI.

147

1965 Oliver feels that he has received a mortal wound,
He will never slake his thirst for revenge.
He strikes now like a true knight in the thick of the press,
He hacks through spears and shields,
Feet, fists, saddles, and sides.
1970 Anyone having seen him dismembering Saracens,
Piling one corpse on top of another,
Would remember a true knight.

L'enseigne Carle n'i volt mie ublïer,
Munjoie escriet e haltement e cler.
1975 Rollant apelet, sun ami e sun per:
"Sire cumpaign, a mei car vus justez!
A grant dulor ermes hoi desevrez." AOI.

148

Rollant reguardet Oliver al visage,
Teint fut e pers, desculuret e pale.
1980 Li sancs tuz clers par mi le cors li raiet,
Encuntre tere en cheent les esclaces.
"Deus!" dist li quens, "or ne sai jo que face.
Sire cumpainz, mar fut vostre barnage!
Jamais n'iert hume ki tun cors cuntrevaillet.
1985 E! France dulce, cun hoi remendras guaste
De bons vassals, cunfundue e chaiete!
Li emperere en avrat grant damage."
A icest mot sur sun cheval se pasmet. AOI.

149

As vus Rollant sur sun cheval pasmet
1990 E Oliver ki est a mort naffret.
Tant ad seinet li oil li sunt trublet,
Ne loinz ne pres ne poet vedeir si cler
Que reconoistre poisset nuls hom mortel.
Sun cumpaignun, cum il l'at encuntret,
1995 Sil fiert amunt sur l'elme a or gemet,
Tut li detrenchet d'ici qu'al nasel,
Mais en la teste ne l'ad mie adeset.
A icel colp l'ad Rollant reguardet,
Si li demandet dulcement e suëf:
2000 "Sire cumpain, faites le vos de gred?
Ja est ço Rollant, ki tant vos soelt amer!
Par nule guise ne m'aviez desfïet!"
Dist Oliver: "Or vos oi jo parler.
Jo ne vos vei, veied vus Damnedeu!
2005 Ferut vos ai, car le me pardunez!"
Rollant respunt: "Jo n'ai nïent de mel,

He does not want to forget Charles's battle cry,
He shouts "Monjoie!" loud and clear.
1975 He calls Roland, his friend and his peer:
"Comrade, sir, do come next to me!
We shall part with great sadness today."   AOI.

148

Roland looks Oliver in the face,
It is wan, livid, colorless, and pale.
1980 Bright blood streaks the length of his body,
It falls to the ground in spurts.
"God!" says the Count, "I don't know what to do now.
Comrade, sir, your valor, what a shame!
There will never be anyone who will measure up to you.
1985 Alas, fair France, how bereft you shall remain
Of worthy knights, how ruined and fallen!
The Emperor will suffer a heavy loss because of this."
Having said this, he faints upon his horse.   AOI.

149

See now Roland, who has fainted upon his horse,
1990 And Oliver, who has suffered a mortal wound.
He has lost so much blood that his eyes are clouded,
He cannot see clearly enough far and near
To be able to recognize any mortal.
Encountering his companion,
1995 He strikes him on his helmet of gold wrought with gems,
He hacks through it completely down to the nasal,
But he did not touch his head.
After this blow, Roland looked at him,
He asked him softly and gently:
2000 "Comrade, sir, are you doing this on purpose?
Look, it's Roland who loves you so!
You haven't challenged me in any way!"
Oliver said: "I hear you speaking now.
I do not see you, may the Lord God see you!
2005 I struck you, please forgive me for this!"
Roland replies: "I have suffered no injury,

Jol vos parduins ici e devant Deu."
A icel mot l'un a l'altre ad clinet,
Par tel amur as les vus desevred!

150

2010 Oliver sent que la mort mult l'angoisset,
Ansdous les oilz en la teste li turnent,
L'oïe pert e la veüe tute.
Descent a piet, al tere se culchet,
Durement en halt si recleimet sa culpe.
2015 Cuntre le ciel ambesdous ses mains juintes,
Si priet Deu que pareïs li dunget
E beneïst Karlun e France dulce,
Sun cumpaignun Rollant sur tuz humes.
Falt li le coer, le helme li embrunchet,
2020 Trestut le cors a la tere li justet,
Morz est li quens, que plus ne se demuret.
Rollant li ber le pluret, sil duluset,
Jamais en tere n'orrez plus dolent hume!

151

Or veit Rollant que mort est sun ami,
2025 Gesir adenz, a la tere sun vis.
Mult dulcement a regreter le prist:
"Sire cumpaign, tant mar fustes hardiz!
Ensemble avum estet e anz e dis,
Nem fesis mal ne jo nel te forsfis.
2030 Quant tu es mor, dulur est que jo vif!"
A icest mot se pasmet li marchis
Sur sun ceval que cleimet Veillantif.
Afermet est a ses estreus d'or fin,
Quel part qu'il alt, ne poet mie chaïr.

152

2035 Ainz que Rollant se seit aperceüt,
De pasmeisuns guariz ne revenuz,
Mult grant damage li est apareüt:

I forgive you this here and before God."
After he said this, they bowed to each other,
See them now parting with such affection!

150

2010 Oliver feels that death is gripping him hard,
Both eyes are rolling in his head,
He loses hearing and vision completely.
He dismounts, he lies down on the ground,
He confesses his sins in a loud voice.
2015 With both hands joined and raised toward heaven,
He prays God to grant him Paradise,
He blessed Charles and fair France,
And his companion Roland above all others.
His heart fails him, his helmet drops forward,
2020 His whole body falls to the ground,
The Count is dead, he lingers no more.
Noble Roland weeps over him and laments over him,
You shall never hear a sadder man on earth!

151

Now Roland sees that his friend is dead,
2025 Lying prone, his face toward the earth.
He began to lament over him very softly:
"Companion, sir, what a pity, you were so brave!
We were together for years and days,
You never did me harm and I did not wrong you.
2030 Now that you are dead, it is painful for me to live!"
After saying this, the Marquis faints
Upon the horse he calls Veillantif.
He is firm in his pure gold stirrups,
No matter where he goes, he cannot fall.

152

2035 Before Roland had regained consciousness,
Recovered from his swoon or come round,
A very great catastrophe befell him:

Morz sunt Franceis, tuz les i ad perdut,
Senz l'arcevesque e senz Gualter de l'Hum.
2040 Repairez est des muntaignes jus;
A cels d'Espaigne mult s'i est cumbatuz,
Mort sunt si hume, sis unt paiens vencut.
Voeillet o nun, desuz cez vals s'en fuit,
Si reclaimet Rollant, qu'il li aiut:
2045 "E! gentilz quens, vaillanz hom, u ies tu?
Unkes nen oi poür, la u tu fus.
Ço est Gualter, ki cunquist Maëlgut,
Li niés Droün, al vieill e al canut!
Pur vasselage suleie estre tun drut.
2050 Ma hanste est fraite e percet mun escut
E mis osbercs desmailet e rumput;
Par mi le cors. . . .
Sempres murrai, mais cher me sui vendut!"
A icel mot l'at Rollant entendut,
2055 Le cheval brochet, si vient poignant vers lui.   AOI.

153

Rollant ad doel, si fut maltalentifs,
En la grant presse cumencet a ferir.
De cels d'Espaigne en ad getet mort .XX.,
E Gualter .VI. e l'arcevesque .V.
2060 Dient paien: "Feluns humes ad ci!
Guardez, seignurs, qu'il n'en algent vif!
Tut par seit fel ki nes vait envaïr
E recreant ki les lerrat guarir!"
Dunc recumencent e le hu e le cri,
2065 De tutes parz le revunt envaïr.   AOI.

154

Li quens Rollant fut noble guerrer,
Gualter de Hums est bien bon chevaler,
Li arcevesque prozdom e essaiet:
Li uns ne volt l'altre nïent laisser.
2070 En la grant presse i fierent as paiens.
Mil Sarrazins i descendent a piet

126

The French are dead, he has lost every one of them,
Except the Archbishop and Gautier de l'Hum.
2040 The latter has come back down from the mountains;
He has fought hard against the men of Spain,
His men are dead, the pagans have vanquished them.
Willy-nilly, he flees through the valleys,
He calls Roland to help him:
2045 "Ah, noble count, worthy man, where are you?
I was never afraid wherever you were.
It is I, Gautier, who captured Maëlgut,
The nephew of old white-haired Droön!
Because of my courage I used to be your trusted friend.
2050 Now my lance is shattered and my shield pierced,
And the metal links of my hauberk broken and torn apart;
Through the middle of my body. . . .
I shall soon die, but I've sold my life dearly!"
When he said this, Roland heard him,
2055 He spurs his horse and comes toward him at full tilt.   AOI.

153

Roland is in a rage and he is furious,
He begins to strike in the thick of the press.
He threw down dead twenty men from Spain,
Gautier six, and the Archbishop five.
2060 The pagans say: "We've got vicious men here!
See to it, my lords, that they don't escape with their lives!
Whoever fails to attack them is the worst kind of scoundrel,
And whoever allows them to save themselves a coward!"
So they raise once again the hue and cry,
2065 They renew their attack against them from all directions.   AOI.

154

Count Roland was a noble warrior,
Gautier de l'Hum is a very good knight,
The Archbishop worthy and well tried:
The one will in no way abandon the other.
2070 They strike against the pagans in the thick of the press.
A thousand Saracens dismount,

E a cheval sunt .XL. millers.
Men escïentre, nes osent aproismer!
Il lor lancent e lances e espiez,
2075 E wigres e darz e museras e agiez e gieser.
As premers colps i unt ocis Gualter,
Turpins de Reins tut sun escut percet,
Quasset sun elme, si l'unt nasfret el chef,
E sun osberc rumput e desmailet,
2080 Par mi le cors nasfret de .IIII. espiez,
Dedesuz lui ocient sun destrer.
Or est grant doel quant l'arcevesque chiet.   AOI.

155

Turpins de Reins, quant se sent abatut,
De .IIII. espiez par mi le cors ferut,
2085 Isnelement li ber resailit sus.
Rollant reguardet, puis si li est curut
E dist un mot: "Ne sui mie vencut!
Ja bon vassal nen ert vif recreüt."
Il trait Almace, s'espee de acer brun,
2090 En la grant presse mil colps i fiert e plus.
Puis le dist Carles qu'il n'en esparignat nul,
Tels .IIII. cenz i troevet entur lui,
Alquanz nafrez, alquanz par mi ferut,
S'i out d'icels ki les chefs unt perdut.
2095 Ço dit la Geste e cil ki el camp fut,
Li ber Gilie, por qui Deus fait vertuz,
E fist la chartre el muster de Loüm.
Ki tant ne set ne l'ad prod entendut.

156

Li quens Rollant gentemet se cumbat,
2100 Mais le cors ad tressuët e mult chalt.
En la teste ad e dulor e grant mal,
Rumput est li temples, por ço que il cornat.
Mais saveir volt se Charles i vendrat,
Trait l'olifan, fieblement le sunat.
2105 Li emperere s'estut, si l'escultat:

And forty thousand are on horseback.
But, I do believe, they dare not approach them!
They throw lances and spears at them,
2075 Wigars, darts, mizraks, agers, and javelins.
With the first volley they killed Gautier,
Pierced Turpin of Reims's shield through and through,
Smashed his helmet and wounded him in the head,
Broke and tore apart the metal links of his hauberk,
2080 Wounded him through the middle with four spears,
And killed his horse from under him.
Now when the Archbishop falls it is a great pity.　　AOI.

155

Turpin of Reims, feeling himself struck down,
Pierced through the middle by four spears,
2085 The noble man quickly leaped back on his feet.
He looks at Roland, then ran up to him
And said these words: "I am not vanquished!
A good fighter will never give up as long as he's alive."
He draws Almace, his sword of burnished steel,
2090 In the thick of the press, he strikes a thousand blows and more.
Afterward Charles said he spared not a one,
He finds four hundred of them around his body,
Some wounded, others pierced through the middle,
And there were some of them who had lost their heads.
2095 So says the Chronicle and the one who was on the battlefield,
Saint Giles, for whom God performs miracles,
He set it down in a charter in the minster of Laon.
Anyone who does not know all this has missed the point.

156

Count Roland is fighting nobly,
2100 But his body is covered with sweat and is very hot.
He has an ache and a great pain in his head,
His temple is burst because he sounded the horn.
But he wants to know if Charles will come,
He draws the oliphant, he sounded it feebly.
2105 The Emperor halted and listened to it:

"Seignurs," dist il, "Mult malement nos vait!
Rollant mis niés hoi cest jur nus defalt,
Jo oi al corner que guaires ne vivrat.
Ki estre i voelt isnelement chevalzt!
2110 Sunez voz grasles tant que en cest ost ad!"
Seisante milie en i cornent si halt,
Sunent li munt e respondent li val.
Paien l'entendent, nel tindrent mie en gab,
Dit l'un a l'altre: "Karlun avrum nus ja!"

157

2115 Dient paien: "L'emperere repairet, AOI.
De cels de France oëz suner les graisles!
Se Carles vient, de nus i avrat perte.
Se Rollant vit, nostre guerre novelet,
Perdud avuns Espaigne, nostre tere."
2120 Tels .IIII. cenz s'en asemblent a helmes,
E des meillors ki el camp qüient estre,
A Rollant rendent un estur fort e pesme.
Or ad li quens endreit sei asez que faire. AOI.

158

Li quens Rollant, quant il les veit venir,
2125 Tant se fait fort e fiers e maneviz!
Ne lur lerat tant cum il serat vif.
Siet el cheval qu'om cleimet Veillantif,
Brochet le bien des esperuns d'or fin,
En la grant presse les vait tuz envaïr,
2130 Enseml'od lui arcevesques Turpin.
Dist l'un a l'altre: "Ça vus traiez, ami!
De cels de France les corns avuns oït.
Carles repairet, li reis poësteïfs!"

159

Li quens Rollant unkes n'amat cuard,
2135 Ne orguillos, ne malvais hume de male part,
Ne chevaler, se il ne fust bon vassal.

"My lords," he said, "things are going very badly for us!
My nephew Roland will be gone from us this day,
I hear by the sound of the horn that he will not live much longer.
Anyone who wants to be there had better ride fast!
2110 Blow your bugles, every single one in this army!"
Sixty thousand horns blow so loud
The mountains resound and the valleys echo.
The pagans hear it and they do not think lightly of it,
One says to the other: "We'll soon have Charles to deal with!"

157

2115 The pagans say: "The Emperor is returning, AOI.
Listen to the bugle calls of the men from France!
If Charles comes, it will mean losses for us.
If Roland lives, our war begins anew,
We have lost Spain, our land."
2120 Four hundred of them assemble, wearing helmets,
Those who consider themselves to be the best on the battlefield,
They make a heavy and savage attack upon Roland.
For his part, the Count now has much to do. AOI.

158

When Count Roland sees them coming,
2125 He makes himself so strong, so fierce, so sharp!
He will not give in to them as long as he is alive.
He sits astride the horse called Veillantif,
He urges him on with his pure gold spurs,
He attacks them all in the thick of the press,
2130 Archbishop Turpin is with him.
One pagan said to the other: "Come on, my friend!
We have heard the bugles of the men from France.
Charles, the mighty king, is returning!"

159

Count Roland never cared for any coward,
2135 Villain, or evil man with a bad character,
Or any knight if he were not a good fighter.

Li arcevesques Turpin en apelat:
"Sire, a pied estes e jo sui a ceval,
Pur vostre amur ici prendrai estal.
2140 Ensemble avruns e le ben e le mal,
Ne vos lerrai pur nul hume de car.
Encui rendruns a paiens cest asalt,
Les colps des mielz, cels sunt de Durendal."
Dist l'arcevesque: "Fel seit ki ben n'i ferrat!
2145 Carles repairet, ki ben nus vengerat."

160

Paien dient: "Si mare fumes nez!
Cum pesmes jurz nus est hoi ajurnez!
Perdut avum noz seignurs e noz pers,
Carles repeiret od sa grant ost, li ber.
2150 De cels de France odum les graisles clers,
Grant est la noise de Munjoie escrier.
Li quens Rollant est de tant grant fiertet,
Ja n'ert vencut pur nul hume carnel.
Lançuns a lui, puis sil laissums ester."
2155 E il si firent darz e wigres asez,
Espiez e lances e museraz enpennez.
L'escut Rollant unt frait e estroët,
E sun osberc rumput e desmailet,
Mais enz el cors ne l'ad mie adeset.
2160 Mais Veillantif unt en .XXX. lius nafret
Desuz le cunte, si l'i unt mort laisset.
Paien s'en fuient, puis sil laisent ester.
Li quens Rollant i est remés a pied. AOI.

161

Paien s'en fuient, curuçus e irez,
2165 Envers Espaigne tendent de l'espleiter.
Li quens Rollant nes ad dunt encalcer,
Perdut i ad Veillantif, sun destrer,
Voellet o nun, remés i est a piet.
A l'arcevesque Turpin alat aider,
2170 Sun elme ad or li deslaçat del chef,

He called Archbishop Turpin:
"My lord, you are on foot and I am on horseback,
For love of you, I shall make a stand here.
2140 We shall endure together the good and the bad,
I shall not abandon you for any man alive.
In a moment we shall pay the pagans back for this attack,
The best blows are those of Durendal."
The Archbishop said: "Damn anyone who will not strike hard!
2145 Charles, who will avenge us well, is returning."

160

The pagans say: "We were born for such misfortune!
What a cruel day has dawned for us this day!
We have lost our lords and our peers,
Brave Charles is returning with his great army.
2150 We hear the clear bugles of the men from France,
The noise from those shouting 'Monjoie!' is great.
Count Roland is so fierce,
He shall never be vanquished by any man alive.
Let's throw our spears at him, then let him be."
2155 So they did this with a rain of darts and wigars,
Spears, lances, and feathered mizraks.
They pierced and punctured Roland's shield,
And shattered and broke the metal links of his hauberk,
But not a spear entered his body.
2160 However, they wounded Veillantif in thirty places
Under the Count, and they left him dead.
The pagans flee, thus letting him be.
Count Roland now remains on foot. AOI.

161

The pagans flee, angry and vexed,
2165 They strive with all their might to reach Spain.
Count Roland does not have any way to pursue them,
He has lost his war-horse Veillantif,
Willy-nilly, he now remains on foot.
He went to help Archbishop Turpin,
2170 He unlaced his golden helmet from his head,

133

Si li tolit le blanc osberc leger.
E sun blialt li ad tut detrenchet,
En ses granz plaies les pans li ad butet.
Cuntre sun piz puis si l'ad enbracet,
2175 Sur l'erbe verte puis l'at suëf culchet.
Mult dulcement li ad Rollant preiet:
"E! gentilz hom, car me dunez cunget!
Noz cumpaignuns, que oümes tanz chers,
Or sunt il morz, nes i devuns laiser.
2180 Joes voell aler querre e entercer,
Dedevant vos juster e enrenger."
Dist l'arcevesque: "Alez e repairez!
Cist camp est vostre, mercit Deu, vostre e mien."

162

Rollant s'en turnet, par le camp vait tut suls,
2185 Cercet les vals e si cercet les munz.
Iloec truvat Gerin e Gerer sun cumpaignun,
E si truvat Berenger e Attun;
Iloec truvat Anseïs e Sansun,
Truvat Gerard le veill de Russillun.
2190 Par uns e uns les ad pris, le barun,
A l'arcevesque en est venuz atut,
Sis mist en reng dedevant ses genuilz.
Li arcevesque ne poet muër n'en plurt,
Lievet sa main, fait sa beneïçun.
2195 Aprés ad dit: "Mare fustes, seignurs!
Tutes voz anmes ait Deus li Glorius!
En pareïs les metet en sentes flurs!
La meie mort me rent si anguissus,
Ja ne verrai le riche empereür!"

163

2200 Rollant s'en turnet, le camp vait recercer,
Sun cumpaignun ad truvet, Oliver.
Encuntre sun piz estreit l'ad enbracet,
Si cum il poet a l'arcevesques en vent,
Sur un escut l'ad as altres culchet,

He took off the light white hauberk.
And he cut his under-tunic all in pieces,
He puts the strips in his great wounds.
Then he embraced him against his breast,
2175 Afterward he laid him softly on the green grass.
Roland begged him very gently:
"Oh, noble man, pray give me leave!
Our companions, whom we held so dear,
Are dead now and we must not abandon them.
2180 I want to go look for them and identify them,
To lay them out and line them up before you."
The Archbishop said: "Go and then return!
This battlefield is yours, thank God, yours and mine."

162

Roland turns and goes away, he wanders through the field all alone,
2185 He searches the valleys and he searches the mountains.
There he found Gerin and his companion Gerier,
And he found Berengier and Atton;
There he found Anseïs and Samson,
He found old Gerard of Roussillon.
2190 The knight took them one by one,
He came back with them to the Archbishop,
He lined them up before his knees.
The Archbishop cannot help crying,
He raises his hand, he gives his blessing.
2195 Afterward he said: "You are to be pitied, my lords!
May God in His Glory have all your souls!
May He place them among the holy flowers!
My own death is causing me such anguish,
I shall never see the mighty Emperor!"

163

2200 Roland turns and goes away, he sets out to search the field,
He found his companion Oliver.
He embraced him tight against his breast,
He comes to the Archbishop as best he can,
He laid him with the others on a shield,

2205 E l'arcevesque les ad asols e seignet.
Idunc agreget le doel e la pitet.
Ço dit Rollant: "Bels cumpainz Oliver,
Vos fustes filz al duc Reiner
Ki tint la marche del Val de Runers.
2210 Pur hanste freindre e pur escuz peceier,
Pur orgoillos veintre e esmaier
E pur prozdomes tenir e cunseiller
E pur glutun veintre e esmaier,
En nule tere n'ad meillor chevaler!"

164

2215 Li quens Rollant, quant il veit mort ses pers
E Oliver, qu'il tant poeit amer,
Tendrur en out, cumencet a plurer.
En sun visage fut mult desculurer.
Si grant doel out que mais ne pout ester,
2220 Voeillet o nun, a tere chet pasmet.
Dist l'arcevesque: "Tant mare fustes, ber!"

165

Li arcevesques, quant vit pasmer Rollant,
Dunc out tel doel unkes mais n'out si grant.
Tendit sa main, si ad pris l'olifan.
2225 En Rencesvals ad un ewe curant,
Aler i volt, sin durrat a Rollant.
Sun petit pas s'en turnet cancelant.
Il est si fieble qu'il ne poet en avant,
N'en ad vertut, trop ad perdut del sanc.
2230 Einz que om alast un sul arpent de camp,
Falt li le coer, si est chaeit avant.
La sue mort l'i vait mult angoissant.

166

Li quens Rollant revient de pasmeisuns,
Sur piez se drecet, mais il ad grant dulur.
2235 Guardet aval e si guardet amunt:

136

2205 And the Archbishop absolved them and crossed them.
Then the sorrow and the pity intensify.
Roland says: "Good comrade Oliver,
You were the son of Duke Renier,
Who held the march of the Valley of Runers.
2210 When it comes to smashing lances and piercing shields,
Vanquishing and dismaying villains,
Aiding and counseling worthy men,
Vanquishing and dismaying evildoers,
There is no finer knight in any land!"

164

2215 Count Roland sees his peers dead
And Oliver, whom he loved so well,
He was moved with pity, he begins to weep.
His face lost all its color.
He suffered such pain that he could no longer stand,
2220 Willy-nilly, he falls to the ground.
The Archbishop said: "You are to be pitied, worthy knight!"

165

When the Archbishop saw Roland faint,
He suffered greater anguish than ever before.
He stretched out his hand and took the oliphant.
2225 At Roncevaux there is a running stream,
He wants to go there, he will give some water to Roland.
He turns and goes away with short, faltering steps.
He is so weak that he cannot go any farther,
He has not the strength to, he has lost too much blood.
2230 In less time than it would take a man to cover a single acre,
His heart fails him and he falls forward.
His death is gripping him hard.

166

Count Roland recovers from his swoon,
He rises to his feet, but he is suffering great pain.
2235 He gazes uphill and he gazes downhill:

Sur l'erbe verte, ultre ses cumpaignuns,
La veit gesir le nobilie barun,
Ço est l'arcevesque, que Deus mist en sun num.
Cleimet sa culpe, si reguardet amunt,
2240 Cuntre le ciel amsdous ses mains ad juinz,
Si priet Deu que pareïs li duinst.
Morz est Turpin, le guerreier Charlun.
Par granz batailles e par mult bels sermons
Cuntre paiens fut tuz tens campiuns.
2245 Deus li otreit seinte beneïçun! AOI.

167

Li quens Rollant veit l'arcevesque a tere:
Defors sun cors veit gesir la buële,
Desuz le frunt li buillit la cervele.
Desur sun piz, entre les dous furceles,
2250 Cruisiedes ad ses blanches mains, les beles.
Forment le pleignet a la lei de sa tere:
"E! gentilz hom, chevaler de bon aire,
Hoi te cumant al Glorius celeste!
Jamais n'ert hume plus volenters le serve.
2255 Des les apostles ne fut hom tel prophete
Pur lei tenir e pur humes atraire.
Ja la vostre anme nen ait sufraite!
De pareïs li seit la porte uverte!"

168

Ço sent Rollant que la mort li est pres,
2260 Par les oreilles fors s'e ist la cervel.
De ses pers priet Deu ques apelt,
E pois de lui a l'angle Gabriël.
Prist l'olifan, que reproce n'en ait,
E Durendal s'espee en l'altre main.
2265 Dun arcbaleste ne poet traire un quarrel,
Devers Espaigne en vait en un guaret.
Muntet sur un tertre, desuz .II. arbres bels,
Quatre perruns i ad, de marbre faiz.

On the green grass, beyond his companions,
He sees the noble warrior lying,
It is the Archbishop, whom God sent in his name.
The Archbishop says his confession, he gazes upward,
2240 He has joined and raised both hands toward heaven,
And he prays God to grant him Paradise.
Charles's warrior Turpin is dead.
By fighting great battles and preaching many fine sermons,
He was always a relentless fighter against the pagans.
2245 May God grant him his holy blessing! AOI.

167

Count Roland sees the Archbishop on the ground:
He sees his entrails spilled outside his body,
His brain is oozing out beneath his forehead.
Over his breast, on the sternum,
2250 He has crossed his beautiful white hands.
Roland laments over him in a loud voice, as is customary in his land:
"Ah, noble man, high-born knight,
I commend you this day to God in His celestial Glory!
No man shall ever serve Him more willingly.
2255 There never was such a prophet since the Apostles
To keep the Faith and to win men over.
May your soul not endure any suffering!
May it find the gate of Paradise open!"

168

Roland feels that death is near,
2260 His brain is coming out through his ears.
He prays God to call his Peers,
And then, for his own sake, he prays the angel Gabriel.
He took the oliphant so as not to incur any blame,
And his sword Durendal with his other hand.
2265 Where no crossbow can shoot a bolt,
He goes in the direction of Spain to a fallow field.
He climbs a hill and halts beneath two beautiful trees.
There are four objects made of marble there.

Sur l'erbe verte si est caeit envers,
2270 La s'est pasmet, kar la mort li est pres.

169

Halt sunt li pui e mult halt les arbres,
Quatre perruns i ad luisant de marbre.
Sur l'erbe verte li quens Rollant se pasmet.
Uns Sarrazins tute veie l'esguardet,
2275 Si se feinst mort, si gist entre les altres.
Del sanc luat sun cors e sun visage,
Met sei en piez e de curre s'astet.
Bels fut e forz e de grant vasselage,
Par sun orgoill cumencet mortel rage.
2280 Rollant saisit e sun cors e ses armes
E dist un mot: "Vencut est li niés Carles!
Iceste espee porterai en Arabe."
En cel tireres li quens s'aperçut alques.

170

Ço sent Rollant que s'espee li tolt,
2285 Uvrit les oilz, si li ad dit un mot:
"Men escïentre, tu n'ies mie des noz!"
Tient l'olifan, que unkes perdre ne volt,
Sil fiert en l'elme, ki gemmet fut a or.
Fruisset l'acer e la teste e les os,
2290 Amsdous les oilz del chef li ad mis fors,
Jus a ses piez si l'ad tresturnet mort.
Aprés li dit: "Culvert paien, cum fus unkes si os
Que me saisis, ne a dreit ne a tort?
Ne l'orrat hume ne t'en tienget por fol.
2295 Fenduz en est mis olifans el gros,
Caiuz en est li cristals e li ors."

171

Ço sent Rollant la veüe ad perdue,
Met sei sur piez, quanqu'il poet s'esvertuet,
En sun visage sa culur ad perdue.

He fell backward on the green grass,
2270 He fainted there, for death is near.

169

The mountains are high and the trees are very high,
There are four shiny marble objects there.
Count Roland faints on the green grass.
A Saracen is watching him all the while,
2275 He feigns death and lies amid the others.
He smeared his body and his face with blood,
He rises to his feet and makes a dash forward.
He was well proportioned, strong, and very brave,
Through pride he embarks upon an act of fatal folly.
2280 He seized Roland's body and his weapons,
And he said these words: "Charles's nephew is vanquished!
I shall carry this sword to Arabia."
But as the Saracen was pulling, the Count came round a bit.

170

Roland feels the Saracen stealing his sword from him,
2285 He opened his eyes and said these words to him:
"I don't believe you're one of our men!"
He holds on to the oliphant, he does not want to part with it for a
    single moment,
And he strikes him on the helmet, whose gold is wrought with gems.
He smashes the steel, the head, the bones,
2290 He knocked both his eyes out of his head,
He tumbled him over dead at his feet.
Afterward he says: "Dirty pagan, whatever possessed you
To seize me rightly or wrongly?
No one will hear of this without thinking you were mad.
2295 My oliphant is split at the wide end now,
The crystal and the gold ornaments have fallen off."

171

Roland notices that his sight is failing him,
He rises to his feet and exerts himself to the utmost,
All color has faded from his face.

2300 Dedevant lui ad une perre byse,
.X. colps i fiert par doel e par rancune.
Cruist li acers, ne freint ne n'esgruignet.
"E!" dist li quens, "seinte Marie, aiue!
E! Durendal, bone, si mare fustes!
2305 Quant jo mei perd, de vos n'en ai mais cure.
Tantes batailles en camp en ai vencues
E tantes teres larges escumbatues
Que Carles tient, ki la barbe ad canue!
Ne vos ait hume ki pur altre fuiet!
2310 Mult bon vassal vos ad lung tens tenue,
Jamais n'ert tel en France l'asolue."

172

Rollant ferit el perrun de sardonie,
Cruist li acers, ne briset ne n'esgrunie.
Quant il ço vit que n'en pout mie freindre,
2315 A sei meïsme la cumencet a pleindre:
"E! Durendal, cum es bele e clere e blanche!
Cuntre soleill si luises e reflambes!
Carles esteit es vals de Moriane,
Quant Deus del cel li mandat par sun agle
2320 Qu'il te dunast a un cunte cataignie:
Dunc la me ceinst li gentilz reis, li magnes.
Jo l'en cunquis e Anjou e Bretaigne,
Si l'en cunquis e Peitou e le Maine;
Jo l'en cunquis Normendie la franche,
2325 Si l'en cunquis Provence e Equitaigne
E Lumbardie e trestute Romaine;
Jo l'en cunquis Baiver e tute Flandres
E Burguigne e trestute Puillanie,
Costentinnoble, dunt il out la fiance,
2330 E en Saisonie fait il ço qu'il demandet;
Jo l'en cunquis e Escoce e Vales Islonde
E Engletere, que il teneit sa cambre;
Cunquis l'en ai païs e teres tantes,
Que Carles tient, ki ad la barbe blanche.
2335 Pur ceste espee ai dulor e pesance,
Mielz voeill murir qu'entre paiens remaigne.
Deus Pere, n'en laiser hunir France!"

2300 There is a dark stone in front of him,
He strikes it ten blows in bitterness and frustration.
The steel grates, but it is not smashed or nicked.
"Oh," said the Count, "Holy Mary, help me!
Oh, Durendal, noble one, you are to be pitied!
2305 Since I am finished, I no longer have you in my care.
I have won so many battles in the field with you
And conquered so many vast lands
Over which white-bearded Charles rules!
May no turn-tail ever possess you!
2310 A very good knight has owned you for a long time,
Never again shall there be such a sword in blessed France."

172

Roland struck the sardonyx stone,
The steel grates, but it does not break or nick.
Seeing that he cannot smash it,
2315 He begins to lament over it to himself:
"Oh, Durendal, how beautiful you are, how clear, how bright!
How you shine and flash against the sun!
Charles was in the valleys of Maurienne
When God instructed him from heaven on high by His angel
2320 To give you to a captain count:
So the great, noble king girded me with it.
With it I conquered Anjou and Brittany,
With it I conquered Poitou and Maine,
With it I conquered Normandy the free,
2325 With it I conquered Provence and Aquitaine,
Lombardy and all Romagna;
With it I conquered Bavaria and all Flanders,
Burgundy, all Poland,
And Constantinople, which rendered homage to him,
2330 And he does as he wishes in Saxony;
With it I conquered Scotland, Iceland,
And England, which he held under his jurisdiction;
With it I conquered so many countries and lands
Over which white-bearded Charles rules.
2335 I feel sad and heavy-hearted for this sword,
I would rather die than have it remain with the pagans.
God, our Father, do not let France be dishonored in this way!"

173

Rollant ferit en une perre bise,
Plus en abat que jo ne vos sai dire.
2340 L'espee cruist, ne fruisset ne ne brise,.
Cuntre ciel amunt est resortie.
Quant veit li quens que ne la freindrat mie,
Mult dulcement la pleinst a sei meïsme :
"E! Durendal, cum es bele e seintisme!
2345 En l'oriet punt asez i ad reliques :
La dent seint Perre e del sanc seint Basilie
E des chevels mun seignor seint Denise,
Del vestement i ad seinte Marie.
Il nen est dreiz que paiens te baillisent,
2350 De chrestïens devez estre servie.
Ne vos ait hume ki facet cuardie!
Mult larges teres de vus avrai cunquises,
Que Carles tent, ki la barbe ad flurie,
E li empereres en est ber e riches."

174

2355 Ço sent Rollant que la mort le tresprent,
Devers la teste sur le quer li descent.
Desuz un pin i est alet curant,
Sur l'erbe verte s'i est culchet adenz.
Desuz lui met s'espee e l'olifan ensumet.
2360 Turnat sa teste vers la paiene gent :
Pur ço l'at fait que il voelt veirement
Que Carles diet e trestute sa gent,
Li gentilz quens, qu'il fut mort cunquerant.
Cleimet sa culpe e menut e suvent,
2365 Pur ses pecchez Deu en puroffrid lo guant.   AOI.

175

Ço sent Rollant de sun tens n'i ad plus,
Devers Espaigne est en un pui agut.
A l'une main si ad sun piz batud :
"Deus, meie culpe vers les tues vertuz
2370 De mes pecchez, des granz e des menuz

173

Roland struck a dark stone,
He whacks off more than I can say.
2340 The sword grates, but neither shatters nor breaks,
It rebounds upward toward heaven.
The Count, seeing that he cannot smash it,
Laments over it softly to himself:
"Oh, Durendal, how beautiful you are and how very holy!
2345 There are many relics in the golden hilt:
Saint Peter's tooth, some of Saint Basil's blood,
Some of my lord Saint Denis's hair,
Some of Saint Mary's clothing.
It is not right for the pagans to own you,
2350 You must be served by Christians.
May no coward ever possess you!
With you I conquered many vast lands
Over which white-bearded Charles rules,
And the Emperor is powerful and mighty as a consequence."

174

2355 Roland feels that death is overcoming him,
It descends from his head to his heart.
He ran beneath a pine tree,
He lay down prone on the green grass.
He places his sword and (also?) his oliphant beneath him.
2360 He turned his head toward the pagan army:
He did this because he earnestly desires
That Charles and all his men say
That the noble Count died as a conqueror.
He beats his breast in rapid succession over and over again,
2365 He proffered his gauntlet to God for his sins.   AOI.

175

Roland feels that his time is up,
He is on a steep hill, his face turned toward Spain.
He beat his breast with one hand:
"Mea culpa, Almighty God,
2370 For my sins, great and small,

Que jo ai fait des l'ure que nez fui
Tresqu'a cest jur que ci sui consoüt!"
Sun destre guant en ad vers Deu tendut,
Angles del ciel i descendent a lui.   AOI.

176

2375 Li quens Rollant se jut desuz un pin,
Envers Espaigne en ad turnet sun vis.
De plusurs choses a remembrer li prist:
De tantes teres cum li bers cunquist,
De dulce France, des humes de sun lign,
2380 De Carlemagne, sun seignor, kil nurrit.
Ne poet muër n'en plurt e ne suspirt,
Mais lui meïsme ne volt mettre en ubli,
Cleimet sa culpe, si priet Deu mercit:
"Veire Patene, ki unkes ne mentis,
2385 Seint Lazaron de mort resurrexis
E Danïel des leons guaresis,
Guaris de mei l'anme de tuz perilz
Pur les pecchez que en ma vie fis!"
Sun destre guant a Deu en puroffrit,
2390 Seint Gabrïel de sa main l'ad pris.
Desur sun braz teneit le chef enclin,
Juntes ses mains est alet a sa fin.
Deus tramist sun angle Cherubin
E seint Michel del Peril,
2395 Ensembl'od els sent Gabrïel i vint.
L'anme del cunte portent en pareïs.

177

Morz est Rollant, Deus en ad l'anme es cels.
Li emperere en Rencesvals parvient.
Il nen i ad ne veie ne senter,
2400 Ne voide tere, ne alne ne plein pied
Que il n'i ait o Franceis o paien.
Carles escriet: "U estes vos, bels niés?
U est l'arcevesque e li quens Oliver?
U est Gerins e sis cumpainz Gerers?

146

Which I committed from the time I was born
To this day when I am overtaken here!"
He offered his right gauntlet to God,
Angels from heaven descend toward him.   AOI.

176

2375   Count Roland lay beneath a pine tree,
He has turned his face toward Spain.
He began to remember many things:
The many lands he conquered as a brave knight,
Fair France, the men from whom he is descended,
2380   Charlemagne, his lord, who raised him.
He cannot help weeping and sighing.
But he does not wish to forget prayers for his own soul,
He says his confession in a loud voice and prays for God's mercy:
"True Father, who never lied,
2385   Who resurrected Saint Lazarus from the dead
And saved Daniel from the lions,
Protect my soul from all perils
Due to the sins I committed during my life!"
He proffered his right gauntlet to God,
2390   Saint Gabriel took it from his hand.
He laid his head down over his arm,
He met his end, his hands joined together.
God sent His angel Cherubin
And Saint Michael of the Peril,
2395   Saint Gabriel came with them.
They bear the Count's soul to Paradise.

177

Roland is dead, his soul is with God in Heaven.
The Emperor reaches Roncevaux.
There is no road or path,
2400   No open ground, no yard, no foot of land
Not covered with a Frenchman or a pagan.
Charles cries out: "Where are you, dear nephew?
Where is the Archbishop and Count Oliver?
Where is Gerin and his companion Gerier?

2405 U est Otes e li quens Berengers,
  Ive e Ivorie, que jo aveie tant chers?
  Que est devenuz li Guascuinz Engeler,
  Sansun li dux e Anseïs li bers?
  U est Gerard de Russillun li veilz,
2410 Li .XII. per, que jo aveie laiset?"
  De ço qui chelt, quant nul n'en respundiet?
  "Deus!" dist li reis, "tant me pois enrager
  Que jo ne fui a l'estur cumencer!"
  Tiret sa barbe cum hom ki est iret,
2415 Plurent des oilz si baron chevaler.
  Encuntre tere se pasment .XX. millers,
  Naimes li dux en ad mult grant pitet.

178

  Il n'en i ad chevaler ne barun
  Que de pitet mult durement ne plurt.
2420 Plurent lur filz, lur freres, lur nevolz
  E lur amis e lur lige seignurs;
  Encuntre tere se pasment li plusur.
  Naimes li dux d'iço ad fait que proz,
  Tuz premereins l'ad dit l'empereür:
2425 "Veez avant de dous liwes de nus,
  Vedeir puëz les granz chemins puldrus,
  Qu'asez i ad de la gent paienur.
  Car chevalchez! Vengez ceste dulor!"
  "E! Deus!" dist Carles, "ja sunt il ja si luinz!
2430 Cunsentez mei e dreiture e honur,
  De France dulce m'unt tolue la flur."
  Li reis cumandet Gebuin e Otun,
  Tedbalt de Reins e le cunte Milun:
  "Guardez le champ e les vals e les munz.
2435 Lessez gesir les morz tut issi cun il sunt:
  Que n'i adeist ne beste ne lion,
  Ne n'i adeist esquier ne garçun;
  Jo vus defend que n'i adeist nuls hom,
  Josque Deus voeilge que en cest camp revengum."
2440 E cil respundent dulcement, par amur:
  "Dreiz emperere, cher sire, si ferum!"
  Mil chevaler i retient des lur.   AOI.

148

2405 Where is Oton and Count Berenger,
Yvon and Yvoire, whom I love so dearly?
What has become of Engelier the Gascon,
Duke Samson and brave Anseïs?
Where is old Gerard of Roussillon,
2410 Where are the Twelve Peers I had left behind?"
But what is the use when no one replies?
"God!" said the King, "how it enrages me
That I wasn't present at the beginning of the battle!"
He tugs his beard like a man who is angry,
2415 His brave knights' eyes are brimming with tears.
Twenty thousand fall to the ground in a swoon,
Duke Naimes feels very great sorrow.

178

Every knight and brave warrior
Sheds bitter tears of sorrow.
2420 They weep for their sons, their brothers, their nephews,
Their friends and their liege lords;
Most of them fall to the ground in a swoon.
Duke Naimes did the wise thing,
He was the first to speak to the Emperor:
2425 "Look ahead of us, at a distance of two leagues,
You can see the dust rising from the main roads,
For they are choked with the pagan army.
Ride now! Avenge this hurt!"
"Oh, God!" said Charles, "they are already so far away!
2430 Grant me justice and honor,
They have ravished the flower of fair France."
The King commands Geboin and Oton,
Tedbald of Reims and Count Milon:
"Guard the battlefield, the valleys, and the mountains.
2435 Let the dead lie exactly as they are now:
Let no beast or lion touch them,
Let no squire or servant boy touch them either;
I forbid you to allow any man to touch them
Until it is God's will that we return to this battlefield."
2440 And the latter replied gently and with affection:
"Just Emperor, dear lord, we shall do it!"
They retain a thousand of their knights.   AOI.

179

Li empereres fait ses graisles suner,
Puis si chevalchet od sa grant ost li ber.
2445 De cels d'Espaigne unt lur les dos turnez,
Tenent l'enchalz, tuit en sunt cumunel.
Quant veit li reis le vespres decliner,
Sur l'erbe verte descent li reis en un pred,
Culchet sei a tere, si priet Damnedeu
2450 Que li soleilz facet pur lui arester,
La nuit targer e le jur demurer.
Ais li un angle ki od lui soelt parler,
Isnelement si li ad comandet:
"Charle, chevalche, car tei ne falt clartet!
2455 La flur de France as perdut, ço set Deus.
Venger te poez de la gent criminel."
A icel mot est l'empere muntet.   AOI.

180

Pur Karlemagne fist Deus vertuz mult granz,
Car li soleilz est remés en estant.
2460 Paien s'en fuient, ben les chalcent Franc.
El Val Tenebrus la les vunt ateignant,
Vers Sarraguce les enchalcent ferant,
A colps pleners les en vunt ociant,
Tolent lur veies e les chemins plus granz.
2465 L'ewe de Sebre, el lur est dedevant:
Mult est parfunde, merveilluse e curant,
Il n'en i ad barge, ne drodmund ne caland.
Paiens recleiment un lur deu, Tervagant,
Puis saillent enz, mais il n'i unt guarant.
2470 Li adubez en sunt li plus pesant,
Envers les funz s'en turnerent alquanz;
Li altre en vunt cuntreval flotant.
Li miez guariz en unt boüd itant,
Tuz sunt neiez par merveillus ahan.
2475 Franceis escrient: "Mare fustes, Rollant!"   AOI.

181

Quant Carles veit que tuit sunt mort paiens,
Alquanz ocis e li plusur neiet—

179

The Emperor orders his bugles to be sounded,
Then the brave man rides off with his great army.
2445 They have made the men of Spain turn tail,
They are in hot pursuit and all join in.
When the King sees the afternoon light waning,
He dismounts on the green grass in a meadow,
He prostrates himself on the ground and prays the Lord God
2450 That He stop the sun for him,
That He postpone nightfall and prolong daylight.
Now there appears to him an angel who regularly speaks with him,
He promptly commands the King:
"Ride, Charles, for you do not lack daylight!
2455 God knows that you have lost the flower of France.
You can now avenge yourself on this crime-ridden people."
When he heard this, the Emperor mounted up.   AOI.

180

God performed a very great miracle for Charlemagne,
For the sun stood still.
2460 The pagans flee, the Franks pursue them relentlessly.
They overtake them in the Val Tenebros,
Spurring on, they pursue them toward Saragossa,
Slaying them with mighty blows.
They cut off their getaway and main escape routes.
2465 The Ebro River is before them now:
It is very deep, fearsome, and rapid,
There is no barge, galley, or lighter.
The pagans cry out to Tervagant, one of their gods,
Then jump in, but they receive no protection.
2470 The men in full armor weigh the heaviest,
Some go swirling down to the bottom;
The others go floating downstream.
The survivors, however, swallowed so much water
That they all drowned in fearful pain.
2475 The French cry out: "You are to be pitied, Roland!"   AOI.

181

Charles sees that all the pagans are dead,
Some killed, but most of them drowned—

Mult grant eschec en unt si chevaler—
Li gentilz reis descendut est a piet,
2480 Culchet sei a tere, sin ad Deu graciet.
Quant il se drecet, li soleilz est culchet.
Dist l'emperere: "Tens est del herberger,
En Rencesvals est tart del repairer.
Noz chevals sunt e las e ennuiez:
2485 Tolez lur les seles, le freins qu'il unt es chefs,
E par cez prez les laisez refreider."
Respundent Franc: "Sire, vos dites bien." AOI.

182

Li emperere ad prise sa herberge.
Franceis descendent en la tere deserte,
2490 A lur chevals unt toleites les seles,
Les freins a or e metent jus les testes,
Livrent lur prez, asez i ad fresche herbe;
D'altre cunreid ne lur poeent plus faire.
Ki mult est las, il se dort cuntre tere.
2495 Icele noit n'unt unkes escalguaite.

183

Li emperere s'est culcet en un pret,
Sun grant espiet met a sun chef li ber.
Icele noit ne se volt il desarmer,
Si ad vestut sun blanc osberc sasfret,
2500 Laciet sun elme, ki est a or gemmet,
Ceinte Joiuse—unches ne fut sa per—
Ki cascun jur muët .XXX. clartez.
Asez savum de la lance parler
Dunt Nostre Sire fut en la cruiz nasfret:
2505 Carles en ad la mure, mercit Deu,
En l'oret punt l'ad faite manuvrer.
Pur ceste honur e pur ceste bontet,
Li nums Joiuse l'espee fut dunet.
Baruns franceis nel deivent ublïer:
2510 Enseigne en unt de Munjoie crier,
Pur ço nes poet nule gent cuntrester.

His knights win a huge mass of booty in the process—
Then the noble King dismounted,
2480 He lies on the ground, he thanked God.
When he rises, the sun has set.
The Emperor said: "It is time to bivouac,
It is too late to return to Roncevaux.
Our horses are tired and exhausted:
2485 Remove their saddles and the bridles from their heads,
And let them refresh themselves in these meadows.
The Franks reply: "Well said, sire."   AOI.

182

The Emperor has pitched camp.
The French dismount in the deserted land,
2490 They have taken the saddles away from their horses,
They remove the golden bridles from their heads,
They turn them loose in the meadows, there is abundant fresh grass there;
They have no other provisions for them.
Anyone who is very tired sleeps on the bare ground.
2495 That night they do not mount guard at all.

183

The Emperor lies down in a meadow,
The brave man sets his great spear down next to his head.
That night he does not wish to take off his armor,
He has put on his shiny saffron hauberk,
2500 Laced on his helmet of gold wrought with gems,
Girded Joyeuse—it has always been without peer—
Which changes color thirty times a day.
We can say a good deal about the Lance
With which Our Lord was wounded on the Cross:
2505 Charles has its tip, thanks be to God,
He had it mounted in the golden pommel of his sword.
Because of this honor and because of this grace,
The name Joyeuse was given to the sword.
French knights must not forget it:
2510 They derive their battle cry "Monjoie!" from it,
That is why no people on earth can withstand them.

184

Clere est la noit e la lune luisant.
Carles se gist, mais doel ad de Rollant,
E d'Oliver li peiset mult forment,
2515 Des .XII. pers e de la franceise gent.
En Rencesvals ad laiset morz sanglenz.
Ne poet muër n'en plurt e nes dement,
E priet Deu qu'as anmes seit guarent.
Las est li reis, kar la peine est mult grant,
2520 Endormiz est, ne pout mais en avant.
Par tuz les prez or se dorment li Franc.
N'i ad cheval ki puisset ester en estant,
Ki herbe voelt, il la prent en gisant.
Mult ad apris ki bien conuist ahan.

185

2525 Karles se dort cum hume traveillet.
Seint Gabrïel li ad Deus enveiet,
L'empereür li cumandet a guarder.
Li angles est tute noit a sun chef.
Par avisiun li ad anunciet
2530 D'une bataille ki encuntre lui ert:
Senefiance l'en demustrat mult gref.
Carles guardat amunt envers le ciel,
Veit les tuneires e les venz e les giels
E les orez, les merveillus tempez;
2535 E fous e flambes i est apareillez,
Isnelement sur tute sa gent chet.
Ardent cez hanstes de fraisne e de pumer
E cez escuz jesqu'as bucles d'or mier,
Fruisent cez hanstes de cez trenchanz espiez,
2540 Cruissent osbercs e cez helmes d'acer.
En grant dulor i veit ses chevalers.
Urs e leuparz les voelent puis manger,
Serpenz e guivres, dragun e averser;
Grifuns i ad, plus de trente millers,
2545 N'en i ad cel a Franceis ne s'agiet.
E Franceis crient: "Carlemagne, aidez!"
Li reis en ad e dulur e pitet,
Aler i volt, mais il ad desturber:

184

The night is clear and the moon is shining.
Charles is lying down, but he is grieving for Roland,
And the memory of Oliver weighs heavily upon him,
2515 That of the Twelve Peers, too, and of the French army.
He has left bloody cadavers at Roncevaux.
He cannot help weeping and making an outcry,
And he prays God to save their souls.
The King is worn out, for his sorrow is very great,
2520 He is asleep, he could not stay awake any longer.
The Franks are sleeping everywhere in the meadows.
No horse is able to remain standing,
Any mount wishing grass takes it lying down.
The man who has suffered greatly has learned a good deal.

185

2525 Charles sleeps like a troubled man.
God sent Saint Gabriel to him,
He commands him to watch over the Emperor.
The angel spent the entire night by his head.
In a vision he told him
2530 Of a battle that will be fought against him:
He showed him very ominous signs of this.
Charles gazed upward toward the sky,
He sees the thunderbolts, the winds, the freezing rain,
The storms, the fearsome tempests;
2535 A ball of fire and flames gathers,
Suddenly it falls on all his men.
It burns the ash and applewood spear shafts
And the shields down to their pure gold bosses,
It smashes the shafts of the sharp spears,
2540 Crushes the hauberks and the steel helmets.
He sees his knights in great agony.
Then bears and leopards try to devour them,
Serpents, vipers, dragons, and devils;
There are more than thirty thousand griffins,
2545 All throw themselves upon the French.
And the French cry out: "Help, Charlemagne!"
The King suffers great pain and distress from this,
He tries to go there, but something prevents him:

Devers un gualt uns granz leons li vint,
2550 Mult par ert pesmes e orguillus e fiers.
Sun cors meïsmes i asalt e requert,
E prenent sei a braz ambesdous por loiter;
Mais ço ne set liquels abat ne quels chiet.
Li emperere n'est mie esveillet.

186

2555 Aprés icel li vien un altre avisiun,
Qu'il ert en France, ad Ais, a un perrun,
En dous chaeines s'i teneit un brohun.
Devers Ardene veeit venir .XXX. urs,
Cascun parolet altresi cume hum.
2560 Diseient li: "Sire, rendez le nus!
Il nen est dreiz que il seit mais od vos,
Nostre parent devum estre a sucurs."
De sun paleis uns veltres i acurt,
Entre les altres asaillit le greignur
2565 Sur l'erbe verte, ultre ses cumpaignuns.
La vit li reis si merveillus estur,
Mais ço ne set liquels veint ne quels nun.
Li angles Deu ço ad mustret al barun.
Carles se dort tresqu'al demain, al cler jur.

187

2570 Li reis Marsilie s'en fuit en Sarraguce,
Suz un olive est descendut en l'umbre.
S'espee rent e sun elme e sa bronie,
Sur la verte herbe mult laidement se culcet.
La destre main ad perdue trestute,
2575 Del sanc qu'en ist se pasmet e angoiset.
Dedevant lui sa muiller Bramimunde
Pluret e criet, mult forment se doluset,
Ensembl'od li plus de .XX. mil humes,
Si maldient Carlun e France dulce.
2580 Ad Apolin en curent en une crute,
Tencent a lui, laidement le despersunent:
"E! malvais deus, por quei nus fais tel hunte?

A huge lion came at him from a wood,
2550 It is extremely ferocious, savage, and fierce.
It seeks out and attacks his very person,
And the two of them grapple with each other;
But Charles cannot determine who is throwing, who is falling.
The King did not awake.

186

2555 After this vision came another
In which he was at Aix, in France, before a pillar,
A bear was being restrained there by two chains.
He saw thirty bears coming from the Ardennes,
Each speaks like a man:
2560 They said to him: "Sire, give him back to us!
It isn't right that he stay with you,
We must come to the aid of our kinsman."
A hound comes running out of the palace,
It attacks the biggest among them
2565 On the green grass, away from his companions.
The King saw a fearsome struggle in his dream,
But he does not know who is triumphing and who is not.
The angel of God shows this to the brave man.
Charles sleeps until the next day, bright and early.

187

2570 King Marsile flees to Saragossa,
He dismounts under an olive tree, in the shade.
He gives up his sword, his helmet, and his byrnie,
He lies down, a grisly sight, on the green grass.
He has lost his right hand completely,
2575 He swoons and writhes with pain from the bleeding.
Before him, his wife Bramimonde
Weeps and wails, and sets up a very loud lament,
And with her more than twenty thousand men
Curse Charles and fair France.
2580 They run to an idol of Apollo in a crypt,
They rail at it, they abuse it in vile fashion:
"Oh, evil god, why do you cover us with such shame?

Cest nostre rei por quei lessas cunfundre?
Ki mult te sert, malvais luër l'en dunes!"
2585 Puis si li tolent ses ceptre e sa curune.
Par mains le pendent sur une culumbe,
Entre lur piez a tere le tresturnent,
A granz bastuns le batent e defruisent.
E Tervagan tolent sun escarbuncle
2590 E Mahumet enz en un fosset butent
E porc e chen le mordent e defulent.

188

De paismeisuns en est venuz Marsilies
Fait sei porter en sa cambre voltice,
Plusurs culurs i ad peinz e escrites.
2595 E Bramimunde le pluret, la reïne,
Trait ses chevels, si se cleimet caitive.
A l'altre mot mult haltement s'escriet:
"E! Sarraguce, cum ies oi desguarnie
Del gentil rei ki t'aveit en baillie!
2600 Li nostre deu i unt fait felonie,
Ki en bataille oi matin le faillirent.
Li amiralz i ferat cuardie
S'il ne cumbat a cele gent hardie
Ki si sunt fiers n'unt cure de lur vies.
2605 Li emperere od la barbe flurie
Vasselage ad e mult grant estultie.
S'il ad bataillie, il ne s'en fuirat mie.
Mult est grant doel que n'en est ki l'ociet!"

189

Li emperere par sa grant poëstet
2610 .VII. anz tuz plens ad en Espaigne estet,
Prent i chastels e alquantes citez.
Li reis Marsilie s'en purcacet asez:
Al premer an fist ses brefs seieler,
En Babilonie Baligant ad mandet—
2615 Ço est l'amiraill, le viel d'antiquitet,
Tut survesquiet e Virgilie e Omer—

Why have you allowed this King of ours to be brought to ruin?
You pay out poor wages to anyone who serves you well!"
2585 Then they tear away the idol's scepter and its crown.
They tie it by the hands to a column,
They topple it to the ground at their feet,
They beat it and smash it to pieces with big sticks.
They snatch Tervagant's carbuncle,
2590 Throw the idol of Mohammed into a ditch,
And pigs and dogs bite and trample it.

188

Marsile has regained consciousness,
He has himself carried into his vaulted room,
Which is painted and decorated in several colors.
2595 Queen Bramimonde weeps over him,
She tears out her hair, she bewails her miserable lot.
In the next breath, she cries out in a loud voice:
"Oh, Saragossa, how despoiled you are today
Of the noble king who once ruled over you!
2600 Our gods committed a great crime
When they failed him in battle this morning.
The Emir will behave in cowardly fashion
If he does not fight this brave people,
Who are so fierce they care not about their own lives.
2605 The Emperor with the white beard
Has courage and great impetuousness.
If he fights a battle, he shall not flee.
It's a great shame there's no one to kill him!"

189

In a demonstration of his great power, the Emperor
2610 Has been in Spain for seven long years,
He captures castles and many cities there.
King Marsile takes the necessary steps:
The first year he commanded his letters to be sealed,
He sent word to Baligant in Babylon—
2615 He is the Emir, a very old man,
He outlived Virgil and Homer—

En Sarraguce alt sucurre li ber.
E s'il nel fait, il guerpirat ses deus
E tuz ses ydeles que il soelt adorer,
2620 Si recevrat seinte chrestïentet,
A Charlemagne se vuldrat acorder.
E cil est loinz, si ad mult demuret.
Mandet sa gent de .XL. regnez,
Ses granz drodmunz en ad fait aprester,
2625 Eschiez e barges e galies e nefs.
Suz Alixandre ad un port juste mer,
Tut sun navilie i ad fait aprester.
Ço est en mai, al premer jur d'ested,
Tutes ses oz ad empeintes en mer.

190

2630 Granz sunt les oz de cele gent averse,
Siglent a fort e nagent e guvernent.
En sum cez maz e en cez haltes vernes,
Asez i ad carbuncles e lanternes.
La sus amunt pargetent tel luiserne
2635 Par la noit la mer en est plus bele.
E cum il vienent en Espaigne la tere,
Tut li païs en reluist e esclairet.
Jesqu'a Marsilie en parvunt les noveles.   AOI.

191

Gent paienor ne voelent cesser unkes,
2640 Issent de mer, venent as ewes dulces.
Laisent Marbrise e si laisent Marbrose,
Par Sebre amunt tut lur naviries turnent.
Asez i ad lanternes e carbuncles,
Tute la noit mult grant clartet lur dunent.
2645 A icel jur venent a Sarraguce.   AOI.

192

Clers est li jurz e li soleilz luisant.
Li amiralz est issut del calan.

That the brave man should come to his aid at Saragossa.
If he fails to do this, Marsile will abandon his gods
And all the idols he customarily adores,
2620 He will become a convert to holy Christianity
And will consent to an accord with Charlemagne.
Baligant is far away, he tarried a good deal.
But now he summons his people from forty kingdoms,
He commanded his great dromonds to be made ready,
2625 Warships, barges, galleys, and boats.
There is a seaport below Alexandria,
He commanded his whole fleet to be fitted out there.
May is here, it is the first day of summer,
He has launched all his forces out to sea.

190

2630 The infidel armies are vast in number,
They proceed under full sail, they row and steer.
At the mastheads and on the high prows
There are many carbuncles and lanterns.
They cast such a glow from on high
2635 That the sea is made more beautiful through the night.
And when they reach the land of Spain,
The entire countryside gleams and is illuminated by them.
The news reaches Marsile.   AOI.

191

The pagan forces have no intention of leaving off,
2640 They leave the sea behind them, they enter fresh waters.
They pass beyond Marbrise and they pass beyond Marbrose,
They head all their ships up the Ebro.
There are many lanterns and carbuncles,
They give off very great light for them all night long.
2645 On the day after Marsile's defeat they arrive at Saragossa.   AOI.

192

The day is clear and the sun is shining.
The Emir disembarks from the lighter.

Espaneliz fors le vait adestrant,
.XVII. reis aprés le vunt siwant,
2650 Cuntes e dux i ad ben, ne sai quanz.
Suz un lorer, ki est en mi un camp,
Sur l'erbe verte getent un palie blanc.
U faldestoed i unt mis d'olifan,
Desur s'asiet li paien Baligant,
2655 Tuit li altre sunt remés en estant.
Li sire d'els premer parlat avant:
"Oiez ore, franc chevaler vaillant!
Carles li reis, l'emperere des Francs,
Ne deit manger se jo ne li cumant.
2660 Par tute Espaigne m'at fait guere mult grant,
En France dulce le voeil aler querant.
Ne finerai en trestut mun vivant
Josqu'il seit mort u tut vif recreant."
Sur sun genoill en fiert sun destre guant.

193

2665 Puis qu'il l'ad dit, mult s'en est afichet
Que ne lairat pur tut l'or desuz ciel
Que il n'alt ad Ais, o Carles soelt plaider.
Si hume li lodent, si li unt cunseillet.
Puis apelat dous de ses chevalers,
2670 L'un Clarifan e l'altre Clarïen:
"Vos estes filz al rei Maltraïen,
Ki messages soleit faire volenters.
Jo vos cumant qu'en Sarraguce algez,
Marsiliun de meie part li nunciez
2675 Cuntre Franceis li sui venut aider.
Se jo truis o, mult grant bataille i ert.
Si l'en dunez cest guant ad or pleiet,
El destre poign si li faites chalcer.
Si li portez cest bastuncel d'or mer
2680 E a mei venget pur reconoistre sun feu.
En France irai pur Carle guerreier,
S'en ma mercit ne se culzt a mes piez
E ne guerpisset la lei de chrestïens,
Jo li toldrai la corune del chef."
2685 Paien respundent: "Sire, mult dites bien."

Espanelis gets off with him on his right,
Seventeen kings follow in his train,
2650 I cannot tell you how many counts and dukes there are.
Beneath a laurel tree, which is in the middle of a field,
They throw down a white silk cloth on the green grass.
They have set up an ivory throne,
The pagan Baligant sits upon it,
2655 All the others have remained standing.
Their lord spoke first:
"Now hear this, noble and worthy knights!
King Charles, the Emperor of the Franks,
Must not eat unless I order him to.
2660 He has waged a very great war against me throughout Spain,
I wish to seek him out now in fair France.
I shall not abandon this idea for the rest of my life
Until he is dead or, being alive, concedes defeat."
He slaps his knee with his right gauntlet.

193

2665 After having said this, he firmly resolved
That for all the gold on earth he would not leave off
Going to Aix, where Charles customarily dispenses justice.
His men advise him, they have counseled him.
Then he called two of his knights,
2670 One is Clarifan and the other Clarien:
"You are sons of King Maltraien,
Who willingly used to deliver messages.
I command you to go to Saragossa,
Inform Marsile on my behalf
2675 That I have come to join forces with him against the French.
If I can only find a place, there will be a very great battle.
Give him this folded gauntlet trimmed with gold,
Make him put it on his right hand.
Take this pure gold rod to him too,
2680 And let him come to me to render homage for his fief.
I shall go to France to wage war against Charles,
If he doesn't crouch at my feet at my mercy
And if he doesn't deny his Christian faith,
I shall snatch the crown from his head."
2685 The pagans reply: "Very well spoken, sire."

163

194

Dist Baligant: "Car chevalchez, barun!
L'un port le guant, li alte le bastun!"
E cil respundent: "Cher sire, si ferum."
Tant chevalcherent que en Sarraguce sunt.
2690   Passent .X. portes, traversent .IIII. punz,
Tutes les rues u li burgeis estunt.
Cum il aproisment en la citet amunt,
Vers le paleis oïrent grant fremur:
Asez i ad de cele gent paienur
2695   Plurent e crient, demeinent grant dolor,
Pleignent lur deus, Tervagan e Mahum
E Apollin, dunt il mie n'en unt.
Dit cascun a l'altre: "Caitifs, que devendrum?
Sur nus est venue male confusiun.
2700   Perdut avum le rei Marsiliun,
Li quens Rollant li trenchat ier le destre poign.
Nus n'avum mie de Jurfaleu le Blunt.
Trestute Espaigne iert hoi en lur bandun."
Li dui message descendent al perrun.

195

2705   Lur chevals laisent dedesuz un olive,
Dui Sarrazin par les resnes les pristrent.
E li message par les mantels se tindrent,
Puis sunt muntez sus el paleis altisme.
Cum il entrerent en la cambre voltice,
2710   Par bel amur malvais saluz li firent:
"Cil Mahumet ki nus ad en baillie,
E Tervagan e Apollin, nostre sire,
Salvent le rei e guardent la reïne!"
Dist Bramimunde: "Or oi mult grant folie!
2715   Cist nostre deu sunt en recreantise.
En Rencesval malvaises vertuz firent,
Noz chevalers i unt lesset ocire.
Cest mien seignur en bataille faillirent,
Le destre poign ad perdut, n'en ad mie,
2720   Si li trenchat li quens Rollant, li riches.
Trestute Espaigne avrat Carles en baillie.

194

Baligant said: "Ride, brave men!
Let one bear the gauntlet, the other the staff!"
And the latter reply: "Dear lord, we'll do it."
They rode on, eventually they reach Saragossa.

2690 They go through ten gates, they pass four bridges
And along the streets where the townspeople live.
Approaching the summit inside the citadel,
They heard a great commotion coming from the palace:
A large number of the pagan people

2695 Are crying and wailing, and giving way to despair,
They lament their gods Tervagant, Mohammed,
And Apollo, whom they have no more.
They said to one another: "Unhappy wretches, what will become of us?
A great misfortune has befallen us.

2700 We have lost King Marsile,
Count Roland cut off his right hand yesterday.
We no longer have Jurfaleu le Blond.
Today all Spain will be at their mercy."
The two messengers dismount at the horse-block.

195

2705 They leave their horses beneath an olive tree,
Two Saracens took them by the reins.
The messengers held each other by the cloak,
Then climbed to the very high place.
Entering the vaulted chamber,

2710 They greeted them (?) malevolently with feigned affection:
"May Mohammed, who has us in his power,
And Tervagant and Apollo, our lord,
Save the King and protect the Queen!"
Bramimonde said: "What rubbish I hear!

2715 Those gods of ours have given up the fight.
At Roncevaux they did us a colossal bad turn,
They allowed our knights to get killed.
They failed my lord in battle,
He lost his right hand, he no longer has it,

2720 Mighty Count Roland severed it from him.
Charles will have all Spain in his power.

Que devendrai, duluruse, caitive?
E! lasse, que n'en ai un hume ki m'ociet!"   AOI.

196

Dist Clarïen: "Dame, ne parlez mie itant!
2725 Messages sumes al paien Baligant.
Marsiliun, ço dit, serat guarant,
Si l'en enveiet sun bastun e sun guant.
En Sebre avum .IIII. milie calant,
Eschiez e barges e galees curant;
2730 Drodmunz i ad, ne vos sai dire quanz.
Li amiralz est riches e puisant,
En France irat Carlemagne querant,
Rendre le quidet u mort o recreant."
Dist Bramimunde: "Mar en irat itant!
2735 Plus pres d'ici purrez truver les Francs,
En ceste tere ad estet ja .VII. anz.
Li emperere est ber e cumbatant,
Meilz voel murir que ja fuiet de camp.
Suz ciel n'ad rei qu'il prist a un enfant,
2740 Carles ne creint nuls hom ki seit vivant."

197

"Laissez ço ester!" dist Marsilies li reis.
Dist as messages: "Seignurs, parlez a mei!
Ja veez vos que a mort sui destreit.
Jo si nen ai filz ne fille ne heir;
2745 Un en aveie, cil fut ocis her seir.
Mun seignur dites qu'il me vienge veeir.
Li amiraill ad en Espaigne dreit:
Quite li cleim, se il la voelt aveir,
Puis la defendet encuntre li Franceis.
2750 Vers Carlemagne li durrai bon conseill,
Cunquis l'avrat d'oi cest jur en un meis.
De Sarraguce les clefs li portereiz,
Pui li dites il n'en irat, s'il me creit."
Cil respundent: "Sire, vus dites veir."   AOI.

What will become of wretched, miserable me?
What a pity there is no one here to kill me!"   AOI.

196

Clarien said: "My lady, don't talk so much!
2725 We are messengers of pagan Baligant.
He will be Marsile's protector, he says,
And he sends him his staff and his gauntlet.
We have four thousand lighters on the Ebro,
Warships, barges, and swift galleys;
2730 I can't tell you how many dromonds there are.
The Emir is mighty and powerful,
He shall seek out Charlemagne in France,
He intends to kill him or force him to concede defeat."
Bramimonde said: "He'll rue the day he goes so far!
2735 You will find the Franks nearer here,
Charles has already been in this land for seven years.
The Emperor is brave and warlike,
He'd rather die than ever flee from the battlefield.
There is no king on earth he considers to be more than a child,
2740 Charles fears no man alive."

197

"Leave off with that!" said King Marsile.
He said to the messengers: "My lords, speak to me!
You see now that I am harassed by death.
I have no son, no daughter, no heir;
2745 I had one, but he was killed yesterday afternoon.
Tell my lord to come see me.
The Emir has rights in Spain:
I renounce in his favor all claim to this land, if he wishes to have it,
But let him defend it against the French.
2750 I will give him some good advice concerning Charlemagne,
One month from today he will have conquered him.
You will take him the keys to Saragossa,
Then tell him he shall not go away, if he believes in me."
They reply: "Sire, you speak the truth."   AOI.

198

2755 Ço dist Marsilie: "Carles l'emperere
Mort m'ad mes homes, ma tere deguastee,
E mes citez fraites e violees.
Il jut anuit sur cel ewe de Sebre,
Jo ai cunté, n'i ad mais que .VII. liwes.
2760 L'amirail dites que sun host i amein,
Par vos li mand bataille i seit justee."
De Sarraguce les clefs li ad livrees.
Li messager ambedui l'enclinerent,
Prenent cunget, a cel mot s'en turnerent.

199

2765 Li dui message es chevals sunt muntet,
Isnelement issent de la citet.
A l'amiraill en vunt esfreedement,
De Sarraguce li presentent les cles.
Dist Baligant: "Que avez vos truvet?
2770 U est Marsilie, que jo aveie mandet?
Dist Clarïen: "Il est a mort naffret.
Li emperere fut ier as porz passer,
Si s'en vuleit en dulce France aler.
Par grant honur se fist rereguarder:
2775 Li quens Rollant i fut remés, sis niés,
E Oliver e tuit li .XII. per,
De cels de France .XX. milie adubez.
Li reis Marsilie s'i cumbatit, li bers,
Il e Rollant el camp furent remés.
2780 De Durendal li dunat un colp tel
Le destre poign li ad del cors sevret.
Sun filz ad mort, qu'il tant suleit amer,
E li baron qu'il i out amenet.
Fuiant s'en vint, qu'il n'i pout mes ester,
2785 Li emperere l'ad enchacet asez.
Li reis vos mandet que vos le sucurez,
Quite vos cleimet d'Espaigne le regnet."
E Baligant cumencet a penser,
Si grant doel ad por poi qu'il n'est desvet.   AOI.

198

2755 Marsile said: "Emperor Charles
Has killed my men, laid waste my land,
Smashed and penetrated my citadels.
Last night he slept here at the edge of Ebro's waters,
I calculated that it is no more than seven leagues from here.
2760 Tell the Emir to lead his army there,
Through you I send him word to give battle there."
He gave them (?) the keys to Saragossa.
The two messengers bowed down before him,
They take their leave and, having done so, they turn and go away.

199

2765 The two messengers have mounted their horses,
They ride quickly from the city.
They go to the Emir in a panic,
They present him the keys to Saragossa.
Baligant said: "What did you find?
2770 Where is Marsile, whom I had sent for?"
Clarien said: "He is mortally wounded.
Yesterday the Emperor was going through the pass,
He wanted to return to fair France.
He commanded his army to be guarded in the rear by knights of
high renown:
2775 His nephew Count Roland remained there,
Oliver, the Twelve Peers,
And twenty thousand knights from France.
Brave Marsile fought them,
He and Roland found themselves face to face on the battlefield.
2780 The latter gave him such a blow with Durendal
That he severed his right hand from his body.
He killed his son, whom he loved so dearly,
And the brave men he had brought with him.
Marsile fled, for he couldn't hold out any longer,
2785 The Emperor pursued him hotly.
The King sends word for you to help him,
He renounces the kingdom of Spain in your favor."
Baligant begins to reflect,
His fury is so great he nearly goes mad.   AOI.

200

2790 "Sire amiralz," dist Clarïens,
"En Rencesvals une bataille out ier.
Morz est Rollant e li quens Oliver,
Li .XII. per, que Carles aveit tant cher;
De lur Franceis i ad mort .XX. millers.
2795 Li reis Marsilie le destre poign i perdit
E l'emperere asez l'ad enchalcet.
En ceste tere n'est remés chevaler
Ne seit ocis o en Sebre neiet.
Desur la rive sunt Francés herbergiez:
2800 En cest païs nus sunt tant aproeciez,
Se vos volez, li repaires ert grefs."
E Baligant le reguart en ad fiers,
En sun curage en est joüs e liet.
Del faldestod se redrecet en piez,
2805 Puis escriet: "Baruns, ne vos targez!
Eissez des nefs, muntez, si chevalciez!
S'or ne s'en fuit Karlemagne li veilz,
Li reis Marsilie enqui serat venget:
Pur sun poign destre l'en liverai le chef.

201

2810 Paien d'Arabe des nefs se sunt eissut,
Puis sunt muntez es chevals e es muls,
Si chevalcherent, que fereient il plus?
Li amiralz, ki trestuz les esmut,
Sin apelet Gemalfin, un sun drut:
2815 "Jo te cumant de tute mes oz . . ."
Puis est munté en un sun destrer brun,
Ensembl'od lui em meinet .IIII. dux,
Tant chevalchat qu'en Saraguce fut.
A un perron de marbre est descenduz
2820 E quatre cuntes l'estreu li unt tenut.
Par les degrez el paleis muntet sus
E Bramidonie vient curant cuntre lui,
Si li ad dit: "Dolente, si mare fui!
A itel hunte, sire, mon seignor ai perdut!"
2825 Chet li as piez, li amiralz la reçut,
Sus en la chambre ad doel en sunt venut.   AOI.

200

2790   "Emir, sire," said Clarien,
      "There was a battle at Roncevaux yesterday.
      Roland died, Count Oliver too,
      And the Twelve Peers, whom Charles loved so dearly;
      Twenty thousand Frenchmen have been slain.
2795   King Marsile lost his right hand there,
      And the Emperor pursued him hotly.
      Every single knight in this land
      Was either slain or drowned in the Ebro.
      The French are bivouacked upon its banks.
2800   They have drawn so near us in this land
      That, if you so desire, returning home will be very difficult for
        them."
      Baligant's look becomes very fierce,
      He is overjoyed and content in his heart.
      He rises to his feet away from the throne,
2805   Then he cries out: "Barons, do not delay!
      Come away from the ships, mount up, and ride!
      If old Charlemagne doesn't flee now,
      King Marsile shall be avenged this day:
      I shall give him a head for the right hand he has lost."

201

2810   The pagans of Arabia came out of the ships,
      Then they mounted horses and mules,
      And they rode off, what else could they do?
      The Emir, who set them all in motion,
      Calls Gemalfin, his trusted friend:
2815   "I put you in command of all my armies . . ."
      Then he mounted one of his brown war-horses,
      He takes four dukes with him,
      He rode until he reached Saragossa.
      He dismounted at a marble horse-block,
2820   And four counts held his stirrup.
      He climbs to the palace by the stairs,
      But Bramimonde comes running up to him.
      She said to him: "Oh, wretched, oh, woe is me!
      Sire, I have lost my lord so disgracefully!"
2825   She falls at his feet, the Emir caught her,
      They went up into the room grief-stricken.   AOI.

202

Li reis Marsilie, cum il veit Baligant,
Dunc apelat dui Sarrazin espans:
"Pernez m'as braz, sim drecez en sedant."
2830 Al puign senestre ad pris un de ses guanz.
Ço dist Marsilie: "Sire reis, amiralz,
Teres tutes ici . . .
E Sarraguce e l'onur qu'i apent.
Mei ai perdut e tute ma gent."
2835 E cil respunt: "Tant sui jo plus dolent,
Ne pois a vos tenir lung parlement.
Jo sai asez que Carles ne m'atent,
E nepurquant de vos receif le guant."
Al doel qu'il ad s'en est turnet plurant.   AOI.
2840 Par les degrez jus del paleis descent,
Muntet el ceval, vient a sa gent puignant.
Tant chevalchat qu'il est premers devant,
De ures ad altres si se vait escriant:
"Venez, paien, car ja s'en fuient Frant!"   AOI.

203

2845 Al matin, quant primes pert li albe,
Esveillez est li eperere Carles.
Sein Gabrïel, ki de part Deu le guarde,
Levet sa main, sur lui fait sun signacle.
Li reis descent, si ad rendut ses armes,
2850 Si se desarment par tute l'ost li altre.
Puis sunt muntet, par grant vertut chevalchent
Cez veiez lunges e cez chemins mult larges.
Si vunt vedeir le merveillus damage
En Rencesvals, la o fut la bataille.   AOI.

204

2855 En Rencesvals en est Carles venuz,
Des morz qu'il troevet cumencet a plurer.
Dist a Franceis: "Segnus, le pas tenez,
Kar mei meïsme estoet avant aler
Pur mun neüd que vuldreie truver.

202

Having seen Baligant, King Marsile
Called two Spanish Saracens:
"Take me in your arms and sit me up."
2830 He took one of his gauntlets with his left hand.
Marsile said: "My lord king, Emir,
All these lands . . .
Together with Saragossa and the fief connected with it.
I have ruined myself and all my people too."
2835 And the latter replies: "I am all the more distressed,
But I cannot hold a lengthy conference with you.
I know very well that Charles is not expecting me,
Nevertheless I do accept the gauntlet from you."
He turned away and left weeping because of his grief.   AOI.
2840 He descends from the palace by the stairs,
He mounts his horse, he comes spurring toward his men.
He rode on, eventually he is in the forefront,
Time and again he cries out:
"Come on, pagans, the Franks are already fleeing!"   AOI.

203

2845 On that same morning, at the first streak of dawn,
Emperor Charles awoke.
Saint Gabriel, who watches over him for God,
Raises his hand and makes the sign of the cross over him.
The King ungirds himself, he has removed his armor,
2850 And the others throughout the army disarm themselves too.
Then they mounted their horses, they ride hard
Along those lengthy roads and those wide highways.
They go see the awesome destruction
At Roncevaux, where the battle took place.   AOI.

204

2855 Charles has arrived at Roncevaux,
He begins to weep over the dead he finds.
He said to the French: "My lords, slacken the pace,
For I must go on ahead by myself,
Because I should like to find my nephew.

2860 A Eis esteie, a une feste anoel,
  Si se vanterent mi vaillant chevaler
  De granz batailles, de forz esturs pleners.
  D'une raisun oï Rollant parler:
  Ja ne murreit en estrange regnet
2865 Ne trespassast ses hume e ses pers,
  Vers lur païs avreit sun chef turnet,
  Cunquerrantment si finereit li bers."
  Plus qu'en ne poet un bastuncel jeter,
  Devant les altres est en un pui muntet.

205

2870 Quant l'empereres vait querre sun nevold,
  De tantes herbes el pre truvat les flors,
  Ki sunt vermeilz del sanc de noz barons!
  Pitet en ad, ne poet muër n'en plurt.
  Desuz dous arbres parvenuz est Carlluns.
2875 Les colps Rollant conut en treis perruns.
  Sur l'erbe verte veit gesir sun nevuld,
  Nen est merveille se Karles ad irur.
  Descent a pied, aled i est pleins curs,
  Entre ses mains ansdous . . .
2880 Sur lui se pasmet, tant par est anguissus.

206

  Li empereres de pasmeisuns revint.
  Naimes li dux e li quens Acelin,
  Gefrei d'Anjou e sun frere Tierri
  Prenent le rei, sil drecent suz un pin.
2885 Guardet a la tere, veit sun nevold gesir,
  Tant dulcement a regreter le prist:
  "Amis Rollant, de tei ait Deus mercit!
  Unques nuls hom tel chevaler ne vit
  Por granz batailles juster e defenir.
2890 La meie honor est turnet en declin."
  Carles se pasmet, ne s'en pout astenir.   AOI.

2860   Once when I was at Aix, at a solemn feast,
      My worthy knights were boasting
      About great battles, about wild melees.
      I heard Roland make a statement:
      He would never die in a foreign land
2865   Without going beyond his men and his peers,
      He would have his head turned toward enemy country,
      The brave knight would meet his end as a conqueror.
      Farther than one can throw a stick,
      Charles climbed a hill ahead of the others.

205

2870   Seeking out his nephew, the Emperor
      Found so many flowering plants in the meadow
      Stained red by the blood of our brave knights!
      He is moved to pity, he cannot help weeping.
      Charles has arrived beneath two trees.
2875   He recognized Roland's blows on three stones.
      He sees his nephew lying on the green grass,
      It is no wonder that Charles is chagrined.
      He dismounts, he hurried over there,
      In his two hands . . .
2880   He is so overcome with grief he swoons over him.

206

      The Emperor regained consciousness.
      Duke Naimes and Count Acelin,
      Geoffrey of Anjou and his brother Thierry
      Take the King and raise him to his feet beneath a pine tree.
2885   He gazes on the ground, he sees his nephew lying there,
      He began to lament over him so softly:
      "Roland, dear friend, may God have mercy on you!
      No man ever saw a knight better able
      To fight great battles to a finish.
2890   My honor has fallen into decline."
      Charles faints, he cannot help himself.   AOI.

207

Carles li reis se vint de pasmeisuns,
Par mains le tienent .IIII. de ses barons.
Guardet a tere, vei gesir sun neüld,
2895 Cors ad gaillard, perdue ad sa culur,
Turnez ses oilz, mult li sunt tenebros.
Carles le pleint par feid e par amur:
"Ami Rollant, Deus metet t'anme en flors,
En pareïs, entre les glorius!
2900 Cum en Espaigne venis mal, seignur!
Jamais n'ert jurn de tei n'aie dulur.
Cum decarrat ma force e ma baldur!
Nen avrai ja ki sustienget m'onur,
Suz ciel ne quid aveir ami un sul!
2905 Se jo ai parenz, n'en i ad nul si proz."
Trait ses crignels, pleines ses mains amsdous.
Cent milie Franc en unt si grant dulur
N'en i ad cel ki durement ne plurt.   AOI.

208

"Ami Rollant, jo m'en irai en France.
2910 Cum jo serai a Loün, en ma chambre,
De plusurs regnes vendrunt li hume estrange,
Demanderunt: 'U est li quens cataignes?'
Jo lur dirrai qu'il est morz en Espaigne.
A grant dulur tendrai puis mun reialme,
2915 Jamais n'ert jur que ne plur ne n'en pleigne."

209

"Ami Rollant, prozdoem, juvente bele,
Cum jo serai a Eis, em ma chapele,
Vendrunt li hume, demanderunt noveles.
Jes lur dirrai, merveilluses e pesmes:
2920 'Morz est mis niés, ki tant me fist cunquere.'
Encuntre mei revelerunt li Seisne
E Hungre e Bugre e tante gent averse,
Romain, Puillain e tuit icil de Palerne
E cil d'Affrike e cil de Califerne.

176

207

King Charles regained consciousness,
Four of his barons are holding him up by his hands.
He gazes on the ground, he sees his nephew lying there,
2895   He is robust of body, but he has lost his color,
His eyes are turned up, they are full of shadows.
Charles laments over him loyally and affectionately:
"Roland, dear friend, may God place your soul among the flowers
In Paradise among the saints in glory!
2900   How unfortunate your coming to Spain, my lord! (?)
I shall grieve for you each day.
How my strength and ardor will fail!
I shall have no one to sustain my honor,
I don't think I have a single friend on earth!
2905   Though I have kinsmen, there are none so worthy."
He tears out his hair by the handful.
A hundred thousand Franks are in such great anguish because of him
That all shed bitter tears.   AOI.

208

"Roland, my friend, I shall go to France.
2910   When I shall be at Laon, in my domain,
Foreigners will come from many kingdoms,
They will ask: 'Where is the Captain Count?'
I shall tell them that he died in Spain.
Henceforth I shall rule my realm in great sorrow,
2915   I shall weep and lament each day."

209

"Roland, my friend, man of honor, noble youth,
When I shall be at Aix, in my chapel,
Men will come, they will ask for news.
I shall tell them the awesome and cruel facts:
2920   'My nephew, through whom I conquered so much, is dead.'
The Saxons will rebel against me,
The Hungarians, the Bulgars, and so many infidel peoples,
The Romans, the Apulians, and all the men of Palermo,
The men of Africa and those of Califerne.

2925 Puis entrerunt mes peines e mes suffraites.
Ki guierat mes oz a tel poëste
Quant cil est morz ki tuz jurz nos cadelet?
E! France, cum remeines deserte!
Si grant doel ai que jo ne vuldreie estre!"
2930 Sa barbe blanche cumencet a detraire,
Ad ambes mains les chevels de sa teste.
Cent milie Francs s'en pasment cuntre tere.

210

"Ami Rollant, de tei ait Deus mercit!
L'anme de tei seit mise en pareïs!
2935 Ki tei ad mort France ad mis en exill.
Si grant dol ai que ne voldreie vivre,
De ma maisnee, ki pur mei est ocise!
Ço duinset Deus, le filz seinte Marie,
Einz que jo vienge as maistres porz de Sirie,
2940 L'anme del cors me seit oi departie,
Entre les lur aluee e mise
E ma car fust delez els enfuïe!"
Ploret des oilz, sa blanche barbe tiret.
E dist dux Naimes: "Or ad Carles grant ire."   AOI.

211

2945 "Sire emperere," ço dist Gefrei d'Anjou,
"Ceste dolor ne demenez tant fort!
Par tut le camp faites querre les noz
Que cil d'Espaigne en la bataille unt mort.
En un carnel cumandez que hom les port."
2950 Ço dist li reis: "Sunez en vostre corn!"   AOI.

212

Gefreid d'Anjou ad sun greisle sunet,
Franceis descendent, Carles l'ad comandet.
Tuz lur amis qu'il i unt morz truvet,
Ad un carner sempres les unt portet.
2955 Asez i ad evesques e abez,

2925 Then my suffering and distress will begin anew.
But who will lead my armies with such power
Now that the one who always commands us is dead?
Ah, France, how deserted you remain!
I have such great anguish that I'd rather be dead!"
2930 He begins to tear his white beard
And, with both hands, the hair from his head.
A hundred thousand Franks fall to the ground in a swoon.

210

"Roland, dear friend, may God have mercy on you!
May your soul be placed in Paradise!
2935 The one who killed you has brought ruin to France.
I have such great anguish that I'd rather be dead,
Because of my household, which has died for me!
May God, the Son of Holy Mary, grant
That before I reach the main pass of Cize
2940 My soul be separated from my body,
Be placed and settled amid theirs,
And my flesh be buried beside them!"
His eyes are brimming with tears, he tears at his white beard.
And Duke Naimes said: "Charles is in anguish now." AOI.

211

2945 "Emperor, sire," said Geoffrey of Anjou,
"Do not afflict yourself so!
Order a search of the entire field for our men
Whom those from Spain killed in the battle.
Command that they be brought to a common grave."
2950 The King said: "Sound your horn for this!" AOI.

212

Geoffrey of Anjou blows his bugle,
The French dismount, Charles has ordered it.
All their friends whom they found dead
They promptly carried to a common grave.
2955 Many bishops and abbots are there,

Munies, canonies, proveires coronez,
Sis unt asols e seignez de part Deu.
Mirre e timonie i firent alumer,
Gaillardement tuz les unt encensez.
2960 A grant honor pois les unt enterrez,
Sis unt laisez, qu'en fereient il el? AOI.

213

Li emperere fait Rollant costeïr
E Oliver e l'arcevesque Turpin.
Devant sei les ad fait tuz uvrir
2965 E tuz les quers en paile recuillir,
Un blanc sarcou de marbre sunt enz mis.
E puis les cors des barons si unt pris,
En quirs de cerf les seignurs unt mis,
Ben sunt lavez de piment e de vin.
2970 Li reis cumandet Tedbalt e Gebuin,
Milun le cunte e Otes le marchis:
"En .III. carettes les guiez . . ."
Bien sunt cuverz d'un palie galazin. AOI.

214

Venir s'en volt li emperere Carles,
2975 Quant de paiens li surdent les enguardes.
De cels devant i vindrent dui messages,
De l'amirail li nuncent la bataille:
"Reis orguillos, nen est fins que t'en alges!
Veiz Baligant, ki aprés tei chevalchet!
2980 Granz sunt les oz qu'il ameinet d'Arabe.
Encoi verrum se tu as vasselage." AOI.
Carles li reis en ad prise sa barbe,
Si li remembret del doel e del damage,
Mult fierement tute sa gent reguardet,
2985 Puis si s'escriet a sa voiz grand e halte:
"Barons franceis, as chevals e as armes!" AOI.

Monks, canons, tonsured priests,
They absolved them and signed them in God's name.
They had myrrh and thymiama kindled,
They censed them all with proper zeal.
2960 Then they buried them with full honors,
And they left them, what else could they do for them? AOI.

213

The Emperor has Roland's body prepared for burial,
Oliver, too, and Archbishop Turpin.
He had them all opened before him,
2965 And all their hearts gathered up in a silk cloth,
They are placed inside a white marble casket.
Then they took the brave knights' bodies,
They wrapped the lords in stag skins,
They are carefully washed with aromatics and with wine.
2970 The King orders Tedbald and Geboin,
Count Milon and the Marquis Oton:
"Escort the three carts bearing them away . . ."
They are completely covered with a silk cloth from Galata. AOI.

214

As Emperor Charles is about to leave,
2975 The vanguard of the pagans bursts upon his sight.
Two messengers came to him from the front ranks,
They announce the battle to him, speaking for the Emir:
"Vile King, it is not fitting that you should go!
See Baligant there, who is riding after you!
2980 The armies he brings from Arabia are vast.
This day we shall see if you have courage." AOI.
King Charles grasped his beard,
He remembers the heartbreak and the destruction,
He looks very fiercely at all his men,
2985 Then he cries out in his strong and loud voice:
"French barons, to horse and to arms!" AOI.

215

Li empereres tuz premereins s'adubet.
Isnelement ad vestue sa brunie,
Lacet sun helme, si ad ceinte Joiuse,
2990   Ki pur soleill sa clartet n'en muet,
Pent a sun col un escut de Biterne,
Tient sun espiet, sin fait brandir la hanste,
En Tencendur, sun bon cheval, puis muntet—
Il le cunquist es guez desuz Marsune,
2995   Sin getat mort Malpalin de Nerbone—
Laschet la resne, mult suvent l'esperonet,
Fait sun eslais, veant cent mil humes,   AOI.
Recleimet Deu e l'apostle de Rome.

216

Par tut le champ cil de France descendent,
3000   Plus de cent milie s'en adubent ensemble.
Guarnemenz unt ki ben lor atalentet,
Cevals curanz e lur armes mult gentes.
Puis sunt muntez e unt grant escïence,
S'il troevent ou, bataille quident rendre.
3005   Cil gunfanun sur les helmes lur pendent.
Quant Carles veit si beles cuntenances,
Sin apelat Jozeran de Provence,
Naimon li duc, Antelme de Maience:
"En tels vassals deit hom aveir fiance!
3010   Asez est fols ki entr'els se demet.
Si Arrabiz de venir ne se repentent,
La mort Rollant lur quid cherement rendre."
Respunt dux Neimes: "E Deus le nos cunsente!"   AOI.

217

Carles apelet Rabel e Guineman.
3015   Ço dist li reis: "Seignurs, jo vos cumant,
Seiez es lius Oliver e Rollant:
L'un port l'espee e l'altre l'olifant,
Si chevalcez el premer chef devant,
Ensembl'od vos .XV. milie de Francs,

215

The Emperor is the first to arm himself.
He quickly puts on his byrnie,
He laces on his helmet, he has girded Joyeuse,
2990 Whose brilliance is not dimmed by the sun,
He hangs a shield from Biterne around his neck,
He holds his spear and brandishes its shaft,
Then he mounted his good horse Tencendor—
He conquered it at the ford below Marsonne,
2995 He threw Malpalin of Narbonne down dead from its back—
He gives him free rein, he spurs him again and again,
He springs forward in full sight of a hundred thousand men,   AOI.
He invokes God and the Apostle of Rome.

216

The men of France dismount everywhere on the field,
3000 More than a hundred thousand arm themselves together.
They have equipment that suits them well,
Their horses are swift and their arms very fine.
Then they mounted; they are very determined
That if an opportunity presents itself they will give battle.
3005 Their pennons hang down to their helmets.
Seeing such fine bearing, Charles
Called Jozeran of Provence,
Duke Naimes, Antelme of Mayence:
"Such brave men deserve our confidence!
3010 Anyone who shows signs of distress in their company is a great fool.
If the Arabs don't change their minds about advancing,
I intend to make them pay dearly for Roland's death."
Duke Naimes replies: "May God grant us this favor!"   AOI.

217

Charles calls Rabel and Guinemant.
3015 The King said: "My lords, I order you
To take up the positions formerly occupied by Oliver and Roland:
Let one carry the sword and the other the oliphant,
Ride on ahead, in the forefront,
With fifteen thousand Franks,

3020 De bachelers, de noz meillors vaillanz.
Aprés icels en avrat altretant,
Sis guierat Gibuins e Loranz."
Naimes li dux e li quens Jozerans
Icez eschieles ben les vunt ajustant.
3025 S'il troevent ou, bataille i ert mult grant.   AOI.

218

De Franceis sunt les premeres escheles.
Aprés les dous establisent la terce:
En cele sunt li vassal de Baivere,
A .XX. milie chevalers la preiserent;
3030 Ja devers els bataille n'ert lessee.
Suz cel n'ad gent que Carles ait plus chere,
Fors cels de France, ki les regnes cunquerent.
Li quens Oger li Daneis, li puinneres,
Les guierat, kar la cumpaigne est fiere.   AOI.

219

3035 Treis escheles ad l'emperere Carles.
Naimes li dux puis establist la quarte
De tels barons qu'asez unt vasselage:
Alemans sunt e si sunt d'Alemaigne,
Vint milie sunt, ço dient tuit li altre.
3040 Ben sunt guarniz e de chevals e d'armes,
Ja por murir ne guerpirunt bataille.
Sis guierat Hermans, li dux de Trace,
Einz i murat que cuardise i facet.   AOI.

220

Naimes li dux e li quens Jozerans
3045 La quinte eschele unt faite de Normans:
.XX. milie sunt, co dient tuit li Franc.
Armes unt beles e bons cevals curanz,
Ja pur murir cil n'erent recreanz.
Suz ciel n'ad gent ki plus poisset en camp.

3020 Young warriors, selected from among our best fighters.
After these men there will be a second division, equal in number.
Geboin and Lorant will lead them."
Duke Naimes and Count Jozeran
Marshall these divisions well.
3025 If an opportunity presents itself, there will be a great battle.   AOI.

218

The first two divisions are made up of Frenchmen.
After these two they marshall the third:
The brave men of Bavaria are in that one,
They estimate that it has twenty thousand knights;
3030 The battle will never be broken off by them.
Charles holds no other people on earth in higher esteem,
Except the men of France, conquerors of his realms.
The fighter, Count Ogier the Dane,
Will lead them, for this company is fierce.   AOI.

219

3035 Emperor Charles now has three divisions.
Next, Duke Naimes marshalled the fourth
With brave knights who have much courage:
They are Germans, they come from Germany,
They are twenty thousand, so say all the others.
3040 They are well equipped with horses and arms,
They will not break off the battle even if it means death.
Herman, Duke of Thrace, will lead them,
He will die before turning coward.   AOI.

220

Duke Naimes and Count Jozeran
3045 Formed the fifth division with Normans:
They are twenty thousand, so say all the Franks.
They have fine arms and good swift horses,
They will not concede defeat even if it means death.
No people on earth can do more in the field.

3050   Richard li velz les guierat el camp,
      Cil i ferrat de sun espiet trenchant.   AOI.

221

      La siste eschele unt faite de Bretuns:
      .XXX. milie chevalers od els unt.
      Icil chevalchent en guise de baron,
3055   Peintes lur hanstes, fermez lur gunfanun.
      Le seignur d'els est apelet Oedun;
      Icil cumandet le cunte Nevelun,
      Tedbald de Reins e le marchis Otun:
      "Guiez ma gent, jo vos en faz le dun!"   AOI.

222

3060   Li emperere ad .VI. escheles faites.
      Naimes li dux puis establist la sedme
      De Peitevins e des barons d'Alverne:
      .XL. milie chevalers poeent estre.
      Chevals unt bons e les armes mult beles.
3065   Cil sunt par els en un val suz un tertre,
      Sis beneïst Carles de sa main destre.
      Els guierat Jozerans e Godselmes.   AOI.

223

      E l'oidme eschele ad Naimes establie,
      De Flamengs est e des barons de Frise.
3070   Chevalers unt plus de .XL. milie,
      Ja devers els n'ert bataille guerpie.
      Ço dist li reis: "Cist ferunt mun servise."
      Entre Rembalt e Hamon de Galice
      Les guierunt tut par chevalerie.   AOI.

224

3075   Entre Naimon e Jozeran le cunte
      La noefme eschele unt faite de prozdomes,
      De Loherengs e de cels de Borgoigne.

3050 Old Richard will lead them into battle,
He will strike there with his sharp spear.   AOI.

221

They formed the sixth division with Bretons:
They have thirty thousand knights with them.
They ride like true knights,
3055 Their spear shafts painted, their pennants fixed to their lances.
Their lord is called Eudon;
The latter commands Count Nevelon,
Tedbald of Reims and the Marquis Oton:
"Lead my men, I grant you this favor!"   AOI.

222

3060 The Emperor has now formed six divisions.
Next, Duke Naimes marshalled the seventh
With Poitevins and brave knights from Auvergne:
They are about forty thousand in number.
They have good horses and very fine arms.
3065 They are off by themselves in a valley below a hill,
Charles blessed them with his right hand.
Jozeran and Godselme will lead them.   AOI.

223

And Naimes marshalled the eighth division,
It is made up of Flemings and brave knights from Frisia.
3070 They have more than forty thousand knights,
The battle will never be broken off by them.
The King said: "They will render the service due to me."
Together Rembald and Hamon of Galicia
Will lead them in proper knightly fashion.   AOI.

224

3075 Together Naimes and Count Jozeran
Formed the ninth division with worthy knights,
Men from Lorraine and men from Burgundy.

.L. milie chevalers unt par cunte,
Helmes laciez e vestues lor bronies;
3080 Espiez unt forz e les hanstes sunt curtes.
Si Arrabiz de venir ne demurent,
Cil les ferrunt, s'il a els s'abandunent.
Sis guierat Tierris, li dux d'Argone.   AOI.

225

La disme eschele est des baruns de France,
3085 Cent milie sunt de noz meillors cataignes.
Cors unt gaillarz e fieres cuntenances,
Les chefs fluriz e les barbes unt blanches,
Osbercs vestuz e lur brunies dubleines,
Ceintes espees franceises e d'Espaigne,
3090 Escuz unt genz, de multes cunoisances.
Puis sunt muntez, la bataille demandent,
Munjoie escrient, od els est Carlemagne.
Gefreid d'Anjou portet l'orieflambe:
Seint Piere fut, si aveit num Romaine,
3095 Mais de Munjoie iloec out pris eschange.   AOI.

226

Li emperere de sun cheval descent,
Sur l'erbe verte se est culchet adenz.
Turnet su vis vers le soleill levant,
Recleimet Deu mult escordusement:
3100 "Veire Paterne, hoi cest jor me defend,
Ki guaresis Jonas tut veirement
De la baleine ki en sun cors l'aveit,
E esparignas le rei de Niniven,
E Daniël del merveillus turment
3105 Enz en la fosse des leons o fut enz,
Les .III. enfanz tut en un fou ardant.
La tue amurs me seit hoi en present!
Par ta mercit, se tei plaist, me cunsent
Que mun nevold pois venger, Rollant!"
3110 Cum ad oret, si se drecet en estant,
Seignat sun chef de la vertut poisant.

They are fifty thousand in number,
Their helmets are laced on and they have donned their byrnies;
3080 They have sturdy spears with short shafts.
If the Arabs do not hesitate to advance
And risk an attack against them, the latter will strike them.
Thierry, Duke of Argonne, will lead them.   AOI.

225

The tenth division is formed with brave knights from France,
3085 They are one hundred thousand chosen from among our best
captains.
They have robust bodies and fierce countenances,
They have hoary heads and white beards,
They have donned their hauberks and their double-mailed byrnies,
They have girded swords made in France and in Spain,
3090 They have fine shields with many distinctive devices.
Then they mounted up, they clamor for battle,
They shout "Monjoie!" and Charles is with them.
Geoffrey of Anjou carries the oriflamme:
It once belonged to Saint Peter and its name was "Romaine,"
3095 But it had taken the new name Monjoie there.   AOI.

226

The Emperor alights from his horse,
He has stretched himself out prone on the green grass.
He turns his face toward the morning sun,
He prays God very fervently:
3100 "True Father, defend me this day,
You who most surely saved Jonah
From the whale who had him in his body,
And spared the King of Nineveh,
And Daniel from terrible agony
3105 In the lions' den where he was,
And the three children burning in a fire.
May your love be with me here today!
Through your mercy, if this be agreeable to you, grant
That I may avenge my nephew Roland!"
3110 Having said his prayer, he rises to his feet,
He signed himself with the powerful sign of the cross.

Muntet li reis en sun cheval curant,
L'estreu li tindrent Neimes e Jocerans.
Prent sun escut e sun espiet trenchant.
3115 Gent ad le cors, gaillart e ben seant,
Cler le visage e de bon cuntenant.
Puis si chevalchet mult aficheement.
Sunent cil greisle e derere e devant,
Sur tuz les altres bundist li olifant.
3120 Plurent Franceis pur pitet de Rollant.

227

Mult gentement li emperere chevalchet,
Desur sa bronie fors ad mise sa barbe.
Pur sue amor altretel funt li altre,
Cent milie Francs en sunt reconoisable.
3125 Passent cez puis e cez roches plus haltes,
E cez parfunz valees, cez destreiz anguisables.
Issent des porz e de la tere guaste,
Devers Espaigne sunt alez en la marche,
En un emplein unt prise lur estage.
3130 A Baligant repairent ses enguardes,
Uns Sulians ki ad dit sun message:
"Veüd avum li orguillus reis Carles,
Fiers sunt si hume, n'unt talent qu'il li faillent.
Adubez vus, sempres avrez bataille!"
3135 Dist Baligant: "Or oi grant vasselage,
Sunez voz graisles, que mi paien le sacet!"

228

Par tute l'ost funt lur taburs suner
E cez buisines e cez greisles mult cler.
Paien descendent pur lur cors aduber.
3140 Li amiralz ne se voelt demurer:
Vest une bronie dunt li pan sunt sasfret,
Lacet sun elme, ki ad or est gemmet,
Puis ceint s'espee al senestre costet.
Par sun orgoill li ad un num truvet:
3145 Par la Carlun dunt il oït parler

The King mounts his swift horse,
Naimes and Jozeran held his stirrup.
He takes his shield and his sharp spear.
3115 His body is well proportioned, robust, and good-looking,
His face is open and of noble mien.
Then he rides off, firm in the saddle.
The trumpets sound in the rear and in front,
The oliphant reverberates louder than all the others.
3120 The French shed tears of pity for Roland.

227

The Emperor rides forth in very noble fashion,
He has exposed his beard to view, on his byrnie.
Out of loyalty to him, the others do the same,
A hundred thousand Franks can be recognized in this way.
3125 They pass by the mountains and the highest rocks,
The deep valleys and the distressful defiles.
They leave the pass and the wasteland,
They entered the Spanish march,
They have halted on a plain.
3130 The men in Baligant's advance party return to him,
Then a Syrian gave his report:
"We have seen evil King Charles,
His men are fierce, they have no intention of failing him.
Arm yourself, you are about to have a battle!"
3135 Baligant said: "I hear now of their great courage,
Sound your trumpets so that my pagans know of it!"

228

They have their drums sound the alarm throughout the army,
The trumpets and the very clear-sounding bugles too.
The pagans dismount to arm themselves.
3140 The Emir does not want to delay:
He puts on a byrnie whose sections are saffron,
He laces on his helmet of gold wrought with gems,
Then he girds his sword at his left side.
In his perversity he found a name for it:
3145 After Charles's sword, which he has heard about

. . . .

Ço ert s'enseigne en bataille campel,
Ses chevalers en ad fait escrier.
Pent a sun col un soen grant escut let:
3150 D'or est la bucle e de cristal listet,
La guige en est d'un bon palie roet.
Tient sun espiet, si l'apelet Maltet:
La hanste grosse cume uns tinels,
De sul le fer fust uns mulez trusset.
3155 En sun destrer Baligant est muntet,
L'estreu li tint Marcules d'Ultremer.
La forcheüre ad asez grant li ber,
Graisles es flancs e larges les costez,
Gros ad le piz, belement est mollet,
3160 Lees les espalles e le vis ad mult cler,
Fier le visage, le chef recercelet,
Tant par ert blancs cume flur en estet;
De vasselage est suvent esprovet.
Deus! quel baron, s'oüst chrestïentet!
3165 Le cheval brochet, li sancs en ist tuz clers,
Fait sun eslais, si tressalt un fosset,
Cinquante pez i poet hom mesurer.
Paien escrient: "Cist deit marches tenser!
N'i ad Franceis, si a lui vient juster,
3170 Voeillet o nun, n'i perdet sun edet.
Carles est fols que ne s'en est alet." AOI.

229

Li amiralz ben resemblet barun:
Blanche ad la barbe ensement cume flur
E de sa lei mult par est saives hom
3175 E en bataille est fiers e orgoillus.
Ses filz Malpramis mult est chevalerus,
Granz est e forz e trait as anceisurs.
Dist a sun pere: "Sire, car cevalchum!
Mult me merveill se ja verrum Carlun."
3180 Dist Baligant: "Oïl, car mult est proz.
En plusurs gestes de lui sunt granz honurs.

. . . .

It was his war cry on the battlefield,
He made his knights shout it.
He suspends his great broad shield from his neck:
3150 Its boss is made of gold and its border of crystal,
Its strap is made of good silk cloth ornamented with circles.
He holds his spear, he calls it Maltet:
Its shaft, which is as big as a club,
A mule would have a full load from its iron tip alone.
3155 Baligant mounted his war-horse,
Marcule of Outremer held his stirrup.
The brave man has a very large crotch,
He is slender in the hips and wide in the sides,
His chest is wide, it is handsomely moulded,
3160 His shoulders are broad and his face is very clear,
His look is fierce, his head is covered with curls,
It was pure white as a flower in summertime;
He has often proved his courage.
God! what a brave knight if only he were a Christian!
3165 He spurs his horse, bright blood spurts out,
He springs forward and leaps over a ditch,
It measures fifty feet across.
The pagans shout: "This man will surely protect the marches!
No Frenchman who fights him
3170 Will escape with his life, like it or not.
Charles is mad not to have gone away."   AOI.

229

The Emir looks a good deal like a true knight:
He has a beard that is white as a flower,
He is very knowledgeable about his religion,
3175 And in combat he is fierce and mean.
His son Malprimes is a very worthy knight,
He is big and strong and takes after his ancestors.
He said to his father: "Let us ride, sire!
I doubt very much we will ever see Charles."
3180 Baligant said: "Oh yes, because he is very worthy.
Great tributes are paid to him in many chronicles.

Il n'en at mie de Rollant sun nevold,
N'avrat vertut ques tienget cuntre nus." AOI.

230

"Bels filz Malpramis," ço li dist Baligant,
3185 "Li altrer fut ocis le bon vassal Rollant
E Oliver, li proz e li vaillanz,
Li .XII. per, qui Carles amat tant,
De cels de France .XX. milie cumbatanz.
Trestuz les altres ne pris jo mie un guant.
3190 Li empereres repairet veirement,
S'il m'at nunciet mes mes, li Sulians,
.X. escheles . . . mult granz.
Cil est mult proz ki sunet l'olifant,
D'un graisle cler racatet ses cumpaignz,
3195 E si cevalcent el premer chef devant,
Ensembl'od els .XV. milie de Francs,
De bachelers que Carles cleimet enfanz.
Aprés icels en i ad ben altretanz,
Cil i ferrunt mult orgoillusement."
3200 Dist Malpramis: "Le colp vos en demant." AOI.

231

"Filz Malpramis," Baligant li ad dit,
"Jo vos otri quanque m'avez ci quis.
Cuntre Franceis sempres irez ferir,
Si i merrez Torleu, le rei persis,
3205 E Dapamort, un altre rei leutiz.
Le grant orgoill se ja puëz matir,
Jo vos durrai un pan de mun païs
Des Cheriant entresqu'en Val Marchis."
Cil respunt: "Sire, vostre mercit!"
3210 Passet avant, le dun en requeillit—
Ço est de la tere ki fut al rei Flurit—
A itel ore unches puis ne la vit,
Ne il n'en fut ne vestut ne saisit.

But he no longer has his nephew Roland,
He will not have the strength to withstand us."   AOI.

230

"Dear son, Malprimes," said Baligant,
3185 "Yesterday the brave knight Roland was slain
And also honorable and worthy Oliver,
The Twelve Peers, whom Charles loved so dearly,
And twenty thousand fighting men from France.
I wouldn't give a cent for all the others.
3190 The Emperor is returning for certain,
My messenger, the Syrian, has informed me of this,
Ten divisions . . . at full strength.
The one who is sounding the oliphant is a man of great worth,
His companion is responding with a clear-sounding bugle,
3195 They are riding in the forefront,
With them, fifteen thousand Franks,
Young men whom Charles calls his children.
After them there is a division certainly equal in number,
They will strike in very vicious fashion.
3200 Malprimes said: "I ask you for the honor of striking the first blow."
    AOI.

231

"My son, Malprimes," Baligant said to him,
"I grant you all that you have asked of me here.
You will proceed now without delay to fight the French,
You will take with you Torleu, the Persian king,
3205 And Dapamort, another Lycian king.
If you can destroy this great evil,
I will give you a portion of my land
From Cheriant to the Val Marchis."
Malprimes replies: "I thank you, sire!"
3210 He comes forward, he accepted the fief—
The land once belonged to King Flori—
But under such circumstances that he never saw it,
He was not invested with it and did not take possession of it
    either.

232

Li amiraill chevalchet par cez oz,
3215   Sis filz le siut, ki mult ad grant le cors.
Li reis Torleus e li reis Dapamort
.XXX. escheles establissent mult tost.
Chevalers unt a merveillus esforz,
En la menur .L. milie en out.
3220   La premere est de cels de Butentrot,
E l'altre aprés de Micenes as chefs gros:
Sur les eschines qu'il unt en mi les dos
Cil sunt seiet ensement cume porc.   AOI.
E la terce est de Nubles e de Blos,
3225   E la quarte est de Bruns e d'Esclavoz,
E la quinte est de Sorbres e de Sorz,
E la siste est d'Ermines e de Mors,
E la sedme est de cels de Jericho,
E l'oitme est de Nigres e la noefme de Gros,
3230   E la disme est de Balide la Fort:
Ço est une gent ki unches ben ne volt.   AOI.
Li amiralz en juret quanqu'il poet
De Mahumet les vertuz e le cors:
"Karles de France chevalchet cume fols.
3235   Bataille i ert, se il ne s'en destolt.
Jamais n'avrat el chef corone d'or."

233

Dis escheles establisent aprés.
La premere est des Canelius les laiz,
De Val Fuït sun venuz en traver.
3240   L'altre est de Turcs e la terce de Pers,
E la quarte est de Pinceneis e de Pers,
E la quinte est de Soltras e d'Avers,
E la siste est d'Ormaleus e d'Eugiez,
E la sedme est de la gent Samuël,
3245   L'oidme est de Bruise e la noefme de Clavers,
E la disme est d'Occian la Desert:
Ço est une gent ki Damnedeu ne sert—
De plus feluns n'orrez parler jamais—
Durs unt les quirs ensement cume fer,

232

The Emir rides in the midst of his armies,
3215 His son, whose body is enormous, follows him.
King Torleu and King Dapamort
Rapidly marshall thirty divisions.
They have a formidable force of knights,
There are fifty thousand in the smallest division.
3220 The first is made up of men from Butentrot,
And the one that comes after, of large-headed men from
    Misnes:
On their spines, along the length of their backs,
They have bristles like pigs.   AOI.
The third is made up of Nubles and Blos,
3225 The fourth of Bruns and Slavs,
The fifth of Sorbres and Sors,
The sixth of Armenians and Moors,
The seventh of men from Jericho,
The eighth of Negroes, the ninth of Gros,
3230 And the tenth of men from Balide la Forte:
These are people who never wanted to do good.   AOI.
The Emir swears as solemnly as he can
By the power and by the body of Mohammed:
"Charles of France is riding like a madman.
3235 There will be a battle if he doesn't turn away.
He will never again wear a golden crown on his head."

233

They marshall ten more divisions next.
The first is made up of ugly Cananaens,
They came across by way of Val Fuit.
3240 The next is made up of Turks and the third of Persians,
The fourth of Pincenois and of Persians,
The fifth of Soltras and Avars,
The sixth of Ormaleus and Eugiés,
The seventh of Samuel's people,
3245 The eighth of men from Bruise, the ninth of Clavers,
And the tenth of men from Occian le Desert:
These are people who do not serve the Lord God—
You will never hear of baser individuals—
Their skins are as tough as iron,

3250 Pur ço n'unt soign de elme ne d'osberc.
En la bataille sunt felun e engrés.   AOI.

234

Li amiralz .X. escheles ad justedes:
La premere est des jaianz de Malprese,
L'altre est de Hums e la terce de Hungres,
3255 E la quarte est de Baldise la Lunge,
E la quinte est de cels de Val Penuse,
E la siste est de . . . Maruse,
E la sedme est de Leus e d'Astrimonies,
L'oidme est d'Argoilles e la noefme de Clarbone,
3260 E la disme est des barbez de Fronde:
Ço est une gent ki Deu nen amat unkes.
Geste Francor .XXX. escheles i numbrent.
Granz sunt les oz u cez buisines sunent.
Paien chevalchent en guise de produme.   AOI.

235

3265 Li amiralz mult par est riches hoem.
Dedavant sei fait porter sun dragon
E l'estandart Tervagan e Mahum
E un ymagene Apolin le felun.
Des Canelius chevalchent envirun,
3270 Mult haltement escrient un sermun:
"Ki par noz deus voelt aveir guarison,
Sis prit e servet par grant afflictiun!"
Paien i bassent lur chefs e lur mentun,
Lor helmes clers i suzclinent enbrunc.
3275 Dient Fanceis: "Sempres murrez, glutun!
De vos seit hoi male confusiun!
Li nostre Deu, guarantisez Carlun!
Ceste bataille seit . . . en sun num!"   AOI.

236

Li amiralz est mult de grant saveir,
3280 A sei apelet sis filz e les dous reis:

3250 For this reason they scorn helmets and hauberks.
In battle they are mean and vicious.   AOI.

234

The Emir formed ten more divisions:
The first is made up of giants from Malprose,
The next of Huns and the third of Hungarians,
3255 The fourth of men from Baldise la Longue,
The fifth of men from Val Peneuse,
The sixth of . . . Marose,
The seventh of men from Leus and Astrimoines,
The eighth of men from Argoilles, the ninth of men from
    Clarbonne,
3260 And the tenth of bearded men from Fronde:
These are a people who never loved God.
The Annals of the Franks list thirty divisions.
The armies where the bugles are ringing out are vast.
The pagans ride forth looking like true knights.   AOI.

235

3265 The Emir is a very powerful man.
He orders his dragon standard to be carried before him,
That of Tervagant and of Mohammed too,
And a statue of vile Apollo.
Ten Cananaens ride around them,
3270 They make a fervent appeal in a very loud voice:
"Let anyone who desires protection from our gods
Pray and serve them in great humility!"
The pagans lower their heads and chins,
They bow their shiny helmets down.
3275 The French say: "You will soon die, scoundrels!
May misfortune rain down upon you this day!
God of ours, protect Charles!
May this battle be . . . in His name!"   AOI.

236

The Emir is extremely cunning,
3280 He summons his son and the two kings:

"Seignurs barons, devant chevalchereiz,
Mes escheles, tutes les guiereiz.
Mais des meillors voeill jo retenir treis:
L'un ert de Turcs e l'altre d'Ormaleis,
3285 E la terce est des jaianz de Malpreis.
Cil d'Ociant ierent esembl'ot mei,
Si justerunt a Charles e a Franceis.
Li emperere, s'il se cumbat od mei,
Desur le buc la teste perdre en deit.
3290 Trestut seit fiz, n'i avrat altre dreit."   AOI.

237

Granz sunt les oz e les escheles beles.
Entr'els nen at ne pui ne val ne tertre,
Selve ne bois asconse n'i poet estre,
Ben s'entreveient en mi la pleine tere.
3295 Dist Baligant: "La meie gent averse,
Car chevalchez pur la bataille quere!"
L'enseigne portet Amborres d'Oluferne.
Paien escrient, Preciuse l'apelent.
Dient Franceis: "De vos seit hoi grant perte!"
3300 Mult haltement Munjoie renuvelent.
Li emperere i fait suner ses greisles
E l'olifan, ki trestuz les esclairet.
Dient paien: "La gent Carlun est bele,
Bataille avrum e aduree e pesme."   AOI.

238

3305 Grant est la plaigne e large la cuntree.
Luisent cil elme as perres d'or gemmees
E cez escuz e cez bronies safrees
E cez espiez, cez enseignes fermees.
Sunent cez greisles, les voiz en sunt mult cleres,
3310 De l'olifan haltes sunt les menees.
Li amiralz en apelet sun frere,
Ço est Canabeus, li reis de Floredee,
Cil tint la tere entresqu'en Val Sevree.
Les escheles Charlun li ad mustrees:

"My lord barons, you will ride in the forefront,
You will lead all my divisions.
But I wish to retain three of the finest for myself:
The first will be made up of Turks, the second of Ormaleus,
3285 And the third of giants from Malprose.
The men of Occiant will be with me,
They will fight Charles and the French.
If the Emperor engages me in combat,
His head will surely be severed from his torso.
3290 Let him be absolutely certain, he will have a right to nothing
     else." AOI.

237

The opposing armies are vast, and the divisions are in fine array.
There is no mountain, valley, or hill between them,
No forest or wood can offer a hiding place,
They see each other clearly in the middle of the open area.
3295 Baligant said: "My good pagans,
Ride now and seek battle!"
Amborre of Oluferne carries the standard.
The pagans cry out its name, "Precieuse!"
The French say: "May you suffer a great loss this day!"
3300 They shout "Monjoie!" anew in a very loud voice.
The Emperor orders his bugles to be sounded,
The oliphant, too, which excites them to a fever pitch.
The pagans say: "Charles's army is in fine fettle,
We shall have a hard and cruel battle." AOI.

238

3305 The plain is vast and the countryside extends far and wide.
The helmets, whose gold is wrought with gems, shine,
As do the shields and the saffron byrnies,
The spears and mounted ensigns.
The bugles ring out, their sound is very clear,
3310 The oliphant's blasts carry far.
The Emperor calls his brother,
Canabeus, King of Floredee,
He ruled the land as far as Val Sevree.
He showed him Charles's divisions:

3315   "Veez l'orgoil de France la loee!
      Mult fierement chevalchet li emperere,
      Il est darere od cele gent barbee.
      Desur lur bronies lur barbes unt getees
      Altresi blanches cume neif sur gelee.
3320   Cil i ferrunt de lances e d'espees.
      Bataille avrum e forte e aduree,
      Unkes nuls hom ne vit tel ajustee."
      Plus qu'om ne lancet une verge pelee,
      Baligant ad ses cumpaignes trespassees.
3325   Une raisun lur a dit e mustree:
      "Venez, paien, kar jon irai en l'estree."
      De sun espiet la hanste en ad branlee,
      Envers Karlun la mure en ad turnee.   AOI.

239

      Carles li magnes, cum il vit l'amiraill
3330   E le dragon, l'enseigne e l'estandart—
      De cels d'Arabe si grant force i par ad,
      De la contree unt purprises les parz,
      Ne mes que tant cume l'empereres en ad—
      Li reis de France s'en escriet mult halt:
3335   "Barons franceis, vos estes bons vassals,
      Tantes batailles avez faites en camps!
      Veez paien, felun sunt e cuart,
      Tutes lor leis un dener ne lur valt.
      S'il unt grant gent, d'iço, seignurs, qui calt?
3340   Ki or ne voelt a mei venir, s'en alt!"
      Des esperons puis brochet le cheval,
      E Tencendor li ad fait .IIII. salz.
      Dient Franceis: "Icist reis est vassals!
      Chevalchez, bers, nul de nus ne vus falt!"

240

3345   Clers fut li jurz e li soleilz luisanz,
      Les oz sunt beles e les cumpaignes granz.
      Justees sunt les escheles devant.
      Li quens Rabels e li quens Guinemans

3315   "See now the wickedness of vaunted France!
       The Emperor is riding forth very fiercely,
       He is in the rear with the bearded men.
       Over their byrnies they have displayed their beards,
       Which are white as snow on ice.
3320   They will strike with their lances and swords.
       We shall have a violent and hard battle,
       No one has ever seen anything like it."
       Farther than a man can throw a shaven stick,
       Baligant has moved ahead of his companies.
3325   He said to them, performing the deed as he spoke:
       "Come along, my pagans, for I am going to move forward."
       He shook the shaft of his spear,
       He turned its point toward Charles.   AOI.

239

       Charles, seeing the Emir
3330   And the dragon ensign and standard—
       There is such a huge force from Arabia
       That it covers the entire countryside,
       Save that area held by the Emperor—
       The King of France cries out in a very loud voice:
3335   "French barons, you are stalwart knights,
       You have fought on so many battlegrounds!
       See the pagans before us, who are evil and cowardly,
       Their whole religion isn't worth a damn.
       They have a huge army, but so what, my lords?
3340   Let any man who doesn't wish to come with me leave at once!"
       Then he urges his horse on with his spurs,
       And Tencendor made four bounds.
       The French say: "The King is courageous!
       Ride on, brave warrior, not a single one of us abandons you!"

240

3345   The day was clear and the sun was shining,
       The armies are in fine array and the companies are vast.
       The lead divisions have joined battle.
       Count Rabel and Count Guinemant

Lascent les resnes a lor cevals curanz,
3350 Brochent a eit, dunc laisent curre Francs,
Si vunt ferir de lur espiez trenchanz.   AOI.

241

Li quens Rabels est chevaler hardiz.
Le cheval brochet des esperuns d'or fin,
Si vait ferir Torleu, le rei persis.
3355 N'escut ne bronie ne pout sun colp tenir:
L'espiet a or li ad enz el cors mis,
Que mort l'abat sur un boissun petit.
Dient Fanceis: "Damnesdeus nos aït!
Carles ad dreit, ne li devom faillir."   AOI.

242

3360 E Guineman justet a un rei leutice,
Tute li freint la targe, ki est flurie;
Aprés li ad la bronie descunfite,
Tute l'enseigne li ad enz el cors mise,
Que mort l'abat, ki qu'en plurt u kin riet.
3365 A icest colp cil de France s'escrient:
"Ferez, baron, ne vos targez mie!
Carles ad dreit vers la gent . . .
Deus nus ad mis al plus verai juïse."   AOI.

243

Malpramis siet sur un cheval tut blanc,
3370 Cunduit sun cors en la presse des Francs.
D'ures en altres granz colps i vait ferant,
L'un mort sur l'altre suvent vait trescevant.
Tut premereins s'escriet Baligant:
"Li mien baron, nurrit vos ai lung tens.
3375 Veez mun fils, Carlun vait querant,
A ses armes tanz barons calunjant,
Meillor vassal de lui ja ne demant.

Give their swift horses free rein,
3350 They spur with all their might, then the Franks let them gallop,
They go to strike with their sharp spears.   AOI.

241

Count Rabel is a stalwart knight.
He urges his horse on with his pure gold spurs,
He goes to strike Torleu, the Persian king.
3355 Neither shield nor byrnie can withstand his blow:
He has thrust his golden spear into his body,
Throwing him down dead on a small bush.
The French say: "May the Lord God help us!
Charles is in the right, we must not fail him."   AOI.

242

3360 And Guinemant fights a Lycian king,
He smashes his shield, which is decorated with a flower design;
Afterward he ripped apart his byrnie,
He plunges his whole ensign into his body,
Throwing him down dead, whether one weeps or laughs
    because of it.
3365 When they see this blow, the men of France shout:
"Strike, brave knights, do not delay!
Charles is in the right against the . . . people!
God has placed us on the side of true justice."   AOI.

243

Malprimes sits astride a pure white horse,
3370 He throws himself into the press of the Franks.
Over and over again he strikes great blows,
Repeatedly he finishes off his adversaries, piling one on top of
    the other.
Baligant is the first to shout:
"My good barons, I've supported you a long time.
3375 See now my son, who is attacking Charles,
Challenging so many fighting men with his arms,
I couldn't ask for a braver knight than he.

Succurez le a voz espiez trenchant!"
A icest mot paien venent avant,
3380   Durs colps i fierent, mult est li caples granz.
La bataille est merveilluse e pesant,
Ne fut si fort enceis ne puis cel tens.   AOI.

244

Granz sunt les oz e les cumpaignes fieres,
Justees sunt trestutes les escheles
3385   E li paien merveillusement fierent.
Deus! tantes hanstes i ad par mi brisees,
Escuz fruisez e bronies desmaillees!
La veïsez la tere si junchee,
L'erbe del camp, ki est verte e delgee,
3390   . . . .
Li amiralz recleimet sa maisnee:
"Ferez, baron, sur la gent chrestïene!"
La bataille est mult dure e afichee,
Unc einz ne puis ne fut si fort ajustee,
3395   Josqu'a la noit n'en ert fins otriee.   AOI.

245

Li amiralz la sue gent apelet:
"Ferez, paien, por el venud n'i estes!
Jo vos durrai muillers gentes e beles,
Si vos durai feus e honors e teres."
3400   Paien respundent: "Nus le devuns ben fere."
A colps pleners de lor espiez i perdent,
Plus de cent milie espees i unt traites.
Ais vos le caple e dulurus e pesmes!
Bataille veit cil ki entr'els volt estre!   AOI.

246

3405   Li emperere recleimet ses Franceis:
"Seignors barons, jo vos aim, si vos crei.
Tantes batailles avez faites pur mei,
Regnes cunquis e desordenet reis!

Help him with your sharp spears!"
When they hear this, the pagans advance,
3380 They strike hard blows, the fighting is very fierce.
The battle is wild and oppressive,
There never was a more violent struggle before or since that
    time. AOI.

244

The armies are vast and the companies fierce,
All the divisions have joined battle,
3385 And the pagans strike in wild fashion.
God! there are so many spear shafts broken in half,
Shields smashed and byrnies' metal links broken!
There you would have seen the ground so littered,
The grass, which is green and tender, in the field
3390 . . . .
The Emir calls upon the members of his household:
"Brave knights, smite the Christian people!"
The battle is very hard and bitter,
There never was a more hotly contested fray before nor since,
3395 It will not be broken off until nightfall. AOI.

245

The Emir calls out to his men:
"Strike, my pagans, you have come for no other reason!
I shall give you noble and fair spouses,
I shall give you fiefs, domains, and lands."
3400 The pagans reply: "We shall do this without fail."
Striking mighty blows, they lose their spears,
Now they have drawn more than a hundred thousand swords.
See now the bitter and cruel fighting!
Anyone wishing to be among them sees a battle! AOI.

246

3405 The Emperor calls out to his Frenchmen:
"My lord barons, I care for you and trust in you.
You have fought so many battles for me,
Conquered so many realms and deposed so many kings!

Ben le conuis que gueredun vos en dei
3410 E de mun cors, de teres e d'aveir.
Vengez voz filz, voz freres e voz heirs
Qu'en Rencesvals furent morz l'altre seir!
Ja savez vos cuntre paiens ai dreit."
Respondent Franc: "Sire, vos dites veir."
3415 Itels .XX. miliers en ad od sei,
Cumunement l'en prametent lor feiz,
Ne li faldrunt pur mort ne pur destreit.
N'en i ad cel sa lance n'i empleit,
De lur espees i fierent demaneis.
3420 La bataille est de merveillus destreit.   AOI.

247

E Malpramis par mi le camp chevalchet,
De cels de France i fait mult grant damage.
Naimes li dux fierement le reguardet,
Vait le ferir cum hume vertudable.
3425 De sun escut li freint la pene halte,
De sun osberc les dous pans li desaffret,
El cors li met tute l'enseigne jalne,
Que mort l'abat entre .VII.C. des altres.

248

Reis Canabeus, le frere a l'amiraill,
3430 Des esporuns ben brochot sun cheval.
Trait ad l'espee, le punt est de cristal,
Si fiert Naimun en l'elme principal,
L'une meitiet l'en fruissed d'une part,
Al brant d'acer l'en trenchet .V. des laz.
3435 Li capelers un dener ne li valt,
Trenchet la coife entresque a la char,
Jus a la tere une piece en abat.
Granz fut li colps, li dux en estonat,
Sempres caïst, se Deus ne li aidast.
3440 De sun destrer le col en enbraçat.
Se li paiens une feiz recuvrast,
Sempres fust mort li nobilies vassal.
Carles de France i vint, kil succurrat.   AOI.

I recognize full well that I owe you a reward for this,
3410 Redeemable with my body, my lands, and my wealth.
Avenge your sons, your brothers, and your heirs,
Who died last night at Roncevaux!
You know full well that I am in the right against the pagans."
The Franks reply: "Sire, what you say is true."
3415 There are twenty thousand of them with him,
Together they give him their word
That they will not fail him even if it means death or anguish.
Every single one of them uses his lance,
They strike immediately with their swords.
3420 The battle is extraordinarily bitter.   AOI.

247

And Malprimes rides throughout the battlefield,
He plays havoc among the men of France.
Duke Naimes looks at him fiercely,
He goes to strike him like a stalwart.
3425 He smashed the upper edge of his shield,
He rips the saffron away from the two sections of his hauberk,
He plunges his whole yellow ensign into his body,
Throwing him down dead among seven hundred others.

248

King Canabeus, the Emir's brother,
3430 Urged his horse on vigorously with his spurs.
He has drawn his sword, its hilt is made of crystal,
He strikes Naimes upon his princely helmet,
He shatters half of it on one side,
He hacks through five of the laces with his steel blade.
3435 The coif does not protect him in the least,
The pagan hacks through the coif down to the skin,
He knocks a piece down to the ground.
The blow was harsh, the Duke was stunned by it,
He would have fallen had God not helped him.
3440 He threw his arms around his war-horse's neck.
If the pagan had struck once more,
The noble knight would have died straightaway.
But Charles of France came and rescued him.   AOI.

249

Naimes li dux tant par est anguissables,
3445 E li paiens de ferir mult le hastet.
Carles li dist: "Culvert, mar le baillastes!"
Vait le ferir par sun grant vasselage:
L'escut li freint, cuntre le coer li quasset,
De sun osberc li desrumpt la ventaille,
3450 Que mort l'abat, la sele en remeint guaste.

250

Mult ad grant doel Carlemagnes li reis,
Quant Naimun veit nafret devant sei,
Sur l'erbe verte le sanc tut cler caeir.
Li empereres li ad dit a cunseill:
3455 "Bel sire Naimes, kar chevalcez od mei!
Morz est li gluz ki en destreit vus teneit,
El cors li mis mun espiet une feiz."
Respunt li dux: "Sire, jo vos en crei.
Se jo vif alques, mult grant prod i avreiz."
3460 Puis sunt justez par amur e par feid,
Ensembl'od els tels .XX. milie Franceis.
N'i ad celoi n'i fierge o n'i capleit.   AOI.

251

Li amiralz chevalchet par le camp,
Si vait ferir le cunte Guneman.
3465 Cuntre le coer li fruisset l'escut blanc,
De sun osberc li derumpit les pans,
Les dous costez li deseivret des flancs,
Que mort l'abat de sun cheval curant.
Puis ad ocis Gebuin e Lorain,
3470 Richart le veill, li sire des Normans.
Paien escrient: "Preciuse est vaillant!
Ferez, baron, nus i avom guarant!"   AOI.

252

Ki puis veïst li chevaler d'Arabe,
Cels d'Occiant e d'Argoillie e de Bascle!

249

Duke Naimes is in very great distress,
3445 And the pagan hastens to strike him.
Charles said: "Scoundrel, you'll rue the day you attacked him!"
He goes to strike him with all his might:
He smashes his shield, he shatters it against his heart,
He rips the ventail from his hauberk,
3450 Throwing him down dead, his saddle remaining empty.

250

King Charlemagne is very profoundly afflicted
When he sees Naimes wounded in front of him
And the bright blood falling on the green grass.
The Emperor said to him quietly:
3455 "Dear Sir Naimes, ride by my side now!
The villain who was pressing you hard is dead,
I plunged my spear into his body once and for all."
The Duke answers: "I believe you, sire.
If I live a bit longer, you will profit a good deal from it."
3460 Then they came together in friendship and loyalty,
And with them twenty thousand Frenchmen.
Every single one of them strikes or fights.   AOI.

251

The Emir rides throughout the field,
He goes to strike Count Guinemant.
3465 He shatters his white shield against his heart,
He tears the sections of his hauberk,
He severs his two sides from his flanks,
Throwing him down dead from his swift horse.
Then he killed Geboin and Lorant,
3470 Old Richard, Lord of the Normans.
The pagans shout: "Precieuse is a worthy sword!
Strike, brave knights, we have a protector here!"   AOI.

252

One could see then the knights of Arabia,
The men of Occiant, of Argoille, and of Bascle!

3475 De lur espiez ben i fierent e caplent,
E li Franceis n'unt talent que s'en algent;
Asez i moerent e des uns e des altres.
Entresqu'al vespre est mult fort la bataille:
Des francs barons i ad mult gran damage,
3480 Doel i avrat, enceis qu'ele departed.   AOI.

253

Mult ben i fierent Franceis e Arrabit,
Fruissent cez hanste e cil espiez furbit.
Ki dunc veïst cez escuz si malmis,
Cez blancs osbercs ki dunc oïst fremir
3485 E cez escuz sur cez helmes cruisir,
Cez chevalers ki dunc veïst caïr
E humes braire, contre tere murir,
De grant dulor li poüst suvenir!
Ceste bataille est mult fort a suffrir.
3490 Li amiralz recleimet Apolin
E Tervagan e Mahumet altresi:
"Mi damnedeu, jo vos ai mult servit,
Tutes tes ymagenes ferai d'or fin."   AOI.

. . . .

3495 As li devant un soen drut, Gemalfin,
Males nuveles li aportet e dit:
"Baligant, sire, mal este oi baillit:
Perdut avez Malpramis, vostre filz,
E Canabeus, vostre frere, est ocis:
3500 A dous Franceis belement en avint.
Li empereres en est l'uns, ço m'est vis,
Granz ad le cors, ben resenblet marchis,
Blanc ad la barbe cume flur en avrill."
Li amiralz en ad le helme enclin
3505 E en après sin enbrunket sun vis,
Si grant doel ad sempres quiad murir.
Sin apelat Jangleu l'Ultremarin.

3475   They strike and fight fiercely with their spears,
       But the French have no intention of leaving;
       Many on both sides die.
       The battle rages on until nightfall:
       There are a great many casualties among the brave Frankish
         knights,
3480   There will be grieving before the battle is broken off.   AOI.

253

       The French and the Arabs strike very hard,
       Shafts and furbished spears shatter.
       Anyone having seen then the battered shields,
       Anyone having heard then the shiny hauberks ringing
3485   And shields crashing on helmets,
       Anyone having seen knights falling
       And men howling and dying on the ground,
       Would remember great sorrow!
       This battle is very hard to endure.
3490   The Emir calls upon Apollo,
       Tervagant and also Mohammed:
       "My lord gods, I have served you very long,
       I shall make all your graven images pure gold."   AOI.
      . . . .
3495   Here now before him is Gemalfin, his trusted friend,
       He brings him bad news and says:
       "My lord Baligant, you suffer misfortune this day:
       You have lost your son Malprimes,
       And your brother Canabeus is dead:
3500   Things have gone well for two Frenchmen.
       The Emperor is one of them, I believe,
       He is very big, he looks very much like a marquis,
       His beard is white as a flower in April."
       At this the Emir bows his head,
3505   And then he lowered his face,
       He was so furious that he thought he would die.
       He called Jangleu of Outremer.

254

Dist l'amiraill: "Jangleu, venez avant!
Vos estes proz e vostre saveir est grant,
3510 Vostre conseill ai . . . tuz tens.
Que vos en semblet d'Arrabiz e de Francs?
Avrum nos la victorie del champ?"
E cil respunt: "Morz estes, Baligant!
Ja vostre deu ne vos erent guarant.
3515 Carles est fiers e si hume vaillant,
Unc ne vi gent ki si fust cumbatant.
Mais reclamez les barons d'Occiant,
Turcs e Enfruns, Arabiz e Jaianz.
Ço que estre en deit, ne l'alez demurant."

255

3520 Li amiraill ad sa barbe fors mise,
Altresi blanche cume flur en espine,
Cument qu'il seit, ne s'i voelt celer mie.
Met a sa buche une clere buisine,
Sunet la cler, que si paien l'oïrent;
3525 Par tut le camp ses cumpaignes ralient.
Cil d'Ociant i braient e henissent,
Arguille si cume chen i glatissent;
Requerent Franc par si grant estultie,
El plus espés ses rumpent e partissent.
3530 A icest colp en jetent mort .VII. milie.

256

Li quens Oger cuardise n'out unkes,
Meillor vassal de lui ne vestit bronie.
Quant de Franceis les escheles vit rumpre,
Si apelat Tierri, le duc d'Argone,
3535 Gefrei d'Anjou e Jozeran le cunte.
Mult fierement Carlun en araisunet:
"Veez paien cum ocient voz humes!
Ja Deu ne placet qu'el chef portez corone,
S'or n'i ferez pur venger vostre hunte!"
3540 N'i ad icel ki un sul mot respundet:

254

The Emir said: "Jangleu, come forward!
You are a man of worth and of great cunning,
3510 I have always . . . your advice.
What think you of the Arabs and the Franks?
Shall we be victorious on the battlefield?"
And the latter replies: "You're dead, Baligant!
Your gods will never save you.
3515 Charles is fierce and his men are worthy,
I have never seen such a warlike people.
But summon the men of Occiant,
The Turks, the Enfruns, the Arabs, and the Giants.
Whatever the future holds, don't delay."

255

3520 The Emir has displayed his beard,
White as a hawthorn flower,
Come what may, he does not want to hide.
He raises a clear-sounding bugle to his mouth,
He sounds it clear, so that the pagans heard it;
3525 His companies rally in every part of the field.
The men of Occiant bray and whinny,
The men of Argoille yelp like dogs;
They attack the Franks with such wild abandon
That they break their ranks and divide their tightest formations.
3530 In this onslaught they threw seven thousand down dead.

256

Count Ogier never acted out of cowardice,
A braver knight than he never donned a byrnie.
When he saw the French divisions breaking,
He called Thierry, the Duke of Argonne,
3535 Geoffrey of Anjou, and Count Jozeran.
He spoke very bluntly to Charles:
"See how the pagans are slaughtering your men!
May it never please God that you should wear a crown on your head
If you do not strike forthwith to avenge our dishonor!"
3540 No one utters a single word:

Brochent ad eit, lor cevals laissent cure,
Vunt les ferir la o il les encuntrent.

257

    Mult ben i fiert Carlemagnes li reis,   AOI.
    Naimes li dux e Oger li Daneis,
3545 Geifreid d'Anjou, ki l'enseigne teneit.
    Mult par est proz danz Ogers li Daneis,
    Puint le ceval, laisset curre ad espleit,
    Si vait ferir celui ki le dragun teneit,
    Qu'Ambure cravente en la place devant sei
3550 E le dragon e l'enseigne le rei.
    Baligant veit sun gunfanun cadeir
    E l'estandart Mahumet remaneir:
    Li amiralz alques s'en aperceit
    Que il ad tort e Carlemagnes dreit.
3555 Paien d'Arabe s'en turnent plus .C.
    Li emperere recleimet ses parenz:
    "Dites, baron, por Deu, si m'aidereiz."
    Respundent Francs: "Mar le demandereiz,
    Trestut seit fel ki n'i fierget a espleit!"   AOI.

258

3560 Passet li jurz, si turnet a la vespree,
    Franc e paien i fierent des espees.
    Cil sunt vassal ki les oz ajusterent,
    Lor enseignes n'i unt mie ublïees:
    Li amiraz Preciuse ad criee,
3565 Carles Munjoie, l'enseigne renumee.
    L'un conuist l'altre as haltes voiz e as cleres,
    En mi le camp amdui s'entr'encuntrerent.
    Si se vunt ferir, granz colps s'entredunerent
    De lor espiez en lor targes roees,
3570 Fraites les unt desuz cez bucles lees.
    De lor osbercs les pans en desevrerent,
    Dedenz cez cors mie ne s'adeserent.

They spur with all their might, they give their horses free rein,
They go strike the pagans wherever they find them.

257

King Charlemagne strikes very hard,   AOI.
As do Duke Naimes, Ogier the Dane,
3545 And Geoffrey of Anjou, who carried the ensign.
Lord Ogier the Dane is very courageous,
He spurs his horse, he lets him run full speed,
He goes to strike the man who held the dragon,
So that Amborre falls with a crash there before him
3550 With the dragon and the royal ensign.
Baligant sees his pennon fall
And Mohammed's standard brought low:
The Emir begins to realize
That he is in the wrong and that Charlemagne is in the right.
3555 More than a hundred of the pagans of Arabia turn to flee.
The Emperor calls to his kinsmen:
"Tell me, my brave knights, in God's name, whether you will help
      me now."
The Franks reply: "You need not have asked,
Let everyone strike with all his might or be damned!"   AOI.

258

3560 The daylight fades away, it is growing dusk,
The Franks and pagans strike with swords.
The leaders who brought the armies together in battle are
      courageous,
They have not forgotten their battle cries:
The Emir shouted "Precieuse!",
3565 Charles, the renowned war cry "Monjoie!"
They recognized each other by their loud and clear voices,
The two men met in the middle of the battlefield.
They go to strike each other, they exchange mighty blows,
Spears beating against shields ornamented with circles,
3570 They smashed them above the wide bosses.
They ripped the sections from their hauberks,
But they did not wound each other's bodies.

Rumpent cez cengles e cez seles verserent,
Cheent li rei, a tere se turnerent,
3575 Isnelement sur lor piez releverent.
Mult vassalment unt traites les espees.
Ceste bataille n'en ert mais destornee,
Seinz hume mort ne poet estre achevee.   AOI.

259

Mult est vassal Carles de France dulce,
3580 Li amiralz, il nel crent ne ne dutet.
Cez lor espees tutes nues i mustrent,
Sur cez escuz mult granz colps s'entredunent.
Trenchent les quirs e cez fuz ki sunt dubles,
Cheent li clou, si peceient les bucles.
3585 Puis fierent il nud a nud sur lur bronies,
Des helmes clers li fuus en escarbunet.
Ceste bataille ne poet remaneir unkes,
Josque li uns sun tort i reconuisset.   AOI.

260

Dist l'amiraill: "Carles, kar te purpenses,
3590 Si pren cunseill que vers mei te repentes!
Mort as mun filz, par le men escïente,
A mult grant tort mun païs me calenges.
Deven mes hom, en fiet le te voeill rendre,
Ven mei servir d'ici qu'en Orïente."
3595 Carles respunt: "Mult grant viltet me semblet,
Pais ne amor ne dei a paien rendre.
Receif la lei que Deus nos apresentet,
Chrestïentet, e pui te amerai sempres;
Puis serf e crei le rei omnipotente!"
3600 Dist Baligant: "Malvais sermun cumences!"
Puis vunt ferir des espees qu'unt ceintes.   AOI.

261

Li amiralz est mult de grant vertut.
Fier Carlemagne sur l'elme d'acer brun,

They break the cinches and turned the saddles over,
The kings fall, they tumbled to the ground,
3575 But they quickly got back on their feet.
They drew their swords very bravely.
This struggle will no longer be averted,
It cannot end until one of the men is dead.   AOI.

259

Charles of fair France is very courageous,
3580 But the Emir neither fears nor stands in awe of him.
They display their naked swords in menacing fashion,
They exchange mighty blows on each other's shields.
They hack through the shields' leather and double thickness of wood,
The nails fall, the bosses shatter.
3585 Then they strike each other's unprotected byrnies,
Sparks fly from the shiny helmets.
This duel will never end,
Until one of them admits he is in the wrong.   AOI.

260

The Emir said: "Think it over, Charles,
3590 You'd be well advised to beg my forgiveness!
You have slain my son, of that I am certain,
You very unjustly challenge my right to this country.
Become my vassal and I shall give it back to you as a fief.
Come serve me from here to the Orient."
3595 Charles replies: "This strikes me as a very contemptible notion,
I must bestow neither peace nor friendship on any pagan.
Accept the religion that God reveals to us,
Namely Christianity, then I shall care for you forthwith;
Then serve and believe in the almighty King!"
3600 Baligant said: "You lead off with malicious words!"
Then they go to strike with the swords they have girded on.   AOI.

261

The Emir is a very strong man.
He strikes Charles on his burnished steel helmet,

Desur la teste li ad frait e fendut;
3605 Met li l'espee sur les chevels menuz,
Prent de la carn grant pleine palme e plus,
Iloec endreit remeint li os tut nut.
Carles cancelet, por poi qu'il n'est caüt,
Mais Deus ne volt qu'il seit mort ne vencut.
3610 Seint Gabrïel est repairet a lui,
Si li demandet: "Reis magnes, que fais tu?"

262

Quant Carles oït la seinte voiz de l'angle,
N'en ad poür ne de murir dutance.
Repairet loi vigur e remembrance,
3615 Fiert l'amiraill de l'espee de France,
L'elme li freint o li gemme reflambent,
Trenchet la teste pur la cervele espandre
E tut le vis tresqu'en la barbe blanche,
Que mort l'abat senz nule recuvrance.
3620 Munjoie escriet pur la reconuisance.
A icest mot venuz i est dux Neimes,
Prent Tencendur, muntet i est li reis magnes.
Paien s'en turnent, ne volt Deus qu'il i remainent.
Or sunt Franceis a icels qu'il demandent.

263

3625 Paien s'en fuient, cum Damnesdeus le volt,
Encalcent Franc e l'emperere avoec.
Ço dist li reis: "Seignurs, vengez voz doels,
Si esclargiez voz talenz e voz coers,
Kar hoi matin vos vi plurer des oilz."
3630 Respondent Franc: "Sire, ço nus estoet."
Cascuns i fiert tanz granz colps cum il poet,
Poi s'en estoerstrent d'icels ki sunt iloec.

264

Granz est li calz, si se levet la puldre.
Paien s'en fuient e Franceis les anguissent,

He smashed and split it on his head;
3605 He brings his sword down on his thick hair,
He whacks off more than a palm's breadth of skin,
The bone there remains completely exposed.
Charles reels, he nearly fell,
But God does not wish him to be killed or vanquished.
3610 Saint Gabriel returned to his side,
And he asked him: "Great King, what are you doing?"

262

Charles, hearing the sacred voice of the angel,
Has no fear, nor is he afraid of dying.
His strength and mindfulness return to him,
3615 He strikes the Emir with the sword of France,
He smashes the helmet where the gems flash,
He hacks through his head, spilling out his brain,
And he cleaves his whole face down to his white beard,
Knocking him down dead beyond all recall.
3620 He shouts "Monjoie!" to express his gratitude.
When he heard this, Duke Naimes came,
He takes hold of Tencendor, the great King has mounted him.
The pagans turn and flee, God does not wish them to remain.
Now the French have a go at those they seek out.

263

3625 The pagans flee, as the Lord God wills it,
The Franks together with the Emperor pursue them.
The King said: "My lords, avenge your sorrows,
Relieve your minds and your hearts,
For I saw your eyes brimming with tears this morning."
3630 The Franks reply: "Sire, that we must do."
Each one strikes blows as hard as he can,
Few of the enemy there escape.

264

The heat is great and the dust rises.
The pagans flee and the French follow close on their heels,

3635 Li enchalz duret d'ici qu'en Sarraguce.
En sum sa tur muntee est Bramidonie,
Ensembl'od li si clerc e si canonie
De false lei, que Deus nen amat unkes,
Ordres nen unt ne en lor chefs corones.
3640 Quant ele vit Arrabiz si cunfundre,
A halte voiz s'escrie: "Aiez nos, Mahum!
E! gentilz reis, ja sunt vencuz noz humes,
Li amiralz ocis a si grant hunte!"
Quant l'ot Marsilie, vers sa pareit se turnet,
3645 Pluret des oilz, tute sa chere enbrunchet.
Morz est de doel, si cum pecchet l'encumbret,
L'anme de lui as vifs diables dunet.   AOI.

265

Paien sunt morz, alquant . . .
E Carles ad sa bataille vencue.
3650 De Sarraguce ad la porte abatue,
Or set il ben que . . . mais defendue.
Prent la citet, sa gent i est venue,
Par poëstet icele noit i jurent.
Fiers est li reis a la barbe canue,
3655 E Bramidonie les turs li ad rendues,
Les dis sunt grandes, les cinquante menues.
Mult ben espleitet qui Damnesdeus aiuet.

266

Passet li jurz, la noit est aserie,
Clers est la lune e les esteiles flambient.
3660 Li emperere ad Sarraguce prise.
A mil Franceis funt ben cercer la vile,
Les sinagoges e les mahumeries.
A mailz de fer e a cuignees qu'il tindrent
Fruissent les ymagenes e trestutes les ydeles,
3665 N'i remeindrat ne sorz ne falserie.
Li reis creit Deu, faire voelt sun servise,
E si evesque les eves beneïssent,
Meinent paien entesqu'al baptisterie.

3635   The pursuit lasts from here to Saragossa.
Bramimonde has climbed to the top of her tower,
Together with her clerics and canons
Of the false religion, which God never loved,
They are not in holy orders, nor have they received the tonsure.
3640   Seeing the Arabs in full rout,
She cries out in a loud voice: "Help us, Mohammed!
Oh, noble King, our men are vanquished now,
The Emir slain so shamefully!"
Hearing this, Marsile turns toward the wall,
3645   Tears come to his eyes, he lowers his whole head.
He died of despair, for sin encumbers him,
He gives his soul to the most hideous devils.   AOI.

265

The pagans are dead, a few . . .
And Charles has won his battle.
3650   He has broken down the gate to Saragossa,
Now he is certain that it is no longer defended.
He takes the citadel, his men have entered it,
They lie there in full force that night.
The white-haired King is fierce,
3655   And Bramimonde surrendered the towers to him,
Ten of them great, fifty of them small.
Whomever the Lord God assists fares very well.

266

The daylight fades away, night has fallen,
The moon is clear and the stars blaze forth.
3660   The Emperor has taken Saragossa.
Orders are given for a thousand Frenchmen to search the city,
The synagogues, and the mosques.
Holding iron hammers and axes,
They smash the statues and all the idols,
3665   No sorcery or false cult will remain there.
The King believes in God, he wishes to serve Him,
His bishops bless the waters,
They lead the pagans to the baptisteries.

S'or i ad cel qui Carle cuntredie,
3670 Il le fait prendre o ardeir ou ocire.
Baptizet sunt asez plus de .C. milie
Veir chrestïen, ne mais sul la reïne:
En France dulce iert menee caitive,
Ço voelt li reis par amur cunvertisset.

267

3675 Passet la noit, si apert le cler jor.
De Sarraguce Carles guarnist les turs,
Mil chevalers i laissat puigneürs,
Guardent la vile a oes l'empereor.
Muntet li reis e si hume trestuz
3680 E Bramidonie, qu'il meinet en sa prisun,
Mais n'ad talent que li facet se bien nun.
Repairez sunt a joie e a baldur.
Passent Nerbone par force e par vigur,
Vint a Burdeles, la citet de ...
3685 Desur l'alter seint Severin le baron
Met l'oliphan plein d'or e de manguns,
Li pelerin le veient ki la vunt.
Passet Girunde a mult granz nefs qu'i sunt.
Entresque a Blaive ad cunduit sun nevold
3690 E Oliver, sun nobilie cumpaignun,
E l'arcevesque, ki fut sages e proz.
En blancs sarcous fait metre les seignurs:
A Seint Romain, la gisent li baron,
Francs les cumandent a Deu e a ses nuns.
3695 Carles cevalchet e les vals e les munz,
Entresqu'a Ais ne volt prendre sujurn.
Tant chevalchat qu'il descent al perrun.
Cume il est en sun paleis halçur,
Par ses messages mandet ses jugeors,
3700 Baivers e Saisnes, Loherencs e Frisuns,
Alemans mandet, si mandet Borguignuns
E Peitevins e Normans e Bretuns,
De cels de France des plus saives qui sunt.
Des ore cumencet le plait de Guenelun.

Now if there is anyone who opposes Charles,
3670 He orders him to be taken prisoner, burned, or put to death.
Well over a hundred thousand are baptized
True Christians, with the sole exception of the Queen:
She will be led captive to fair France,
The King wishes her to become a convert out of devotion.

267

3675 The night passes and the day dawns bright.
Charles manned the towers of Saragossa,
He left a thousand fighting men there,
They guard the city in the Emperor's name.
The King mounts up, as do all his men
3680 And Bramimonde, whom he leads away as his captive,
But he intends to do well by her.
They returned joyfully and jubilantly.
In passing they took Nerbonne by force and by storm,
They came to Bordeaux, the city of . . .
3685 On noble Saint Seurin's altar
He places the oliphant filled with gold and with mangons,
The pilgrims who travel there still see it.
He crosses the Gironde in the great ships that are there.
He brought his nephew all the way to Blaye,
3690 Together with his noble companion Oliver
And the Archbishop, who was wise and worthy.
He orders the lords to be placed in white caskets:
The brave knights lie in the church of Saint-Romain,
The Franks commended them to God and His names.
3695 Charles rides through valleys and over mountains,
He does not wish to interrupt his march before reaching Aix.
He rode on, eventually he descends at the horse-block.
When he is in his majestic palace,
He summons his judges by messenger,
3700 Bavarians, Saxons, men of Lorraine, and Frisians,
He summons Germans and he summons Burgundians,
Poitevins, Normans, and Bretons,
The wisest men in France.
Now begins the trial of Ganelon.

268

3705 Li empereres est repairet d'Espaigne
E vient a Ais, al meillor sied de France,
Muntet el palais, est venut en la sale.
As li Alde venue, une bele damisele,
Ço dist al rei: "O est Rollant le catanie,
3710 Ki me jurat cume sa per a prendre?"
Carles en ad e dulor e pesance,
Pluret des oilz, tiret sa barbe blance:
"Soer, cher amie, de hume mort me demandes.
Jo t'en durai mult esforcet eschange,
3715 Ço est Loewis, mielz ne sai a parler,
Il est mes filz e si tendrat mes marches."
Alde respunt: "Cest mot mei est estrange.
Ne place Deu ne ses seinz ne ses angles
Aprés Rollant que jo vive remaigne!"
3720 Pert la culor, chet as piez Carlemagne,
Sempres est morte, Deus ait mercit de l'anme!
Franceis barons en plurent e si la pleignent.

269

Alde la bel est a sa fin alee.
Quidet li reis que el se seit pasmee,
3725 Pitet en ad, sin pluret l'emperere;
Prent la as mains, si l'en ad relevee,
Desur les espalles ad la teste clinee.
Quant Carles veit que morte l'ad truvee,
Quatre cuntesses sempres i ad mandees.
3730 A un muster de nuneins est portee,
La noit la guaitent entresqu'a l'ajurnee.
Lunc un alter belement l'enterrerent,
Mult grant honur i ad li reis dunee. AOI.

270

Li emperere est repairet ad Ais.
3735 Guenes li fels, en caeines de fer,
En la citet est devant le paleis.
A un estache l'unt atachet cil serf,
Les mains li lient a curreies de cerf.

268

3705 The Emperor has returned from Spain,
He comes to Aix, the capital of France,
He climbs up to the palace, he has entered the hall.
Now Alda, a fair damsel, came to him,
She said to the King: "Where is Roland, the captain,
3710 Who gave me his solemn word he would take me to wife?"
Charles feels sad and heavy-hearted over this,
His eyes are brimming with tears, he tugs his white beard:
"Sister, dear friend, you ask me about a dead man.
I shall give you a very powerful individual to take his place,
3715 I mean Louis, I don't know what more I can say,
He is my son and he will rule my marches."
Alda replies: "This offer seems strange to me.
May it not please God, his angels and his saints
That I remain alive after Roland!"
3720 She loses her color, she falls at Charlemagne's feet,
She died on the spot, may God have mercy on her soul!
The brave French knights weep over it and lament her.

269

Fair Alda has met her end.
The King thinks she has fainted,
3725 He is moved to pity, the Emperor weeps over it;
He takes her by the hands, he has raised her up,
Her head drops on her shoulder.
Charles, seeing that she was already dead,
Immediately summoned four countesses,
3730 She is borne away to a convent for nuns,
They watch over her all night long until daybreak.
They buried her in noble fashion alongside an altar,
The King made a very great endowment to the convent in her
    honor. AOI.

270

The Emperor has returned to Aix.
3735 Wicked Ganelon, in iron chains,
Is in the citadel in front of the palace.
The serfs have tied him to a stake,
They bind his hands with deerhide thongs.

Tres ben le batent a fuz e a jamelz,
3740 N'ad deservit que altre ben i ait.
A grant dulur iloec atent sun plait.

271

Il est escrit en l'ancïene geste
Que Carles mandet humes de plusurs teres.
Asemblez sunt ad Ais, a la capele.
3745 Halz est li jurz, mult par est grande la feste,
Dient alquanz del baron seint Silvestre.
Des ore cumencet le plait e les noveles
De Guenelun, ki traïsun ad faite.
Li emperere devant sei l'ad fait traire.   AOI.

272

3750 "Seignors barons," dist Carlemagnès li reis,
"De Guenelun car me jugez le dreit!
Il fut en l'ost tresque en Espaigne od mei,
Si me tolit .XX. milie de mes Franceis
E mun nevold, que jamais ne verreiz,
3755 E Oliver, li proz e li curteis;
Les .XII. pers ad traït por aveir."
Dist Guenelon: "Fel seie se jol ceil!
Rollant me forfist en or e en aveir,
Pur que jo quis sa mort e sun destreit;
3760 Mais traïsun nule n'en i otrei."
Respundent Franc: "Ore en tendrum cunseill."

273

Devant le rei la s'estut Guenelun.
Cors ad gaillard, el vis gente color,
S'il fust leials, ben resemblast barun.
3765 Veit cels de France e tuz les jugeürs,
De ses parenz .XXX. ki od lui sunt.
Puis s'escriat haltement, a grant voeiz:
"Pur amor Deu, car m'entendez, barons!
Seignors, jo fui en l'ost avoec l'empereür,

3740

They thrash him soundly with sticks and rods,
He deserved no other treatment.
He awaits his trial there in great pain.

271

3745

It is written in the venerable chronicle
That Charles summons vassals from many lands.
They have assembled at Aix, in the chapel.
It is a holy day, the feast is very solemn,
Some say it is noble Saint Silvester's Day.
Now begin the allegations and the countercharges
Concerning Ganelon, who committed the act of treason.
The Emperor had him dragged before him.   AOI.

272

3750

3755

3760

"My lord barons," said King Charlemagne,
"Now give me a verdict concerning Ganelon!
He was with me in the army all the way to Spain,
He took twenty thousand of my Frenchmen away from me,
My nephew, whom I shall never see again,
And noble and worthy Oliver;
He betrayed the Twelve Peers for gain."
Ganelon said: "I'll be damned if I hide it!
Roland wronged me in a matter concerning gold and wealth,
Which is why I sought his death and his suffering;
But I submit no treason was committed here.
The French reply: "We shall hold a council for this purpose now."

273

3765

Ganelon stood there before the King.
He is robust of body, he has high color in his face,
If he were loyal, he would appear to be a worthy knight.
He sees the men of France, all the judges,
And thirty of his kinsmen who are with him.
Then he cried out aloud in a booming voice:
"For the love of God, hear me now, brave knights!
My lords, I was with the Emperor in the army,

3770 Serveie le par feid e par amur.
Rollant sis niés me coillit en haür,
Si me jugat a mort e a dulur.
Message fui al rei Marsiliun,
Par mun saveir vinc jo a guarisun.
3775 Jo desfiai Rollant le poigneor
E Oliver e tuiz lur cumpaignun;
Carles l'oïd e si nobilie baron.
Venget m'en sui, mais n'i ad traïsun."
Respundent Francs: "A conseill en irums."

274

3780 Quant Guenes veit que ses granz plaiz cumencet,
De ses parenz ensemble od li i out trente.
Un en i ad a qui li altre entendent,
Ço est Pinabel del Castel de Sorence.
Ben set parler e dreite raisun rendre,
3785 Vassals est bons por ses armes defendre.   AOI.
Ço li dist Guenes: "En vos . . .
Getez mei hoi de mort e de calunje!"
Dist Pinabel: "Vos serez guarit sempres.
N'i ad Francés ki vos juget a pendre,
3790 U l'emperere les noz dous cors en asemblet,
Al brant d'acer que jo ne l'en desmente."
Guenes li quens a ses piez se presente.

275

Bavier e Saisnes sunt alet a conseill,
E Peitevin e Norman e Franceis;
3795 Asez i ad Alemans e Tiedeis,
Icels d'Alverne i sunt li plus curteis.
Pur Pinabel se cuntienent plus quei.
Dist l'un a l'altre: "Bien fait a remaneir!
Laisum le plait e si preium le rei
3800 Que Guenelun cleimt quite ceste feiz,
Puis si li servet par amur e par feid.
Morz est Rollant, jamais nel revereiz,
N'ert recuvret por or ne por aveir,

3770 I served him in good faith and in friendship.
His nephew Roland conceived a hatred for me,
He marked me for death and suffering.
I was sent as a messenger to King Marsile,
I came back safely by using my head.
3775 I issued a formal challenge to that fighter Roland,
To Oliver and to all their companions;
Charles and his noble knights heard it.
I avenged myself, but there is no treason here."
The Franks reply: "We shall meet in council."

274

3780 Ganelon now sees his great trial beginning.
There were thirty of his kinsmen with him.
There is one the others listen to,
It is Pinabel of Castel de Sorence.
He is a skillful speaker and knows how to argue convincingly.
3785 He is a brave warrior well able to defend his arms.   AOI.
Ganelon said to him: "On you . . .
Free me this day from death and this grave charge!"
Pinabel said: "You will be saved forthwith.
No Frenchman condemns you to hang
3790 Without the Emperor opposing the two of us, the judge and me,
And without my giving him the lie with a steel blade."
Count Ganelon throws himself at his feet.

275

Bavarians and Saxons have gone off to deliberate,
Poitevins, Normans, and Frenchmen too;
3795 There are many Germans and Teutons,
The men of Auvergne render the best services in council.
They keep very quiet because of Pinabel.
One said to the other: "We'd do well to desist!
Let's dismiss the charge and implore the King
3800 To let Ganelon off this time,
And let him serve him henceforth in friendship and in good faith.
'Roland is dead, you'll never see him again,
He can't be recovered for gold or for any other compensation.'

Mult sereit fols ki . . . se cumbatreit."
3805 N'en i ad celoi nel graant e otreit,
Fors sul Tierri, le frere dam Geifreit.   AOI.

276

A Charlemagne repairent si barun,
Dient al rei: "Sire, nus vos prium
Que clamez quite le cunte Guenelun,
3810 Puis si vos servet par feid e par amor.
Vivre le laisez, car mult est gentilz hoem.
Ja por murir n'en ert veüd gerun,
Ne por aveir ja nel recuverum."
Ço dist li reis: "Vos estes mi felun!"   AOI.

277

3815 Quant Caries veit que tuz li sunt faillid,
Mult l'enbrunchit e la chere e le vis,
Al doel qu'il ad si se cleimet caitifs.
Ais li devant uns chevalers,
Frere Gefrei, a un duc angevin.
3820 Heingre out le cors e graisle e eschewid,
Neirs les chevels e alques bruns,
N'est gueres granz ne trop nen est petiz.
Curteisement a l'emperere ad dit:
"Bels sire reis, ne vos dementez si!
3825 Ja savez vos que mult vos ai servit.
Par anceisurs dei jo tel plait tenir:
Que que Rollant a Guenelun forsfesist,
Vostre servise l'en doüst bien guarir!
Guenes est fels d'iço qu'il le traït,
3830 Vers vos s'en est parjurez e malmis.
Pur ço le juz jo a pendre e a murir
E sun cors metre . . .
Si cume fel ki felonie fist.
Se or ad parent ki m'en voeille desmentir,
3835 A ceste espee, que jo ai ceinte ici,
Mun jugement voel sempres guarantir."
Respundent Franc: "Or avez vos ben dit."

Anyone who would fight ... would be quite mad."
3805 Everyone grants or accedes to this,
With the sole exception of Thierry, Lord Geoffrey's brother.   AOI.

276

Charlemagne's brave knights return to him,
They say to the King: "Sire, we implore you
To let Count Ganelon off,
3810 Let him serve you henceforth in good faith and in friendship.
Let him live, for he is a man of very high birth.
Even though he were to die, that wouldn't make amends (?),
Nor could we ever recover him for any compensation."
The King said: "You are compounding this felony against me!"
AOI.

277

3815 When Charles sees that all have failed him,
His head and his face sink down,
Because of the vexation he feels, he bewails his miserable lot.
Now a knight came before him,
Brother of Geoffrey, a duke of Anjou.
3820 He was spare of build, slight and slender,
Black hair and a bit tanned,
He is not very big and not very small.
With a demonstration of profound attachment he said to the
    Emperor:
"Dear lord King, do not show such signs of distress!
3825 You know very well that I have served you long.
Out of loyalty to my ancestors I must pass this judgment:
Even if Roland had wronged Ganelon,
The fact that he was serving you was sufficient to safeguard him!
Ganelon committed a felony because he betrayed him,
3830 He perjured himself and broke his oath of fealty to you.
For this reason I condemn him to hang and to die,
And let his body be placed ...
Like a criminal who has committed a felony.
Now if he has a kinsman who wishes to give me the lie,
3835 With this sword, which I have girded on here,
I shall back up my decision forthwith."
The Franks reply: "Well said."

278

Devant lu rei est venuz Pinabel,
Granz est e forz e vassals e isnel—
3840 Qu'il fiert a colp, de sun tens n'i ad mais—
E dist al rei: "Sire, vostre est li plaiz,
Car cumandez que tel noise n'i ait!
Ci vei Tierri, ki jugement ad fait,
Jo si li fals, od lui m'en cumbatrai."
3845 Met li el poign de cerf le destre guant.
Dist li empereres: "Bons pleges en demant."
.XXX. parenz l'i plevissent leial.
Ço dist li reis: "E jol vos recrrai."
Fait cels guarder tresque li dreiz en serat.   AOI.

279

3850 Quant veit Tierri qu'or en ert la bataille,
Sun destre guant en ad presentet Carle.
Li emperere l'i recreit par hostage,
Puis fait porter .IIII. bancs en la place,
La vunt sedeir cil kis deivent cumbatre.
3855 Ben sunt malez, par jugement des altres,
Sil purparlat Oger de Denemarche;
E puis demandent lur chevals e lur armes.

280

Puis que il sunt a bataille justez,   AOI.
Ben sunt cunfés e asols e seignez;
3860 Oënt lur messes e sunt acuminiez,
Mult granz offrendes metent par cez musters.
Devant Carlun andui sunt repairez.
Lur esperuns unt en lor piez calcez,
Vestent osberc blancs e forz e legers,
3865 Lur helmes clers unt fermez en lor chefs,
Ceinent espees enheldees d'or mier,
En lur cols pendent lur escuz de quarters,
En lur puinz destres unt lur trenchanz espiez;
Puis sunt muntez en lur curanz destrers.
3870 Idunc plurerent .C. milie chevalers

234

278

Pinabel came before the King,
He is big and strong, brave and agile—
3840 Anyone he strikes, his sands have run out—
And he said to the King: "Sire, you're presiding over this trial,
So order this commotion to cease!
I see Thierry here, who has passed judgment,
I declare his decision to be false and I'll fight him on account of it."
3845 He places his right deerskin gauntlet in the King's hand.
The Emperor said: "I require worthy hostages."
Thirty kinsmen pledge themselves to Charles as surety.
The King said: "With this guarantee I'll place Ganelon in your custody."
He has the hostages kept under guard until justice is done.　　AOI.

279

3850 When Thierry sees that there will be a duel now,
He presents his right-hand gauntlet to Charles.
Having received hostages, the Emperor sets Thierry free,
Then he orders four benches brought to the place,
Those who are to fight the duel go sit there.
3855 Formal challenges are exchanged to the judges' satisfaction,
Ogier of Denmark acted as a go-between;
Then they ask for their horses and their arms.

280

Afterward, set for the duel,　　AOI.
They made a good confession, they were absolved and blessed;
3860 They hear mass and they received communion,
They place very large offerings in the churches.
The two of them reappeared before Charles.
They have strapped their spurs to their feet,
They don shiny, strong, and light hauberks,
3865 They have laced their bright helmets on their heads,
They gird on swords with pure gold hilts,
They hang their quartered shields from their necks,
They have sharp spears in their right hands;
Then they mounted their swift war-horses.
3870 Now a hundred thousand knights weep,

Qui pur Rollant de Tierri unt pitiet.
Deus set asez cument la fins en ert.

281

Dedesuz Ais est la pree mult large,
Des dous baruns justee est la bataille.
3875 Cil sunt produme e de grant vasselage
E lur chevals sunt curanz e aates.
Brochent les bien, tutes les resnes lasquent,
Par grant vertut vait ferir l'uns li altre.
Tuz lur escuz i fruissent e esquassent,
3880 Lur osbercs rumpent e lur cengles depiecent,
Les alves turnent, les seles cheent a tere.
.C. mil humes i plurent, kis esguardent.

282

A tere sunt ambdui li chevaler,   AOI.
Isnelement se drecent sur lur piez.
3885 Pinabels est forz e isnels e legers.
Li uns requiert l'altre, n'unt mie des destrers.
De cez espees enheldees d'or mer
Fierent e caplent sur cez helmes d'acer.
Granz sunt les colps as helmes detrencher,
3890 Mult se dementent cil franceis chevaler.
"E! Deus," dist Carles, "le dreit en esclargiez!"

283

Dist Pinabel: "Tierri, car te recreiz!
Tes hom serai par amur e par feid,
A tun plaisir te durrai mun aveir,
3895 Mais Guenelun fai acorder al rei!"
Respont Tierri: "Ja n'en tendrai cunseill,
Tut seie fel se jo mie l'otrei!
Deus facet hoi entre nus dous le dreit!"   AOI.

Moved to pity for Thierry and because of Roland.
God knows very well how this will end.

281

The meadow is very wide below Aix,
The duel of the two brave knights is all set.
3875   They are men of worth and of great courage,
And their horses are swift and spirited.
They spur them hard, they give them the reins,
They go to strike each other with all their might.
They smash and shatter their shields completely,
3880   They rip their hauberks and their cinches to pieces,
The side pieces turn, the saddles fall to the ground.
A hundred thousand men, who are watching them, weep.

282

Both knights are on the ground,   AOI.
They quickly get back on their feet.
3885   Pinabel is strong, swift, and agile.
They attack each other, they no longer have war-horses.
With swords whose hilts are made of pure gold
They strike and beat down on the steel helmets.
The blows are heavy enough to cut through the helmets,
3890   The French knights show signs of great distress.
"Oh, God," said Charles, "let justice blaze forth!"

283

Pinabel said: "Thierry, concede defeat!
I shall be your vassal in friendship and in good faith,
I shall give you what I have to your heart's content,
3895   But reconcile Ganelon with the King!"
Thierry replies: "I shall not give this matter any thought,
I'll be damned if I consent to it in the least!
Let God this day show which one of us is in the right!"   AOI.

284

Ço dist Tierri: "Pinabel, mult ies ber,
3900 Granz ies e forz, e tis cors ben mollez,
De vasselage te conoissent ti per.
Ceste bataille car la laisses ester,
A Carlemagne te ferai acorder.
De Guenelun justise ert faite tel,
3905 Jamais n'ert jur que il n'en seit parlet."
Dist Pinabel: "Ne placet Damnedeu!
Sustenir voeill trestut mun parentet,
N'en recrerrai pur nul hume mortel,
Mielz voeill murir que il me seit reprovet."
3910 De lur espees cumencent a capler
Desur cez helmes, ki sunt a or gemez,
Cuntre le ciel en volet li fous tuz clers.
Il ne poet estre qu'il seient desevrez,
Seinz hume mort ne poet estre afinet.   AOI.

285

3915 Mult par est proz Pinabel de Sorence,
Si fiert Tierri sur l'elme de Provence,
Salt en li fous, que l'erbe en fait esprendre.
Del brant d'acer la mure li presentet,
Desur le frunt li ad faite descendre,
3920 Par mi le vis li ad faite descendre:
La destre joe en ad tute sanglente,
L'osberc del dos josque par sum le ventre.
Deus le guarit, que mort ne l'acraventet.   AOI.

286

Ço veit Tierris que el vis est ferut,
3925 Li sancs tuz clers en chiet el pred herbus.
Fiert Pinabel sur l'elme d'acer brun,
Jusqu'al nasel li ad fait e fendut.
Del chef li ad le cervel espandut,
Brandit sun colp, si l'ad mort abatut.
3930 A icest colp est li esturs vencut.
Escrient Franc: "Deus i ad fait vertut!

284

Thierry said: "Pinabel, you are very brave,
3900 You are big and strong and your body is well built,
Your peers recognize you for your courage.
Leave off fighting this duel,
I shall reconcile you with Charlemagne.
But such justice shall be done to Ganelon
3905 That no day shall pass without it being mentioned."
Pinabel said: "May it not please the Lord God!
I wish to sustain all my kinsmen,
I shall not concede defeat for any man alive,
I'd rather die than incur blame for this."
3910 They begin to strike with their swords
On helmets that are of gold wrought with gems,
Bright sparks fly heavenward.
They cannot be pulled apart,
It cannot end until one of the men is dead.   AOI.

285

3915 Pinabel of Sorence is very courageous,
He strikes Thierry on his helmet made in Provence,
A spark leaps from it, setting the grass on fire.
He brings the point of his steel blade to bear on him,
He made it come down on his forehead,
3920 He made it come down across his face:
His right cheek is all bloody now,
His hauberk, too, from his back to the top of his stomach.
God saved him from being struck dead.   AOI.

286

Thierry sees that he is struck in the face,
3925 Bright blood falls on the grassy meadow.
He strikes Pinabel on his burnished steel helmet,
He smashed it and split it down to the nasal.
He spilled his brain from his head,
He delivers his blow, he struck him down dead.
3930 With this blow the battle is won.
The Franks shout: "God performed a miracle!

239

Asez est dreiz que Guenes seit pendut
E si parent, ki plaidet unt pur lui." AOI.

287

Quant Tierris ad vencue sa bataille,
3935 Venuz i est li emperere Carles,
Ensembl'od lui de ses baruns quarante,
Naimes li dux, Oger de Danemarche,
Geifrei d'Anjou, e Willalme de Blaive.
Li reis ad pris Tierri entre sa brace,
3940 Tert lui le vis od ses granz pels de martre,
Celes met jus, puis li afublent altres,
Mult suavet le chevaler desarment.
Fait en une mule d'Arabe,
Repairet s'en a joie e a barnage,
3945 Vienent ad Ais, descendent en la place.
Des ore cumencet l'ocisïun des altres.

288

Carles apelet ses cuntes e ses dux:
"Que me loëz de cels qu'ai retenuz?
Pur Guenelun erent a plait venuz,
3950 Pur Pinabel en ostage renduz."
Respundent Franc: "Ja mar en vivrat uns!"
Li reis cumandet un soen veier, Basbrun:
"Va, sis pent tuz a l'arbre de mal fust!
Par ceste barbe dunt li peil sunt canuz,
3955 Se uns escapet, morz ies e cunfunduz."
Cil li respunt: "Qu'en fereie joe el?"
Od .C. serjanz par force les cunduit.
.XXX. en i ad d'icels ki sunt pendut.
Ki hume traïst sei ocit e altroi. AOI.

289

3960 Puis sunt turnet Bavier e Aleman
E Peitevin e Bretun e Norman.
Sor tuit li altre l'unt otrïet li Franc

It is just that Ganelon be hanged
Together with his kinsmen who upheld his suit." AOI.

287

After Thierry had won his duel,
3935 Emperor Charles came to him,
Together with forty of his brave knights,
Duke Naimes, Ogier of Denmark,
Geoffrey of Anjou, and William of Blaye.
The King embraced Thierry,
3940 He wipes his face with his great marten furs,
He puts them aside, then they put others on him,
They disarm the knight very gently.
They mounted him (?) on a mule from Arabia,
He returns joyfully in the company of brave knights,
3945 They come to Aix, they dismount in the square.
Now begins the execution of the others.

288

Charles calls his counts and his dukes:
"What do you advise me to do with those I have detained?
They came to support Ganelon's suit
3950 And to pledge themselves as hostages."
The Franks reply: "Not a damn one of them shall live!"
The King commands his provost marshal Basbrun:
"Go and hang them all from the accursed gallows tree!
By this beard whose hair is grizzled,
3955 If a single one of them escapes, you are dead and done for."
The latter replies: "What else would I do?"
With a hundred sergeants he leads them away forcibly.
Thirty of them are hanged.
Anyone who betrays a man brings on his own death and that of
others too. AOI.

289

3960 The Bavarians and the Germans went away,
The Poitevins, too, and the Bretons and the Normans.
The Franks insisted more than all the others

Que Guenes moerget par merveillus ahan.
Quatre destrers funt amener avant,
3965 Puis si li lient e les piez e les mains.
Li cheval sunt orgoillus e curant,
Quatre serjanz les acoeillent devant
Devers un ewe ki est en mi un camp.
Guenes est turnet a perdicïun grant:
3970 Trestuit si nerf mult li sunt estendant
E tuit li membre de sun cors derumpant,
Sur l'erbe verte en espant li cler sanc.
Guenes est mort cume fel recreant,
Hom ki traïst altre nen est dreiz qu'il s'en vant.

290

3975 Quant li empereres ad faite sa venjance,
Sin apelat ses evesques de France,
Cels de Baviere e icels d'Alemaigne:
"En ma maisun ad une caitive franche.
Tant ad oït e sermuns e essamples,
3980 Creire voelt Deu, chrestïentet demandet.
Baptizez la, pur quei Deus en ait l'anme."
Cil li respundent: "Or seit faite par marrenes,
Asez cruiz e linees dames."
As bainz ad Ais mult sunt granz les c . . .
3985 La baptizent la reïne d'Espaigne,
Truvee li unt le num de Juliane.
Chrestïene est par veire conoisance.

291

Quant l'emperere ad faite sa justise
E esclargiez est la sue grant ire,
3990 En Bramidonie ad chrestïentet mise.
Passet li jurz, la nuit est aserie,
Culcez s'est li reis en sa cambre voltice.
Seint Gabrïel de part Deu li vint dire:
"Carles, sumun les oz de tun emperie!
3995 Par force iras en la tere de Bire,

242

That Ganelon die with excruciating pain.
They have four war-horses brought forward,
3965 Then they tie his feet and his hands.
The horses are fiery and swift,
Four sergeants urge them on
Toward a stream that crosses a field.
Ganelon went to his utter perdition:
3970 All his ligaments are stretched as taut as can be,
And his whole body is torn limb from limb,
The bright blood spatters on the green grass.
Ganelon died as befits a dirty miscreant,
Any man who betrays another must not be allowed to brag about it.

290

3975 Having wreaked his vengeance, the Emperor
Called his bishops from France,
Those from Bavaria and those from Germany:
"There is a noble prisoner in my house.
She has heard so many sermons and exempla
3980 That she wishes to believe in God, she asked to become a convert to
         Christianity.
Baptize her so that God may have her soul."
They reply: "Now let her be baptized and have godmothers,
Suitably noble and high-born ladies."
At the baths at Aix, the . . . are very large,
3985 There they baptize the Queen of Spain,
They found for her the name of Juliana.
She is a Christian out of sheer conviction.

291

When the Emperor has dispensed his justice,
And his great wrath has been appeased,
3990 He has Bramimonde christened.
The daylight fades away, night has fallen,
The King has gone to bed in his vaulted room.
Saint Gabriel came from God to tell him:
"Charles, summon the armies of your Empire!
3995 You shall invade the land of Bire,

243

Reis Vivïen si succuras en Imphe,
A la citet que paien unt asise,
Li chrestïen te recleiment e crient."
Li emperere n'i volsist aler mie:
4000 "Deus!" dist li reis, "si penuse est ma vie!"
Pluret des oilz, sa barbe blanche tiret.
Ci falt la geste que Turoldus declinet.

You shall aid King Vivien at Imphe,
The city the pagans have besieged,
The Christians implore and cry out for you."
The Emperor would rather not go there:

4000 "God!" said the King, "my life is so full of suffering!"
His eyes are brimming with tears, he tugs his white beard.
Here ends the story that Turoldus tells.

Notes to the Manuscript

v. 1. *empere*] *emperere*. The abbreviation for *-er* was either accidentally omitted by the scribe or effaced. Cf. MANUSCRIPT, vv. 16, 168, 214, 3790, ánd 3846. On this type of error, see Samaran, p. 34.

v. 16. *eperes*] *epereres*. See MANUSCRIPT, v. 1. On the initial vowel, see OXFORD TEXT, ENGLISH TRANSLATION, v. 42 (cf. v. 2846).

v. 118. *la cuntenance*] *le cuntenant*. Most editors emend because of the masculine form of the adjective in the assonance. Cf. v. 3116.

v. 124. *aurez*] *aürer*. An error due to inattention on the part of the scribe. Cf. v. 429.

v. 147. *Voet*. The scribe almost certainly wrote *Voelt*, but the end of the word was erased and the revisor changed what appears to be an *l* into a *t*.

v. 158. *Chares*] *Charles*. An error due to inattention on the part of the scribe.

v. 168. *emperes*] *empereres*. See MANUSCRIPT, v. 1.

v. 171. *neu*] *neüld*. The manuscript reads *neu* followed by an erasure. Samaran, p. 43: "très probablement *neuold*"; Whitehead, p. 120: "ne/u (uld?)/." I accept Segre's emendation. In the oblique case, the word for 'nephew' is often written *nevold* or *nevuld* in this copy. On the value of the symbol *l* here, see Bédier, *Commentaires*, p. 259; Pope, *From Latin to Modern French*, par. 698; cf. Moignet, p. 281.

v. 197. *anz pleins*] *anz ad pleins*. Most editors emend in this fashion because the verb is missing in this phrase. Other passages in this copy provide close but, unfortunately, not exact equivalents: v. 2 (Set anz tuz pleins ad estet en Espaigne); v. 266 (En cest païs avez estet set anz); v. 2610 (.VII. anz tuz plens ad en Espaigne estet); v. 2736 (En ceste tere ad estet ja .VII. anz).

v. 202. *paienueiat*] *paiens enveiat*. This haplography is noted by Samaran, p. 33.

v. 203. *Chancuns*] *Chascuns*. An error due to inattention on the part of the scribe.

v. 214. *empere*] *emperere*. See MANUSCRIPT, v. 1.

v. 261. *blarcher*] *blancher*. The scribe confused *n* with *r*. Samaran, p. 34.

v. 269. *en espaigne*] *espan*. Jenkins: "The scribe of O (*en espaigne*) did not recognize the word here, but has it correctly at vv. 612, 2828." See also William S. Woods, "*Sarrazins Espans* in the *Roland*, vv. 269, 612, 2828," *Romance Studies Presented to W. Morton Dey* (Chapel Hill: University of North Carolina Press, 1950), pp. 193–96.

v. 283. *out 7*] *out les oilz*. The emendation is supported by Châteauroux and Venice VII. Bédier, *Commentaires*, p. 196; Segre.

v. 290. *contrire*] *contraire*. The emendation is made by all editors to avoid a faulty assonance.

v. 300. *degerie*] *de legerie*. The form *degerie* is almost certainly due to haplography (Samaran, p. 38) and the emendation to *de legerie*, supported by vv. 206, 513, and 1726 (on the parallel between vv. 206, 300, and 513, see COMMENTARY, 4) in this copy, and by Châteauroux, v. 424 (= Oxford, v. 300), *lezerie*, is made by all editors. Venice IV and Venice VII read *felonie* and *trecherie*, respectively, neither of which appears possible here, on paleographical grounds.

v. 310. *qu'aler*. Whitehead, p. 120: "The erased word (probably *que*, not *qu*) was written close up to *aler*." There does not appear to be enough room for the *e*, however, and all other editors read *qu'aler*.

v. 354. *nercs*] *n'ert*. An error due to inattention on the part of the scribe.

v. 367. *messag*] *messages*. The abbreviation sign was inadvertently omitted by the scribe. Samaran, p. 34.

v. 378. *7 duc*] *e cil duc*. A scribal error due to haplography. Cf. v. 2924.

v. 414. *lempereur*] *Marsiliun*. Emperor is a title reserved in every case for Charles throughout the *Song of Roland*. The emendation, which is made by all editors, also finds support in Châteauroux and Venice VII, and in the assonance.

v. 526. *Tanz ad*] *Tanz colps ad*. The emendation is made by all editors on the basis of vv. 541, 554. For discussion of other suggested changes in this line, see Segre, pp. 101–2.

vv. 580–581. These two lines are conflated in the Oxford manuscript and are separated by all editors. The second hemistich in Venice IV reads: *ço dis li roi Marsilie*.

vv. 603–605. The revisor added a number of words at the end of each line (v. 603: *il plus*; v. 604: *nest seuus*; v. 605: *si illi est*), none of which are accepted by any editor. *Rollant* in v. 605 constitutes a faulty assonance. For conjectures, see Segre.

v. 623. *uos*] *nos*. A scribal error due to similarity of *u* and *n*. Venice IV has the erroneous reading; cf., however, v. 630.

v. 640. *n'en out*. The scribe first wrote *neuit*, then expunctuated the last three letters and added *nout* above the line. The original reading, supported by Venice IV, is preferred by Jenkins, Whitehead, and Segre.

v. 647. *guen*] *Guenelun*. The emendation is made by all editors. Cf. Venice IV: *Marsilio abraça Gaynelon a l'espalle*; Châteauroux: *Marsilions fu droit en son esté, / Guene tint, si la mout esgardé*.

v. 711. *Halbercs vestuz e*. After these words the scribe wrote *tres bien*, and the revisor added *fermer*, corrected to read *fermez*. As it now stands in this manuscript, the second hemistich makes no sense and is rejected by all editors. For conjectures, see Segre.

v. 719. *al*] *as*. A scribal error due to inattention or, possibly, to similarity of *l* and *s* (another example [v. 1428] is cited by Samaran, p. 34).

v. 738. *Par mi cel host*. The revisor added the words *suuent a menu reguarded*, a second hemistich no editor accepts. For conjectures, see Segre.

v. 844. *Guens*] *Guenes*. An error due to inattention on the part of the scribe.

v. 919. *saiust*] *s'ajustet*. On this scribal error, see Segre.

v. 990. *li .xii. salient*] *li .XII. per s'alient*. The word *per* is found in all other versions of the poem except Cambridge, which has *ly fier*. The Saracen Peers are referred to indirectly in v. 877 and explicitly in v. 1308.

v. 1013. *lempleit*] *i empleit*. A scribal error due to the similarity of *i* and *l*.

v. 1120. *de lance*] *de la lance*. A scribal error due to haplography (cf. Châteauroux: Fer da la lance). Some editors propose the emendation *ta*, which is also defensible.

v. 1215. *datliun 7 balbiun*] *Dathan e Habirun*. All editors except Moignet emend to *Dathan e Abirun*. Numbers 16:1–35, the ultimate source of these names (which also appear in medieval curses), Foulet, *Glossaire* [Index des noms propres], p. 505), reads (in the Latin): *Datan et Abiron*. Châteauroux and Venice VII provide slight variants of the correct form. Moignet reads *Dathun*; however, on the confusion of *a* and *u* here, see Samaran, p. 34, and MANUSCRIPT, v. 1452. Cf. also OXFORD TEXT, ENGLISH TRANSLATION, v. 2249. Moignet retains the form *Balbiun*, but his translation recognizes *Abiron* (E. Abiram) to be the correct rendering. The initial *b* was doubtless a misreading of *h*, the latter being a common hypercorrection in Old French. Cf. v. 1333: *hunc* (see also Flutre, *Table des noms propres*, s.v. *Aalis, Abilant[t], Aimeri, Alain*, etc.). The error is noted in passing by Samaran, p. 38. There is a possible reminiscence of the punishment meted out to Dathan and Abiram in vv. 3947–3959; see COMMENTARY, 47.

v. 1244. *que uoeillet*] *que tant voeillet.* An omission due to inattention on the part of the scribe. Some editors emend to *que voeillet plus.* The words *tant* and *plus* are found in Paris and Cambridge, respectively, but in variant phrasings.

v. 1261. *Engelers*] *E Gerins.* Gerin, not Engelier, is Gerier's companion. Cf. vv. 107, 174, and 1269.

v. 1271. *ment*] *met.* An error due to inattention on the part of the scribe.

v. 1274. *olilier*] *Oliver.* For other similar instances of dittography, see Samaran, p. 33. The revisor may have attempted to erase this obvious scribal error.

v. 1279. *Que labat*] *Que mort l'abat.* The emendation is based on Venice IV. Some editors insert the missing word after *l'abat.*

v. 1297. *gualter*] *Otes.* Oton, not Gautier, is Berengier's companion. Cf. vv. 795 and 1304.

v. 1306. *escut*] *espiet.* An error due to inattention on the part of the scribe. The correct reading is found in Venice IV and Cambridge.

v. 1343. *7 brace*] *e la brace.* An identical error (*7 br . . . = 7 br . . .*) in v. 1372 suggests haplography here (*la + br*). For comparable errors, see Samaran, p. 33.

v. 1344. *lespalles*] *les espalles.* A scribal error due to haplography. Samaran, p. 33.

v. 1372. *7 bronie*] *e la bronie.* See MANUSCRIPT, v. 1343 above. Some editors emend to *e sa bronie.*

v. 1376. *receif*] *reconois.* The scribe inadvertently omitted the abbreviation sign over the *c* (recois; cf. MANUSCRIPT, v. 1993), puzzling the revisor, who thereupon erased the last three letters and wrote *eif* over the line. Bédier, *Commentaires,* pp. 212–13; Samaran, p. 45. Segre's reading (reonois) is a misprint.

v. 1428. *de paris*] *del Peril.* All editors agree that the scribe confused the *l* of *Peril* with a long *s.* The correct form is found in vv. 152 and 2394. On this toponym, see Dufournet, *Cours sur Roland,* p. 165.

v. 1429. *tresquas de*] *tresqu'as porz de.* The emendation is based on Châteauroux, Venice VII, Paris, and Cambridge. Cf. v. 2626, the only other instance in this copy where *port* means a haven for ships. Foulet, *Glossaire*; Aebischer, "Halt sunt li pui," p. 1. Cf. OXFORD TEXT, ENGLISH TRANSLATION, v. 583.

v. 1433. *ses*] *s'espoënt.* All other versions provide a variant of the form *s'espoent,* but everything after *ses* is missing here. The revisor added *spant* above the line. Editors emend to *s'espaent* or *s'espoent,* the latter finding some support in v. 1599.

v. 1441. *Dist nostre*] *Dist l'arcevesques: "Nostre.* In the margin the revisor wrote the abbreviation for *Rollant.* All other versions provide the correct reading.

v. 1452. *Lacent*] *Luisent.* The emendation is based on Venice IV. For a similar confusion of *a* and *u,* see MANUSCRIPT, v. 1215.

v. 1460. *forte aduree*] *forte e aduree.* All editors agree that the conjunction, which is found in Venice IV and Paris, was inadvertently omitted by the scribe.

v. 1488. *sespee*] *sun helme.* Climborin's helmet, presented to Ganelon in v. 629, is mentioned here in all other versions of the poem.

v. 1499. *aounfundre*] *a cunfundre.* For a similar confusion of letters, see Samaran, p. 34.

v. 1586. *i*] *Li.* A space provided by the scribe for the initial *L* was inadvertently left blank.

v. 1599. *espaent*] *espoënt.* According to Samaran, p. 45, the scribe wrote *espoent,* but the *o* was erased by the revisor, who then added an *a* over the space. See MANU-SCRIPT, v. 1433.

v. 1605. *se*] *le.* On the confusion of *l* and long *s,* see Samaran, p. 34.

v. 1610. *La labaille est meilluse*] *La bataille est merveilluse. La labaille* results from a confusion of letters, *meilluse* from the omission of an abbreviation sign. For similar instances of both kinds of errors, see Samaran, pp. 33–34.

v. 1612. *Trent*] *Trenchent*. In transcribing this word, the copyist evidently skipped from the first *en* to the second. Samaran, p. 33. Cf. MANUSCRIPT, v. 1737. The abbreviation sign over the *e* may have been added by the revisor in an attempt to correct this mistake.

v. 1645. *sarraz*] *Sarrazins*. An error resulting from the omission of an abbreviation sign. Samaran, p. 34.

v. 1731. *vemes*] *veïmes*. The emendation, supported in part by Venice IV's *veiste*, is made by all editors.

v. 1737. *arceues*] *arcevesques*. The scribe skipped from the first *es* to the second. Cf. MANUSCRIPT, v. 1612.

v. 1769. *cucumbatant*] *cumbatant*. The abbreviation 9 for *cum-*, rather than a titulus, was erroneously superscribed over the *u*. For similar dittographies, see Samaran, p. 33.

v. 1779. *arissant*] *aparissant*. A haplography of the type characterized by Samaran, p. 33, as *saut du même au même*. The correct reading is found in Châteauroux and Venice VII.

v. 1782. *ki osast*] *ki l'osast*. This emendation, made by most editors, finds support in Venice IV (olsasse). Above the line, between *osast* and *querre*, the revisor added the letters *re*. This does not appear to be an error for *le*, for the normal position of the direct object is before the principal verb, not before the infinitive it governs. Foulet, *Glossaire*, p. 413.

v. 1823. The line that follows this verse in the Oxford copy (Morz est Turpin, le guerreier Charlun) is inserted after v. 2241 by all editors. For a discussion of this scribal error, see Jenkins; Alfred Ewert and Mario Roques, "L'accident du vers 2242 de la *Chanson de Roland*," *Romania* 59 (1933): 81–83; Samaran, pp. 35–36.

v. 1850. *caignes*] *cataignes*. On this haplography (*ca* + *ta* [=*ca*]), see Samaran, p. 33.

v. 1926. *7 mors*] *e vos cors*. The revisor added *e vos* above the line between the word *calengez* and the Tironian sign. The *m* of *mors* has been retouched, and Félix Lecoy, "Notules sur le texte du *Roland* d'Oxford," *Mélanges Rita Lejeune*, 2:794–95 (summary in Dufournet, *Cours sur Roland*, p. 33), suggests that the scribe's *c* was turned into an *m* by the revisor. The reading *cors* is supported by Châteauroux, Venice VII, Paris, Cambridge, and Lyon. Lecoy notes that the Oxford copy uses the form *morz* throughout. I accept Lecoy's emendation but propose a slightly different explanation: I believe the scribe inadvertently telescoped *uos* and *cors* (uors), a haplography (cf. Samaran, p. 33) the revisor noticed and decided to correct by adding another leg in front of the *u* and a horizontal stroke over this letter to form an *m*.

v. 1993. *recoistre*] *reconoistre*. See MANUSCRIPT, v. 1376.

v. 2052. *Par mi le cors*. The line reads: *Par mi le cors hot une lance ferut*, but the words *une* and *ferut*, above the line (the latter over an erasure), and the letter *h* of *hot* are by the revisor. Samaran, p. 21. Also, the scribe wrote *lances*, but the final letter has been erased. Segre. For conjectures, see Segre.

v. 2058. *get*] *getet*. A haplography noted by Samaran, p. 33.

v. 2063. *guar*] *guarir*. The scribe appears to have written *guarder*, but, having erased his error, forgot to complete the word. It is possible, however, that an original *guarir* was altered by the revisor. Samaran, p. 46; Segre (see also the latter's note to v. 2065).

v. 2120. *asemble*] *asemblent*. An error due to inattention on the part of the scribe.

v. 2147. *pes*] *pesmes*. A haplography noted by Samaran, p. 33.

v. 2194. *beicun*] *beneïçun*. This error, a *saut du même au même*, is cited by Samaran, p. 33.

v. 2242. See MANUSCRIPT, v. 1823.

v. 2246. *laruesque*] *l'arcevesque*. A haplography of the type noted by Samaran, p. 33. The scribe's eye evidently confused *c* and *u*, which led him to omit the first member of the pair *ce* + *ue*.

v. 2250. *blanches les*] *blanches mains, les.* An error due to inattention on the part of the scribe.

v. 2267. *un arbre bele*] *.II. arbres bels.* The emendation is supported by Venice IV, Châteauroux, Venice VII, and the Flemish translation. See also v. 2874. The scribe's error doubtless stems from a misreading of an original *.ii.* for *un.* A similar confusion in numbers produced the mistake in v. 2875 (see COMMENTARY, 24). For bibliography and discussion, see Jenkins; Segre.

v. 2268. *faite*] *faiz.* The emendation is made by all editors.

v. 2302. *freint nesgruignet*] *freint ne n'esgruignet.* A common haplography (*ne* + *ne*) of the type noted by Samaran, p. 33. See MANUSCRIPT, v. 2400. Whitehead, p. 125, cites the parallel with v. 2313.

v. 2322. *cunquis namon*] *cunquis e Anjou.* The correct form is found in Paris and Cambridge. For bibliography and discussion, see Segre.

v. 2400. *alne plein*] *alne ne plein.* For an identical haplography, see MANUSCRIPT, v. 2302.

v. 2412. *enra er*] *enrager.* The scribe wrote *enrager*, which the revisor read as *emager* because the letters *nr* can easily be mistaken for *m* in this copy (cf. Samaran, p. 34 and n. 1: confusion of *n* and *r*). The revisor evidently assumed the word *esmaier* was intended so he added an *s* above the line, after the initial letter *e*, and erased the *g*, which can still be seen faintly in the space between the *a* and the *e*. All editors since Francisque Michel have also read the scribe's *nr* as *m* and have rendered the word as *esmaer* or emended it to *esmaier.* The correct form (enragier) is found in Lyon, v. 1593 (cf. Venice IV, v. 2571: inraçer; Châteauroux, v. 4195: enrajez; Paris, v. 2734: enraigier), variants of the cognate *esragier* in Venice VII, Laisse 239, v. 16 (esrajez), and Cambridge, v. 2068 (esrager). Cf. Oxford, v. 286 (esrages) and vv. 747, 2279 (rage). On the meaning of *rage* and its cognates, cf. OXFORD TEXT, ENGLISH TRANSLATION, vv. 280 (anguisables), 304 (doel, ire), 747 (mortel rage), and 2414 (iret). Aebischer, *Rolandiana Borealia*, p. 222, points out that the rending of garments mentioned in the *Karlamagnús Saga*, Châteauroux, and Venice VII has no textual basis in the Bodleian manuscript or in Venice IV. However, the biblical gesture (see COMMENTARY, 5, note 11) is consistent with an expression of anger (enragier). Bloch and Wartburg, *Dictionnaire*, s.v. rage, provides the date 1160 (i.e., *Enéas*) for *enrager.* On the use of *poeir* in this verse, see OXFORD TEXT, ENGLISH TRANSLATION, v. 2412.

v. 2466. *merueille*] *merveilluse.* The scribe may have inadvertently omitted the abbreviation sign for *us* (⁹). The correct form is found in Venice IV, Châteauroux, and Venice VII.

v. 2512. *luisante*] *luisant.* Most editors emend in order to eliminate the false assonance. All other copies have the correct form. Cf. Bédier, *Commentaires*, p. 254.

v. 2516. *sangenz*] *sanglenz.* An error due to inattention on the part of the scribe.

v. 2539. *Fruisez*] *Fruisent.* The correct form is found in Paris (*Croissent* in Châteauroux and Venice VII results from the telescoping of vv. 2539 and 2540). Bédier, *Commentaires*, p. 227: "On ne sait si l'on a affaire à une faute de copiste ou à une légère négligence du poète." See also Segre.

v. 2563. *uers les altres*] *uns veltres i.* This emendation, initially proposed by Stengel, was accepted by Bédier and Whitehead. For discussion and other conjectures, see Jenkins; Segre; Dufournet, *Cours sur Roland*, p. 76. All editors agree that *veltres* (cf. Venice IV: *veutre*) is the correct form.

v. 2641. *marbrose ... marbrise*] *Marbrise ... Marbrose.* In order to avoid the false assonance, all editors transpose these place-names, which were accidentally inverted by the scribe.

v. 2667. *il ainz*] *il n'alt.* An error due to inattention on the part of the scribe. The emendation is based on Châteauroux and Venice VII. Jenkins; Segre.

v. 2679. *cestuncel*] *cest bastuncel*. An error termed *saut du même au même* (cest [bast]uncel) by Samaran, p. 33. See also Jenkins; Segre.

v. 2688. *fi*] *si*. This scribal error, first noted by Segre, may have resulted from unconscious anticipation of the following word. Cf. Whitehead, p. 124, with reference to the *l* of *rubostl*: "probably due to the *ll* of *exill*" (v. 1862).

v. 2716. *uaises*] *malvaises*. The revisor transformed the *is* into a *u* and added an *m* above the line between *Rencesval* and this word. Most editors assume the revisor was correcting the word to read *muaues* (i.e., *muaves* = *mauvés*), but Samaran, p. 48, suggests that the *u* is actually *iz* and that the latter was intended for *m[al]vaizes*. At any rate, the original scribe's error was doubtless a *saut du même au même* (Rencesval [mal]vaises). Samaran, p. 33; Whitehead, p. 126.

v. 2764. *cuiget*] *cunget*. An error due to inattention on the part of the scribe.

v. 2768. *sarrace*] *Sarraguce*. An error due to inattention on the part of the scribe. The emendation is based on Châteauroux and Venice VII.

v. 2809. *ches*] *chef*. The similarity of long *s* and *f* explains this slip of the pen. For comparable errors, see Samaran, p. 34.

v. 2843. *uns*] *ures*. The scribe doubtless wrote *ures*, which was evidently misunderstood by the revisor, who deleted this word and inserted *uns* over the erasure. The correct reading is found in Paris and London, British Museum, Add. MS. 41295 G. On the latter copies and the related phrasing in Venice IV (D'alora), see Segre.

v. 2883. *henri*] *Tierri*. Editors agree that this is the same character as the one who will figure in the trial of Ganelon, vv. 3806 ff. The correct reading is found in Venice IV, Paris, Cambridge, and London, British Museum, Add. MS. 41295 G. Jenkins; Bédier, *Commentaires*, p. 192; Segre; Dufournet, *Cours sur Roland*, p. 32. Moignet does not emend but notes, p. 210, that a correction is indicated.

v. 2893. *.iii.*] *.IIII.* The correct reading is found in Venice IV. Cf. also vv. 2882–2883. Jenkins; Whitehead; Segre.

v. 2927. *est ki*] *est morz ki*. An error due to inattention on the part of the scribe. The missing word is found in Venice IV and Paris.

v. 2943. *bare*] *barbe*. Anglo-Norman preconsonantal *r* is sometimes effaced (cf. OXFORD TEXT, ENGLISH TRANSLATION, v. 316), thus the form *babe* might be expected, but not *bare*. Throughout this copy the word appears as *barbe* or *barbes*.

v. 2983. *7 damage*] *e del damage*. The emendation is made by all editors on the basis of Venice IV.

v. 3014. *rabe*] *Rabel*. The nominative form *Rabels* is found in vv. 3348 and 3352. The reading is supported by Venice IV, Châteauroux, and Venice VII.

v. 3022. *guinemans*] *Loranz*. The scribe appears to have erroneously repeated the last word in the first line of this laisse. The correct name is found in v. 3469 and in Venice IV.

v. 3029. *.xx. cheualers*] *.XX. milie chevalers*. An error due to inattention on the part of the scribe. The correct reading is found in Venice IV, Paris, and Cambridge. For discussion relative to the number *.XX.*, see Segre.

v. 3069. *est des*] *est e des*. The abbreviation for *est* (.ē.) may have caused a haplography (*e* + *e*). For similar errors, see Samaran, p. 33.

v. 3302. *trestutuz*] *trestuz*. This dittography is cited by Samaran, p. 33.

v. 3340. *Ki errer uoelt*] *Ki or ne voelt*. The confusion of *n* and *r* is noted by Samaran, p. 34. Most editors now agree that this emendation, based on Châteauroux and Venice VII, is indicated. Earlier editors believed *errer* meant 'to ride'. Jenkins still prefers that explanation. See, however, Bédier, *Commentaires*, p. 236; Segre.

v. 3365. *sescririent*] *s'escrient*. The scribe added a superscribed *i* (= *ri*) over the *c*. On this dittography, see Samaran, p. 33. The error probably results from a tear in the manuscript, which forced the scribe to divide the word at this point.

v. 3371. *duuns es*] *D'ures en.* The scribe wrote *du . . . s en.* The letters after the *u* were then erased by the revisor, who added *un* above the line and altered the *n* of the *en* to read *es.* Samaran, p. 49, believes the erased letters were *un* (see also Short, "The Oxford Manuscript of the *Chanson de Roland,*" p. 224, n. 1), but *ure* seems more plausible. Lecoy, "Notules sur le texte du *Roland* d'Oxford," p. 797; Segre; Dufournet, *Cours sur Roland*, p. 34. See MANUSCRIPT, v. 2843; cf. also Segre, v. 2014 (*Durement en halt*] *D'ures en altres*) and the latter's note.

v. 3395. *la nen*] *la noit n'en.* There is a tear in the manuscript between *la* and *nen.* All editors agree that the missing word is either *mort*, found in Venice IV, or *nuit*, which occurs in Cambridge and Paris. Segre points out that *nuit* fits the context because the battle lasts until dusk (vv. 3478, 3560; cf. also v. 3658). One may add a further argument on paleographical grounds: *mort* in Venice IV may be an error for *noit*, the prevalent form in the Oxford manuscript and the orthography proposed here.

v. 3428. *mort entre*] *mort l'abat entre.* An error due to inattention on the part of the scribe. All editors emend on the basis of Venice IV: *mort l'abat.* Cf. also Paris.

v. 3482. *cil hanste*] *cez hanste.* The word *hanste* is feminine, and a plural was doubtless intended. The scribe seems to have been anticipating the word *cil* in the second hemistich. For *hanste* = *hanstes*, see OXFORD TEXT, ENGLISH TRANSLATION, v. 44. The demonstrative adjective should be the feminine nominative plural *celes*, but such a change produces a hypermetric line. Therefore, editors emend to *cez*, the nominative feminine plural of *cest*, a form found in all other copies of the poem. Cf. also MANUSCRIPT, v. 2539.

v. 3593. *en fedeltet voeill*] *en fiet le te voeill.* Editors justify this emendation chiefly on paleographical grounds and by comparison with vv. 432 and 472. See Segre. Bédier, *Commentaires*, p. 238, termed the passage a *locus desperatus*, and it is true that the phrasing in several other copies of the poem is at variance with the proposed reading. However, Paris (en fief le te randrommez) and Conrad (Ich lihe dir Yspania) are reasonably close. Cf. the explanation provided by Moignet, p. 252 ("on peut entendre, à la rigueur: 'je veux te réduire à la fidélité', en admettant qu'un pronom *te* ait été omis après *fedeltet*").

v. 3595. *sembl* = *semblet.* The last two letters of this word were accidently trimmed off when the volume was assembled.

v. 3679. *Mandet*] *Muntet.* An error due to inattention on the part of the scribe. All editors emend on the basis of Venice IV, Châteauroux, Venice VII, and Paris.

v. 3790. *empere*] *emperere.* See MANUSCRIPT, v. 1.—*asemblent*] *asemblet.* An error due to inattention on the part of the scribe.

v. 3791. *brarant*] *brant.* The scribe realized his error, a dittography of the type noted by Samaran, p. 33, but erased only the *r*, leaving *b arant.*

v. 3796. *daluernene*] *d'Alverne.* This dittography is noted by Samaran, p. 33.

v. 3806. *frerere*] *frere.* This dittography is noted by Samaran, p. 33.

v. 3846. *emperes*] *empereres.* See MANUSCRIPT, v. 1.

Notes to the Oxford Text, English Translation

v. 3. *altaigne.* Bédier renders this word as 'hautaine', whereas Foulet, *Glossaire*, defines it more prosaically as 'haut'. See INTRODUCTION, 15, C, and note 323.

v. 8. *Mahumet, Apollin.* For a summary of the various etymologies and explanations of the trinity of pagan gods (Tervagant is mentioned for the first time in v. 611), see Jenkins, notes to vv. 8, 611; Frappier, *Chansons de geste*, 2:122. An illustration of Remigius of Auxerre's *Commentary on Martianus Capella*, dated c. 1100, depicts Apollo riding a cart and carrying, in his left hand, what appears to be a bouquet of little busts of the Three Graces (*see Fig. 34*); see Panofsky and Saxl, "Classical Mythology," pp. 254–55, fig. 39; Panofsky, *Renaissance and Renascences*, p. 85, fig. 53. Cf. the idol held by Idolatria in the *Hortus Deliciarum*; Cames, *Allégories*, pl. XXXI, fig. 49. For a caricature of Mohammed in a Latin translation of the Koran, dated 1162, see Le Goff, *Civilisation*, p. 190. Idols of the pagan gods figure in hagiographic literature and play an important role in Turoldus's poem (vv. 2619, 3268, 3493, 3664). The image of the falling idols constitutes a significant point of contact (COMMENTARY, 43).

v. 9. *AOI.* These mysterious letters continue to puzzle and fascinate scholars. For bibliography and discussion, see Jenkins, note to v. 9; Robert Bossuat, *Manuel bibliographique de la littérature française du moyen âge* (Melun: Librairie d'Argences, 1951), items 799–802; *Supplément* (*1949–53*) (Paris: Librairie d'Argences, 1955), item 6172; *Second Supplément* (*1954–60*) (Paris: Librairie d'Argences, 1961), items 7209, 7244, 7245; Horrent, *La Chanson de Roland*, pp. 330–33; Riquer, *Chansons de geste*, p. 104, n. 131; Henry and Renée Kahane, "Magic and Gnosticism in the 'Chanson de Roland'," *Romance Philology* 12 (1958/59): 216–31; C. Storey, "AOI in the *Chanson de Roland*," *Essays Presented to C. M. Girdlestone* (Newcastle upon Tyne: University of Durham, 1960), 311–17; Frances and Cornelius Crowley, "Le problème de l'étymologie de AOI dans la *Chanson de Roland*," *Cahiers de civilisation médiévale* 3 (1960): 12–13; Erich von Richthofen, "Style and Chronology of the Early Romance Epic," *Saggi e ricerche in memoria di Ettore Li Gotti* (Palermo: Centro di studi filologici e linguistici siciliani, 1962), 3:83–93; Daniel Devoto, "L'AOI dans la *Chanson de Roland*," an unpublished paper read at the Second International Congress of the Société Rencesvals, held at Venice in 1961 (summary in *Bulletin bibliographique de la Société Rencesvals* 3 [1963]: 92, item 260); Ramón Menéndez Pidal, "El *aoi* del manuscrito Rolandiano de Oxford," *Revista de Filología Española* 46 (1963): 173–77; Moignet, p. 31; H. J. Green, "The Etymology of AOI and AE," *MLN* 85 (1970): 593–98; Guy R. Mermier, "The *Chanson de Roland*'s Mysterious AOI," *The Michigan Academician* 5 (1973): 481–91. I favor the interpretation proposed by André de Mandach, "The So-Called AOI in the *Chanson de Roland*," *Symposium* 11 (1957): 303–15. Mandach argues convincingly that the three letters (often actually *Aoi.*) represent *Am.*, an abbreviation for *Amen*.

v. 12. *culched.* The same verb also indicates an attitude of helplessness in vv. 2573, 3992. In vv. 2013, 2358, 2449, 2480, 3097, it is a posture of prayer, and in vv. 2175, 2204, and 2496, one of repose (cf. v. 2481, setting of the sun).

v. 15. *pecchet.* On the meaning of the term here and in v. 3646, see Foulet, *Glossaire* ('calamité'); Jones, *Ethos*, pp. 30–31; Payen, *Le Motif du repentir*, p. 214, n. 5.

v. 20. *saive.* This word is generally transcribed as *savie*; the correct orthography is found in Segre. Foulet, *Glossaire*, p. 356: "Le verbe qui suit *cum* peut être sous-entendu; il faut alors comprendre 'comme fait', 'comme on fait', 'comme il convient à'." On the services due to the lord, summarized in the words *auxilium* and *consilium*, see Ganshof, *Feudalism*, pp. 86–93. The meaning of *saive* in this and other passages is discussed in COMMENTARY, 2 and 5.

v. 23. *de Castel de Valfunde.* Some editors emend the first *de* to *del* on the basis of v. 3783; Whitehead proposes *de Castel del Valfunde*. On the fall of final *l* in proclitics, see Bédier, *Commentaires*, p. 259; Whitehead, p. xiv; and cf. OXFORD TEXT, ENGLISH TRANSLATION, vv. 1619 and 2126.

v. 25. *chevaler.* Foulet, *Glossaire*: "[Le mot] est pris comme adjectif pour indiquer toutes les qualités qui conviennent au chevalier modèle." Georges Gougenheim, "De 'chevalier' à 'cavalier'," *Mélanges Ernest Hoepffner*, pp. 117–26; Jones, pp. 25–26; Burgess, *Vocabulaire pré-courtois*, pp. 108–9.

v. 26. *Prozdom i out.* Jenkins: "Here *i* is for *en lui.*"

v. 28. *orguillus, fier.* Often used for insults in Old French literature, both terms refer here to insane cruelty and fierceness, rather than to pride. Cf. OXFORD TEXT, ENGLISH TRANSLATION, v. 474. Similarly, in vv. 228, 292, 389, and 1773, *orguill* / *orgoilz* / *orgoill* means 'madness'. Jones, pp. 65–67 (cf. v. 56: *pesmes*; p. 31); Calin, *Epic Quest*, p. 17; Georges Gougenheim, "*Orgueil et fierté* dans la *Chanson de Roland*," *Mélanges Jean Frappier*, 1: 365–73; Burgess, "*Orgueil* and *Fierté*," pp. 103–22. Cf., however, OXFORD TEXT, ENGLISH TRANSLATION, v. 578.

v. 29. *amistez.* The feudal term *amer* and its cognates are discussed by Jones, pp. 36–45 (but cf. Christian *amur* in v. 3674 [p. 170]).

v. 34. *soldeiers.* In Turoldus's day the summoning of the *arrière ban*, that is, the levy of every able-bodied man, did occur in crises, but feudal monarchs most frequently called upon vassals who owed them limited military service. This *ost banie* (v. 211) was very often augmented with mercenaries. Smail, *Crusading Warfare*, pp. 88, 92–93, 97.

v. 40. *S'en volt ostages.* On this type of phrase, see Robert-Léon Wagner, *Les phrases hypothétiques commençant par 'si' dans la langue française, des origines à la fin du XVIe siècle* (Paris: Droz, 1939), p. 463; *Huon de Bordeaux*, p. 395, note to vv. 83, 84.

v. 42. *Enveius.* Editors generally emend to *Enveiuns*, for it is assumed that the titulus over the *u* was either accidentally omitted by the scribe (Samaran, p. 34) or effaced. However, the form may be genuine. On the denasalization of Anglo-Norman vowels, see Bédier, *Commentaires*, p. 255; Moignet, p. 282. Cf. Whitehead, p. xiii, and the note at the beginning of this volume.

v. 44. *le = les.* On the fall of final *s*, especially in proclitics, see Bédier, *Commentaires*, pp. 261–62; Whitehead, p. xiv; Moignet, p. 282.

v. 47. *Pa = Par.* Effacement of *r* in final position is discussed by Bédier, *Commentaires*, p. 260; Whitehead, p. xiv; Moignet, p. 282.

v. 49. *L'ost . . . desfere.* For the verb, see Tobler and Lommatzsch, 2:1579. However, perhaps 'raise the siege' is meant (cf. Godefroy, 2: 582–83, s.v. desfaire le siege).

v. 57. *trecher = trencher.* See OXFORD TEXT, ENGLISH TRANSLATION, v. 42.

v. 59. *clere.* Jonin, "La 'Clere' Espagne de Blancandrin," pp. 85–96, renders this passage as 'la belle, la brillante Espagne'. However, he explains that, for the Saracens, Spain is not "claire et riante" but "opulente, éclatante de richesse," and that, for Turoldus, these riches are profane and superficial. Cf. COMMENTARY, 8, note 10.

v. 63. *Balaguet.* Jenkins, note to v. 63: "No doubt Balaguer, in Catalonia, on the Segre"; Paul Aebischer, "Les graphies toponymiques 'Sebre' et 'Balaguet' de la 'Chanson de Roland', Ms. Digby," *Boletín de la Real Academia de Buenas Letras de Barcelona* 28 (1959/60): 185–209; Mandach, *Naissance*, 1:154.

v. 69. *feluns.* In Turoldus's poem this word and its cognates at times refer to a grave crime, but more often than not they are, as in the present instance, ambiguous derogatory expressions. Jones, pp. 28–30; Ménard, *Le Rire*, pp. 129–30.

v. 71. *Cordres*. Possibly Córdoba, although this city is very distant from Saragossa; Jenkins; Foulet, *Glossaire*; Delbouille, *Genèse*, p. 124; Lejeune and Stiennon, 1: 121; Menéndez Pidal, *La Chanson de Roland*, pp. 159, 271, 367–70; Mandach, 1: 68; Jonin, "La 'Clere' Espagne de Blancandrin," pp. 93–95.

v. 72. *olives*. The *s* may have been added by the revisor (cf. vv. 80, 93), which would be an argument in favor of deleting it here. Lecoy, "Notules sur le texte du *Roland* d'Oxford," p. 793. However, Segre notes this form in other manuscripts of the poem.

v. 86. *par amur e par feid*. Jones, p. 44: "it is used ... to connote political [and] emotional ties"; p. 73: "It would seem that the twelfth-century Franks drew little distinction between fealty and religious faith, both of which were rendered by the Latin word *fides*."

v. 108. *altres*. The expression here and in v. 673 is synonymous with *chevalers*; Mireaux, *La Chanson de Roland*, pp. 169–70; Menéndez Pidal, p. 372. Cf. OXFORD TEXT, ENGLISH TRANSLATION, v. 673.

v. 113. *leger*. Moignet translates as 'fous', a meaning that corresponds to the notion discussed in COMMENTARY, 3, note 6; see, however, Dufournet, *Cours sur Roland*, p. 31, n. 1. Jenkins, note to v. 70, mentions a parallel passage in the *Aeneid*.

v. 115. *faldestoed*. The *sella plicabilis* or *currulis*, used by the Holy Roman Emperors in their travels, was, as its name implies, a folding throne and was ornamented with monster heads and paws. A symbol of imperial power, it begins to appear in portraits about A.D. 400. Cames, *Byzance*, pp. 36–38. Charles's throne is said by Turoldus to be made of gold; Baligant's, in v. 2653, of ivory.

v. 118. *Gent*. The epithet *gent* means 'handsome, well-proportioned', but it is linked to the notion of noble birth. Jones, p. 63.

v. 121. *par amur e par bien*. What is intended, no doubt, is 'with a show of friendship and good will'. Sincerity is far from the Saracens' thoughts here. Cf. v. 2710.

v. 126. *salvetet*. Timothy D. Hemming, "Restrictions lexicales dans la chanson de geste," *Romania* 89 (1968): 97, n. 2, erroneously states that this term is missing in the *Roland*.

v. 147. *Voet par hostages*. To the various proposals reviewed by Segre, add Nitze, "Two *Roland* Passages: Verses 147 and 1723" ('He or I promise [VL *voto, *votat*] by hostages'), and William S. Woods, "*La Chanson de Roland*, Line 147," *Romance Philology* 5 (1951/52): 35–38 (an ellipsis for "He pledged it, or it is guaranteed [VL *votatu*] by hostages"). Cf. Whitehead, p. 120: " 'he will do it by giving hostages' or 'he wishes it to be done by an exchange of hostages' involves a violent ellipsis, but it is far from an impossible reading."

v. 149. *Pa = Par*. See OXFORD TEXT, ENGLISH TRANSLATION, v. 47.

v. 152. *seint Michel del Peril*. See Lejeune, "Le Mont-Saint-Michel-au-Péril-de-la-Mer," pp. 414–15, 424–26.

v. 156. *guarir*. On the meaning, cf. v. 1133 ("Asoldrai vos pur voz anmes guarir").

v. 167. *errer*. Jenkins: 'travel', 'proceed', hence, 'be guided'.

v. 176. *proz*. Moignet: 'le preux'; Owen: 'valiant'. OFr. *proz* means 'useful, worthy', which in combat situations naturally means 'valiant'. However, Oliver's usefulness in the present circumstance (a council) plainly consists in giving advice, thus the meaning 'wise', associated here with *gentilz* 'noble'. Cf. v. 172 (Moignet: 'le preux', Owen: 'noble') and see OXFORD TEXT, ENGLISH TRANSLATION, v. 576.

v. 179. *Des ore cumencet le cunseill que mal prist*. The first-hemistich locution is repeated in vv. 3704, 3747, and 3946 and marks important divisions in the narrative. Cf. *Erec*, v. 1796: *Ici fenist li premiers vers* (see Roques's comment, p. ix, n. 1). In the second hemistich *que mal prist* is rendered variously as follows: Jenkins: 'which made a bad beginning', 'which was the beginning of misfortune'; Whitehead: '[went] wrong'; Köhler, " 'Conseil des barons',", p. 11 : 'mit der das Unheil begann' or '. . . die er (Karl) unglücklicherweise einberief'; Moignet: 'qui tourna mal'.

v. 190. *tendrat ses marches*. Lejeune, "La signification du nom 'marche'," p. 269: Il ne faut pas traduire, comme l'a fait Bédier, 'il sera chrétien, c'est de moi qu'il tiendra ses terres'. Car le mot 'terres', ici, est beaucoup trop général. Le roi Marsile n'a pas à se mettre sous la dépendance totale du roi des Francs, même s'il se fait chrétien. Ce qu'il promet à Charles, et ceci est fort naturel, c'est d'abord de lui payer tribut (d'où l'énumération des dons qu'il veut lui faire v. 182–186); il re-connaîtra aussi sa suzeraineté pour une certaine catégorie de terres, les marches, c'est-à-dire les terres en bordure de son royaume sarrasin.

v. 191. *curages*. On the heart as the seat of intellectual functions, see Brault, "Chré-tien de Troyes' *Lancelot*," p. 143. Cf. INTRODUCTION, 16, B. For additional information about the heart in medieval literature and thought, see John Leyerle, "The Heart and the Chain," *Harvard English Studies* 5 (1974): 113–45 (*The Learned and the Lewed: Studies in Chaucer and Medieval Literature*, ed. Larry D. Benson).

v. 198. *Noples*. Cf. v. 1775. For the identification Noples = Pamplona, see Aebischer, *Textes norrois et littérature française du moyen âge*, p. 54; Sholod, *Charlemagne in Spain*, p. 36.

v. 200. *Sezilie*. For various proposals (*Cecilie, Sebilie*), see Jenkins; Bédier, *Com-mentaires*, p. 520; Menéndez Pidal, p. 160; Segre.

v. 209. *chef = chefs*. See OXFORD TEXT, ENGLISH TRANSLATION, v. 44.

v. 210. *guer*. Editors customarily emend to *guere* or *guerre*. However, see Whitehead, p. xiii (fall of unaccented *e* in final position); Moignet.

v. 219. *Mult fierement*. Moignet: 'très fièrement'; Owen: 'full of pride'. But see OXFORD TEXT, ENGLISH TRANSLATION, v. 28.

v. 220. *bricun*. Jenkins: "Apparently the word is not used here as an insult, for Ganelon applies it also to himself, and Roland shows no sign of resenting it. It seems better, therefore, to understand the opening sentence as a sort of deprecatory formula, appropriate in addressing the great Emperor in a public assembly." However, Ganelon uses the strong term *fols* in v. 229, and Jones, p. 59, considers *bricun* to be a "word of opprobrium." Ménard, *Le Rire*, p. 130: "Est-ce un hasard si Ganelon est le seul à user de *bricon* (220)? En ne prêtant pareille injure à nul autre guerrier, n'est-ce point une façon de signaler le traître, de l'isoler de la masse des combattants?" See also pp. 132, 720.

v. 221. *Ne mei ne altre*. Jenkins, note to v. 220: 'Do not heed the advice of any insignificant fellows (like Roland or myself)'; Moignet: 'moi ou un autre'; Owen: 'Or me, or any man'.

v. 223. *jointes ses mains*. On the rite of commendation, see Ganshof, *Feudalism*, pp. 26–27; Dufournet, *Cours sur Roland*, p. 156.

v. 228. *orguill*. See OXFORD TEXT, ENGLISH TRANSLATION, vv. 28, 578.

v. 231. *vassal*. Dufournet, *Cours sur Roland*, pp. 142–51, provides a complete listing of the various meanings for this word in the *Song of Roland* that have to do, essentially, with physical courage. See also Foulet, *Glossaire*; Jones, pp. 22–23.

v. 234. *Saveir i ad, mais qu'il seit entendut*. Moignet: 'il y a là de la sagesse, à condition qu'il soit entendu'; Owen: 'There's wisdom in it, if you pay it heed'. For bibliography, see COMMENTARY, 4, note 27.

v. 248. *saives*. Cf. vv. 279, 294.

v. 255. *Nu = Nun*. See OXFORD TEXT, ENGLISH TRANSLATION, v. 42.

v. 262. *jugez*. Foulet, *Glossaire*, lists four meanings for this verb: (1) 'juger, décider'; (2) 'faire tomber une mission sur quelqu'un'; (3) 'désigner par jugement' (includes the present example); and (4) 'condamner'.

v. 264. *renc.* See COMMENTARY, 22 (v. 2192).

v. 270. *Sin vois vedeir alques de sun semblant.* Jenkins: 'my idea is to see something of what he looks like'; Whitehead: 'discover his attitude'; Moignet: 'Ainsi je vais un peu voir l'air qu'il a'; Owen: 'So as to see what sort of face he shows'.

v. 275. *marche.* The word appears only in the Oxford copy. The other versions indicate that the Emperor simply urges the selection of a worthy or courageous man. Lejeune, "La signification du nom 'marche'," pp. 271–72:

[Charles] demande qu'on lui choisisse non un Franc, mais un homme de la région frontière. Et il le demande avec quelque insistance: 'Choisissez-moi donc' ou 'Choisissez-moi plutôt un baron de ma région frontière'. Quelle région frontière, quelle marche? 'Ma marche' signifie ici, naturellement, la Marche d'Espagne.... si, à ce moment, Roland l'impulsif désigne nommément son parâtre, Ganelon, c'est évidemment que ce dernier n'est pas un Franc, mais un homme de la Marche.... Au lieu de concevoir Ganelon comme une sorte de Goth, voire de Gascon, comme le voulait la version d'Oxford, le moyen âge dut réinventer, plus tard, un Ganelon l'Allemand ou un Ganelon 'de Maiance'.

v. 277. *parastre.* Jenkins: "*Parrastre* may mean not only 'step-father', but also 'a poor imitation of a father'."

v. 280. *anguisables.* After reviewing earlier discussions of this word ('anguished', 'distressed', 'exasperated', 'offended'), Horrent, p. 215, n. 3, concluded that the context suggests the meaning 'désespéré'. Riquer, *Chansons de geste*, p. 98, prefers the interpretation 'offended' proposed by Pellegrini, "L'ira di Gano," pp. 161–62. Lejeune, "Le péché de Charlemagne et la *Chanson de Roland*," p. 361, n. 65, points out that words ending in *-able* (Lat. *-abilis*) often mean 'causing' (e.g., *épouvantable* 'ce qui épouvante', *irritable* 'ce qui cause de l'irritation'), thus *anguisable* 'qui cause de l'angoisse'. But this is surely too narrow an interpretation of the possible connotations this suffix can have (Jean Dubois, *Etude sur la dérivation suffixale en français moderne et contemporain* [Paris: Larousse, 1962], p. 18: "*-able* 'qui a la possibilité'"). It would also force the meaning of the same term in v. 3444 (Naimes li dux tant par est anguissables), where the sense is clearly 'distressed'. Other scholars, believing that Turoldus does not paint Ganelon all black, insist that anger, rather than fear, characterizes the traitor's reaction. Burger, "Le rire," p. 9; Köhler, "'Conseil des barons'," p. 21. On this false premise, see INTRODUCTION, 19, G. I see no reason for excluding an element of fear here— Ganelon's blind and sudden rage can only be explained as the response of an individual beset by complicated emotions (Dufournet, *Cours sur Roland*, p. 68)—but etymologically, at any rate, *anguisables* primarily indicates 'choking with anger'. In the other versions Ganelon experiences anger, anxiety, rage, or fear, the latter two being found together in the corresponding passage of the fourteenth-century Welsh *Campeu Charlymaen* (see Segre).

v. 283. *Vairs.* Jenkins: 'steel-blue' or 'keen', 'expressive'; Colby, *Twelfth-Century French Literature*, pp. 41–42, 54, 178: 'sparkling'. As an example of the latter sense, Greimas, *Dictionnaire*, cites Wace: *Les ioex ot vairs conm a serpens*. Greimas also provides the meaning 'Changeant, avec sens péjor' for the term as used by Conon de Béthune: *Fausse, plus vaire ke pie*. Ménard, *Le Rire*, p. 544, observes that, in Philippe de Tripoli's *Secretum secretorum*, shifty eyes are suspicious (talis homo est fraudulentus, latro, infidelis) and associated with Envy in Guillaume de Lorris's *Roman de la Rose* (see also Fleming, *The Roman de la Rose*, p. 33). Unfortunately, a pejorative meaning does not correspond to what follows in vv. 284–285, although appearances are at times deceiving (INTRODUCTION, 10, B, 2). Since the second hemistich makes it clear that Ganelon had a fierce look on his face, it seems reasonable to conclude that his eyes flashed with anger.

v. 285. *esguardent.* The verb here means 'to look at with amazement, wonder, perhaps even fear'; see also vv. 2274, 3882, and cf. *reguarder*.

v. 288. Jenkins adds a question mark at the end of this line and observes: "Ganelon is (or pretends to be) incredulous: has he heard aright?"

v. 290. *muvra = muvrai*. On the reduction of *ai* to *a* in Anglo-Norman, see Bédier, *Commentaires*, p. 257; Whitehead, p. xiii.

v. 294. *Mai = Mais*. See OXFORD TEXT, ENGLISH TRANSLATION, v. 44.

v. 300. *Einz i frai un poi de legerie*. Jenkins: 'but first, before I go (*ainz*), you must allow me to act and talk rather foolishly [the threat of vv. 289–91]'. On the effacement of Anglo-Norman interconsonantal mute *e* (*frai = ferai*), see Pope, *From Latin to Modern French*, par. 1290.

v. 304. *doel, ire*. Jones, pp. 83, 86: 'dismay, chagrin'. For *ire*, see OXFORD TEXT, ENGLISH TRANSLATION, v. 2414.

v. 307. *fals jugement*. This locution is discussed by Köhler, "'Conseil des barons'," pp. 21–25. For other legal terms in the *Song of Roland*, see Jones, p. 45. Menéndez Pidal, p. 96, n. 1, considers this line to be "insipide et inutile".

v. 316. *Guadez = Guardez*. On the fall of *r* in preconsonantal position, see Bédier, *Commentaires*, p. 260; Whitehead, p. xiv; Moignet, p. 282.

v. 317. *Tro = Trop*. This is the only occurrence of the fall of final *p* in this copy noted by Bédier, *Commentaires*, p. 261; Whitehead, p. xiv; Moignet, p. 282. See, however, OXFORD TEXT, ENGLISH TRANSLATION, v. 1948 (col = colp). In Old French *trop* can mean 'very much' or 'too much'. Ménard, *Syntaxe*, par. 302. On the parallel with v. 327, see Köhler, "'Conseil des barons'," p. 25.

v. 325. *por qu'il*. Most editors emend to *por ço qu'il* on the basis of Venice IV and VII; Whitehead lets the form stand. Bédier emends; cf., however, Foulet, *Glossaire*, p. 453: "*por ço que* 'parce que' 285 [=324], 2102; *por que*, même emploi, 286 [=325]."

v. 333. *dut*. Moignet: "*deveir* signifie 'être sur le point de', et, aux temps passés, il peut servir à signifier que tel fait a *failli* se produire." He translates: 'quand il eut à le prendre'.

v. 348. *L'estreu li tint*. Medieval illustrations of mounting at times show the rider facing the horse's tail; the groom holds the stirrup on the opposite side of the horse. Denholm-Young, *History and Heraldry*, p. 27 and n. 2. Holding the stirrup was a mark of respect deriving from the vassal's *reverentia*. Ganshof, *Feudalism*, p. 82.

v. 351. *En la cort*. The line is hypermetric and many editors emend to *en cort*, a reading supported by v. 446 (Châteauroux and Venice VII have *A cort*). Whitehead and Moignet retain the present phrasing, found in vv. 231 and 775. The latter do not, however, have any metrical irregularity.

v. 359. *Mielz est que sul moerge*. Similar expressions appear in vv. 1091, 1475, 1701, 2336, and 3909; cf. also vv. 447–449.

v. 362. *mun ami e mun per*. Pinabel is Ganelon's kinsman (vv. 3781–3783). Jenkins: "*mon ami* may mean simply 'my friend,' but it may also have the technical sense of 'member of my household'." See also Jones, p. 38. Elsewhere, however, the poet states that this relationship exists between Roland and Oliver (v. 1975: sun ami e sun per).

v. 366. *une olive*. Moignet: 'oliveraie'.

v. 368. *lu = lui*. On Anglo-Norman reduction of *ui* to *u*, see Pope, *From Latin to Modern French*, par. 1160.

v. 376. *Jamais*. I cannot see the point of writing this word as *ja mais* or *jamais* in accordance with the scribe's whim, a practice adopted by many editors since Bédier (see Foulet, *Glossaire*, p. 408).

v. 384. *brunie*. Jenkins: 'a tunic of leather or strong cloth on which were sewed small plates or rings of metal'. Knudson, "La brogne," argues convincingly that *broigne* was simply a synonym for hauberk, that is, the coat of mail.

v. 389. *devreit*. Jenkins: 'should certainly some day'. Identical meaning in v. 1149.

v. 400. *L'emperere meïsmes ad tut a sun talent.* Some editors consider *L'emperere* to be the subject of this sentence; Moignet: 'L'empereur même obtient de lui tout à sa guise'; Owen: 'The emperor himself has all he wants'. This interpretation finds some support in the variant reading provided by Venice VII and Châteauroux (Li enperere fait tot le ses commant). However, the notion that Charles is under Roland's sway fits the context better; see COMMENTARY, 4. Note, too, the following parallel use in the *Roman d'Alexandre*:

> Chivalers aime e honore forment,
> Quant que il a tot lor met em present;
> Tant per es larges ne prisa ne argent,
> Les chivalers teneit toz a talent.

Henry, *Chrestomathie*, p. 90, vv. 36–39 (Glossaire: *tenir a talent* 'traiter selon son désir'). *The Medieval French Roman d'Alexandre*, III, *Version of Alexandre de Paris. Variants and Notes to Branch I*, ed. Alfred Foulet, Elliott Monographs in the Romance Languages and Literatures 38 (Princeton: Princeton University Press; Paris: Presses Universitaires de France, 1949), p. 63, lists the following variant for v. 47 (= Henry, v. 39): *As c. quil servent a t.* For further discussion, see Bédier, *Commentaires*, pp. 201–2; Segre, p. 76; Glyn S. Burgess, "La Chanson de Roland, Line 400," *Romance Notes* 13 (1971): 165–67; idem, "*Talent* in Early Old French (to 1150)," *Romania* 95 (1974): 447–49; William W. Kibler, "Again *La Chanson de Roland*, Verse 400," *Romance Notes* 14 (1972): 621–23; Dufournet, *Cours sur Roland*, pp. 36–37.

v. 418. *fesime* = *fesimes.* See OXFORD TEXT, ENGLISH TRANSLATION, v. 44.

v. 446. *avrai . . . portee.* Jenkins notes the use of the future perfect tense here for the present perfect (see also p. cxxxii and cf. v. 2352) and suggests that the meaning is 'when all is said and done', 'when history shall have given her verdict'.

v. 451. *Tuit, li meillor.* Many editors emend *Tuit* to *Tant,* but not Bédier, Jenkins, and Whitehead. Moignet: 'Les meilleurs'; Owen: 'the leading'. I suggest that the Saracens who urge Marsile to restrain himself are 'the shrewdest' because they perceive the game Ganelon is playing. Cf. v. 449.

v. 452. *ses* = *s'est.* On the effacement of final *t*, see Bédier, *Commentaires*, p. 261; Moignet, p. 281.

v. 455. *Vos doüssez.* The revisor added *le* above the line between these two words. The pronoun is unnecessary and results in a hypermetric line.

v. 456. *Sire.* The Caliph, according to Jenkins.

v. 474. *orguillos.* See OXFORD TEXT, ENGLISH TRANSLATION, v. 28.

v. 481. *sumer.* On this beast of burden, see Dufournet, *Cours sur Roland*, pp. 86–87.

v. 491. *Haltoïe.* Possibly a scribal error for *Haltilie* (Samaran, pp. 34, 38), a form found in Châteauroux and Venice VII; cf. also v. 209. However, variants of this sort are not uncommon in this manuscript. Bédier, *Commentaires*, p. 270, n. 2.

v. 509. *E Guenes l'ad pris.* Many editors emend to *Guenelun prist.* For discussion, see Bédier, *Commentaires*, p. 203; Segre. Moignet keeps the original reading but affirms that the subject of the next line must be Blancandrin. Although Marsile orders Blancandrin to fetch Ganelon, Turoldus may have had the traitor grasp the Saracen's hand and lead him to the pagan king to show that he was eager to get on with the betrayal.

v. 514. *por ferir.* Jenkins: 'even to the point of striking (you)'.

v. 533. *bontet.* Jones, p. 54: "I prefer to translate *bontet* as 'bounty' or 'largess' rather than as 'virtues', as Bédier does." Jones, pp. 19–21, 25, 55, and 63 (followed by Burgess, *Vocabulaire pré-courtois*, pp. 107, 110–11), restricts the meaning to the semantic area of 'good warrior', that is, an individual having strength and physical courage. Jones's assertion is based upon the false premise that eleventh-century feudal culture valued only these qualities in a vassal or a sovereign. Jones, p. 54, n. 48, does concede that, in v. 2507, *bontet* means 'bounty of God' (Moignet: 'grâce'; Owen: 'grace'). In view of the association of Charles and God, it follows that the Emperor's virtues reflect divine goodness and perfection.

v. 556: *ier = iert*. See OXFORD TEXT, ENGLISH TRANSLATION, v. 452.

v. 566. *a Franceis*. Whitehead, p. xiv, n. 4: "probably *a* (< *ad*) and not an error for *as*." Cf. Moignet, p. 62, note. The latter adds: "Le vers pourrait s'entendre comme assertif, et non interrogatif."

v. 576. *E Oliver, li proz e li curteis*. The line is repeated verbatim in v. 3755. Cf. also vv. 1164, 3796, and 3823. According to Jones, p. 62, the epithet *curteis* means the same as *proz*, that is, 'courageous', and is related to the concept of brave service at court (v. 446). See also Burgess, *Vocabulaire pré-courtois*, pp. 21–22. However, *proz* and the expressions with which it is associated are not restricted to this meaning. OXFORD TEXT, ENGLISH TRANSLATION, v. 176.

v. 578. *orguill*. The meaning here is 'pride' and the image is related to that of Pride's Fall in the *Psychomachia*. Cf. Burgess, "*Orgueil* and *Fierté*," pp. 106, 107, and see OXFORD TEXT, ENGLISH TRANSLATION, v. 28.

v. 583. *porz de Sizer*. Cf. v. 719. On the identification of this mountain pass, see Foulet, *Glossaire*, pp. 520–21; Menéndez Pidal, p. 86. The term *porz* appears twenty-one times in Turoldus's epic in this meaning and seems to have originated in the Pyrenees region. Aebischer, "Halt sunt li pui," p. 1; Delbouille, *Genèse*, pp. 125 ff.

v. 591. *Nel di por ço*. Jenkins: "This line appears to mean: 'I do not promise, however, that you will not suffer severely'. OF *nel di por ce* has at times the effect of mod. *non que*, Eng. 'not but that'"; Bédier, *Commentaires*, p. 205: 'je ne dis pas'; Whitehead: 'nevertheless'; Moignet: 'je ne dis pas pour cela'.

v. 593. *estoertrat*. E. G. R. Waters, "Gleanings from MS. Digby 23," *Modern Language Review* 25 (1930): 97. Samaran, p. 44, suggests *estuertrat*. Whitehead, p. 120, notes the form *estoerstrent* in v. 3632.

v. 600. *Tere Major*. On the etymology, see Bédier, *Commentaires*, pp. 146–47, 303. Elsewhere in the *Song of Roland*, this expression always represents Charlemagne's Empire (vv. 818, 952, 1489, 1616, 1784). Could it mean Spain here (cf. Venice IV: Trestuta Spagna)? For discussion, see Jenkins; Segre.

v. 601. *Quan = Quant*. See OXFORD TEXT, ENGLISH TRANSLATION, v. 452. Cf. v. 1932.

v. 602. *venir*. It is possible to emend to *uvrir* on the basis of Châteauroux, Venice IV, and Venice VII, but the present reading can also be justified. Geoffrey Mellor, "*Roland* 602 (O: Puis si cumencet a venir ses tresors)," *MLN* 72 (1957): 111–13 (*ses tresors* is interpreted as the subject of the verb); Raphael Levy, "Interpretations of *venir* in *Roland* 602 and *Perceval* 6428," *Zeitschrift für romanische Philologie* (1961): 342–45; Moignet: "*Venir* semble avoir valeur factitive de 'faire venir'." A treasure chest was an attribute of Avarice. Panofsky, *Renaissance and Renascences*, p. 95 (cf. Katzenellenbogen, *Allegories*, p. 13, n. 1 [a purse]).

v. 608. *si s'en est forsfait*. Owen: 'and succumbed to sin'. Cf. vv. 3758, 3827.

v. 611. *Tervagan*. See OXFORD TEXT, ENGLISH TRANSLATION, v. 8. On the etymology of this term, see Wathelet-Willem, *Recherches*, 1: 595, n. 411 (bibliography).

v. 612. *Sarrazins espans*. On this expression, see MANUSCRIPT, v. 269.

vv. 613–615. The phrasing parallels that of contemporary oaths of fealty. Ganshof, *Feudalism*, pp. 34–35.

v. 615. *murrat*. The subject of this verb is the direct object in v. 613. On the *apo koinou* construction, see Ménard, *Syntaxe*, par. 217.

v. 637. *nusches*. Jenkins, p. 348: 'breast-pin, brooch, necklace'; Mortier: 'colliers'.

v. 641. *hoese*. Ronald C. Johnston, "*Hoese* 'Boot' in the *Chanson de Roland*, Line 641," *Modern Language Review* 58 (1963): 391–92.

v. 662. *Galne*. Almost certainly a scribal error for *Valterne* (the possibility becomes more apparent when the word is written with the standard abbreviation for -*er*), the city is said to have been conquered by Roland in v. 663 (cf. Valterne, in v. 199). The proposed emendation, supported by Châteauroux, Venice VII, and the Norse translation (cf. Venice IV: Valente; see also vv. 931, 1291), is made by several editors but rejected by Jenkins, Bédier, Whitehead, and Moignet. For discussion, see Delbouille, *Genèse*, p. 124; Menéndez Pidal, pp. 159, 424; Segre.

v. 666. *treüd*. Owen 'truce'. OFr. *treu*, *triu* (Lat. *tributum*) 'tribute' is not the same as *trive*, *trieve*, *trie* (Germ. *trinwa 'safety, security'), although ME. *trewes*, plural of *trewe* 'agreement' (OE. *treow* 'fidelity') is often associated with the first of these terms.

v. 673. *altres*. See OXFORD TEXT, ENGLISH TRANSLATION, v. 108.

v. 675. *veisdie*. The term sometimes has a favorable connotation despite its presumed etymology (Lat. *vitium*, according to Moignet, p. 70; Jenkins, p. 376, suggests Lat. *vegetum*), but the context here clearly indicates deceit.

v. 719. *porz de Sizer*. See OXFORD TEXT, ENGLISH TRANSLATION, v. 583.

v. 722. *estrussee*. Jenkins, p. 324, s.v. estrosser: 'break into pieces'; Foulet, *Glossaire*: " 'Briser'. Mais on ne comprend guère *brandie* après *estrussee*." For conjectures, see Segre.

v. 723. *escicles* = *esclices*. The noun is derived from OFr. *esclicier* (Germ. *slizzan 'to slice').

v. 727. *uers*. Many editors believe that the word should read *urs*, or that *uers* = *vers* 'boar'. Jenkins, note to vv. 725 ff.; E. Lerch, "Le 'verrat' dans la *Chanson de Roland*: une correction inutile," *Romania* 64 (1938): 398–405; Segre; Dufournet, *Cours sur Roland*, pp. 75–76. In his review of Steinmeyer, in *Romanic Review* 57 (1966): 56, W. T. H. Jackson notes that boars do not bite, they slash. Marcelle Thiébaux, "The Mouth of the Boar as a Symbol in Medieval Literature," *Romance Philology* 22 (1969): 287–89, points out that the boar was often associated with Satan. However, see Bédier, *Commentaires*, p. 207; Foulet, *Glossaire*, p. 494 (citing, inter alia, *Chanson de Guillaume*, v. 577, where the meaning seems to be 'boar', not 'bear' [Dufournet, pp. 75–76; Wathelet-Willem, *Recherches*, 2: 1209 (v. 578)]); Moignet.

v. 730. *veltres*. On the meaning ('hunting dog'), see Frappier, *Chansons de geste*, 2: 78, n. 1; Dufournet, *Cours sur Roland*, pp. 91–92.

v. 731. *le* = *les*. See OXFORD TEXT, ENGLISH TRANSLATION, v. 44.

v. 732. *al premer*. The meaning of this expression is discussed by Segre. On the form *uer* = *uers*, see OXFORD TEXT, ENGLISH TRANSLATION, v. 44.

v. 735. *Il ne sevent*. Cf. vv. 2553, 2567. Braet, "Fonction et importance du songe," p. 410.

v. 746. *vifs diables*. For several observations relative to the meaning of this expression, see the discussion following Antonio Ubieto Arteta's unpublished paper, "Una nota para la cronología de la 'Chanson de Roland'," at the Third International Congress of the Société Rencesvals, held at Barcelona in 1964, as reported in *Bulletin bibliographique de la Société Rencesvals* 4 (1967): 100. In the present instance, calling someone a living devil is tantamount to saying that Satan has entered his body, a notion made more explicit in the next verse. See also COMMENTARY, 6 (v. 602). Foulet, *Glossaire*, defines *vifs* in vv. 746 and 3647 as "une espèce de superlatif péjoratif."

v. 747. *mortel rage*. The same expression is used in v. 2279 with respect to the Rash Saracen's fatal act of folly. Rage, now usually understood to mean violent or uncontrolled anger, was often equated with insanity or possession in the Middle Ages. Madness, then as now, was not without its comic aspects, especially when it referred to a lover having taken leave of his senses (Ménard, *Le Rire*, pp. 178–83, 235–36, 247, 466, 720). In *Enéas*, v. 1270, Dido's passion is described as a *mortel rage*. However, the state to which Charles alludes is no laughing matter. It is *rage au coeur*, synonymous with mortal sin and caused by the devil (cf. Charlot in *La Chevalerie Ogier*, vv. 8746–8749, cited by Payen, *Le Motif du repentir*, p. 213). Ganelon is to be compared to the demoniacs encountered by Christ in the country of the Gadarenes (Matthew 8:28–34; Luke 8:26–39). In medieval iconography a possessed person was often shown with his hair standing on end like the devil (Réau, II, 2: 379). This suggests that Ganelon is the figure on the extreme left in the illustration of the *Pinrat* in Conrad (*see Fig. 43*), rather than the clean-shaven young man sitting next to the tree, as tentatively proposed by Lejeune and Stiennon, 1: 124–25.

v. 763. *culvert, put aire.* On the meaning of *culvert* when used as an insult, see Jones, p. 59; Ménard, *Le Rire*, p. 129. The allusion to Ganelon's ancestry is not to be taken literally; Jones, p. 20; Ménard, pp. 129, 136–37, 695. The rhymed versions did, however, develop the latter notion and, in a different passage, stated that the traitor was descended from Caesar's assassins. COMMENTARY, 47, note 5.

v. 764. *place.* Georges Gougenheim, "*Place* dans la *Chanson de Roland*: Recherche d'un contenu sémantique," *Bulletin des Jeunes Romanistes* 9 (1964): 1–4.

vv. 796–797. Many editors switch the position of the final word in these two verses, on the basis of Venice IV and Cambridge.

v. 805. *purpernez les deserz e les tertres.* On the maneuver, see Bancourt, "'Sen' et 'chevalerie'," p. 628.

v. 813. *pesme.* Jenkins, p. 354, indicates that this adjective modifies *le jur.* See, however, Jones, p. 31.

v. 817. *lius = lieues.* Elsewhere in this manuscript, the word for 'leagues' is written *liwes* (vv. 1756, 2425, 2759), eliminating possible confusion with the medieval equivalent of MFr. *lieux.*

v. 820. *le remembret.* The verb calls for the dative (Foulet, *Glossaire*), consequently, all editors emend *le* to *lur.* Cambridge, Châteauroux, and Venice VII have the supposedly correct form, but cf. Venice IV: *E li e remembra.* Perhaps *le = les* (see OXFORD TEXT, ENGLISH TRANSLATION, v. 44) and the latter is functioning as a dative. Pope, *From Latin to Modern French*, par. 1251, refers to this use in the northern (*sic*, for northeastern) region, but lists it as a late (fourteenth-century) development in Anglo-Norman. See COMMENTARY, 32 (vv. 2710, 2762).

v. 821. *pulcele = pulceles.* Cf. OXFORD TEXT, ENGLISH TRANSLATION, v. 44. Leo Spitzer, "Pucelle," *Romania* 72 (1951): 103–4, cites this example to support his contention that OFr. *pucele* is an aristocratic word.

vv. 822, 825. *pitet.* See INTRODUCTION, 16, A; OXFORD TEXT, ENGLISH TRANSLATION, v. 3871.

v. 830. *Suz sun mantel en fait la cuntenance.* Bédier, *Commentaires*, pp. 208–9, agrees with Littré's gloss: '*en fait la cuntenance* [d'homme affligé]'. Leo Spitzer, "Le vers 830 du *Roland*," *Romania* 68 (1944/45): 471–77: 'sous son manteau il cache son angoisse', i.e., 'il en prend son parti'; Whitehead: "*en faire la cuntenance* conceal one's emotion (?)"; Moignet: 'Sous son manteau, il a la contenance de ses sentiments' (in note, p. 80: "il a la contenance que lui vaut son inquiétude, étant donné la situation et les présages qu'il a eus"); Owen: 'Hiding his anguished face beneath his cloak'. Vance, *Reading the Song of Roland*, p. 41, writes of Charlemagne's "regard for the potency of the spoken word" and desire to forestall the tragedy by not verbalizing it. Turoldus's locution may be ambiguous, but the Emperor's gesture is not. Foulet, *Glossary of the First Continuation*, p. 180, terms it "un signe de grande douleur ou d'angoisse." Conrad, v. 2737, has Marsile hiding beneath his cloak in order to weep; similar gestures are recorded in *Thèbes*, v. 8139; *Yvain*, vv. 3960–3961; *La Folie Tristan de Berne* (ed. Ernest Hoepffner, 2d ed., Publications de la Faculté des lettres de l'Université de Strasbourg, Textes d'étude 3 [Paris: Les Belles Lettres, 1949]), v. 210; *La Folie Tristan d'Oxford*, v. 478. Cf. 1 Kings 19:13 (Elijah's encounter with God).

v. 839. *estrange marche*. Moignet: 'marche étrangère'; Owen: 'foreign soil'. Cf., however, Harrison: 'hostile land'. Lejeune, "La signification du nom 'marche'," p. 267: "L'endroit où est resté Roland est considéré ici non pas comme la marche de la *Francia*, mais bien comme la marche du pays sarrasin, d'où l'adjectif *estrange*, étrangère. La réflexion de Charlemagne, laconique, est destinée à montrer combien la position de Roland est périlleuse." See also INTRODUCTION, 17.

v. 840. *escange*. Jones, p. 43: "When Charlemagne dreams that he is going to lose Roland, his chief regret is that he will be unable to replace him. . . . In other words, he seems sadder at being bereft of his defender than at being bereaved of his nephew." See, however, COMMENTARY, 44 (v. 3714).

v. 842. *.C. milie*. See COMMENTARY, 35 and note 17.

vv. 849–850. *almaçurs, cunturs*. Jenkins: "Arabic *al mansûr* 'the victorious', surname of Mohammed ibn-Ali-Abir"; Horrent, pp. 289–90; Moignet: "*Cunturs* < *comitores*, lat. médiéval: titre féodal."

v. 852. *taburs*. Saracen drums constitute one of the rare bits of local color in the *Song of Roland*. Foulet, *Glossaire*, p. 481; Smail, *Crusading Warfare*, p. 76.

v. 862. *belement en riant*. Ménard, *Le Rire*, p. 31, n. 44, asserts that the meaning here is 'en souriant aimablement' or 'en souriant doucement', rather than 'en riant de bon coeur' (see also p. 35, n. 69), but this implies too benign a view of Aelroth.

v. 869. *pans*. The portions of territory that make up a feudal domain.

v. 870. *porz d'Espaigne, Durestant*. Many scholars suggest that *Espaigne* may be a scribal error due to dittography (cf. v. 869). Venice IV (li porti d'Aspre) offers a workable alternate reading. Jenkins; Delbouille, *Genèse*, p. 123; Segre. However, the expression does occur elsewhere in this manuscript (vv. 824, 1103, 1152). *Durestant* is generally considered to be a Spanish city (for possible identifications, see Jenkins), but Lejeune, "Le Mont-Saint-Michel-au-Péril-de-la-Mer," p. 432, citing Flutre, *Table des noms propres*, p. 232, proposes Wijk te Duurstede in Holland. See also Wathelet-Willem, *Recherches*, 1:622–23.

v. 871. *recrerrunt*. Jones, p. 53: "Bédier renders the words *si recrerrunt si Francs* as 'les Français se rendront', yet surrender is not necessarily implied." Various shadings of meaning are provided by Foulet, *Glossaire*.

v. 886. *de males arz*. Jenkins, p. 291: 'crafty, wily'. Cf. v. 1392: *artimal* 'necromancy'. The notion of calling down the devil is doubtless involved here, as well as in v. 918 (male vode).

v. 888. Most editors assume that at least one line, containing Corsalis's *vantance*, is missing here. For discussion, see Segre, pp. 172–73.

v. 889. *Brigant*. The assonance is false, and many editors emend to *Brigal* on the basis of v. 1261. See, however, Bédier, *Commentaires*, p. 270.

v. 892. *Rencesvals*. On the spelling of this word, see INTRODUCTION, note 341.

v. 894. *Balaguez*. Cf. OXFORD TEXT, ENGLISH TRANSLATION, v. 63.

v. 901. *juër*. Most editors emend to *guier*, a variant found in Venice IV, Venice VII, and Châteauroux. However, Moignet believes *juër* may simply be an Anglo-Norman graph for the same word. For discussion and bibliography, see Segre.

v. 918. *male vode*. See OXFORD TEXT, ENGLISH TRANSLATION, v. 886.

v. 934. *orguill*. See OXFORD TEXT, ENGLISH TRANSLATION, v. 28.

v. 957. *beltet*. Paul Aebischer, *Rolandiana et Oliveriana. Recueil d'études sur les chansons de geste*, Publications romanes et françaises 92 (Geneva: Droz, 1967), p. 266: 'courage, vigueur, vertus chevaleresques' (see also Dufournet, *Cours sur Roland*, p. 194). But, as pointed out by Zumthor, *Langue et techniques poétiques*, pp. 191–92, the phrase suggests courtliness. Cf. Burgess, *Vocabulaire pré-courtois*, p. 120 (referring to vv. 955–957): "Ces vers servent d'ouverture au monde courtois, où la devise est, peut-être, sans beauté, pas d'amour."

v. 969. *France en ert hunie.* Jones, p. 48, notes the close connection between defeat and shame in this passage. Margariz's phrase will be echoed by Oliver in v. 1734. Gérard, "L'axe Roland-Ganelon," p. 449. Cf. also vv. 1927, 2337.

v. 979. *dun = dunt.* See OXFORD TEXT, ENGLISH TRANSLATION, vv. 452, 2265.

v. 993. *sapide.* The last four letters were written by the revisor over an erasure. The correct Anglo-Norman form would be *sapei(d)e.* Moignet.

v. 1017. *Oliver est desur un pui.* Over an erasure, the revisor wrote *haut muntez,* which results in a false assonance. Venice IV reads: *Oliver monta desor o pei altor,* suggesting that the revisor read *halçur* (= *altor*) at the end of this verse as *haut,* then added the last word of v. 1028.

v. 1018. *su.* The revisor added a *z,* which is emended by all editors to *r.* However, it is not clear that there was an erasure (see Whitehead, p. 120; Segre, p. 191) and the scribe may have written *su.* On the latter form, see OXFORD TEXT, ENGLISH TRANSLATION, v. 47.

v. 1032. *safrez.* On the meaning of this word, see Dufournet, *Cours sur Roland,* p. 31.

v. 1036. *E = En.* See OXFORD TEXT, ENGLISH TRANSLATION, v. 42.

v. 1037. *Cum il einz pout.* Moignet: 'Le plus vite qu'il peut' (in note, p. 94: "'comme il put tout d'abord, au plus tôt', d'où 'dès qu'il put', 'du plus vite qu'il put'").

v. 1048. *Ja pur murir.* The locution, which also appears in vv. 1096, 1909, 3041, 3048, and 3812, was studied by F. J. Tanquerey, "Ancien français *por les membres trenchier,*" *Romania* 64 (1938): 1–17.

v. 1088. *Mis talenz en est graigne.* For possible meanings, see Burgess, "*Talent* in Early Old French," pp. 449–51.

v. 1094. *meveillus.* See OXFORD TEXT, ENGLISH TRANSLATION, v. 316.

v. 1099. *veez en alques.* Jenkins: 'you already see not a few of them'; Foulet, *Glossaire:* "'voyez-en un certain nombre', c'est-à-dire 'voyez, les voilà en nombre'"; Whitehead, p. 131: 'just look at them'; Moignet: 'voyez combien ils sont' (in note, p. 98: "*Alques* est ici pronom: 'quelques-uns'").

v. 1100. *trop.* See OXFORD TEXT, ENGLISH TRANSLATION, v. 317.

v. 1123. The first hemistich reads *E purrunt dire,* but the conjunction, which is in the margin, and the third word, which is over an erasure, are by the revisor. For conjectures, see Segre.

v. 1136. *decendent.* The scribe wrote *cendent,* an inattention the revisor remedied by adding *de* (not *des,* as in Moignet) above the line.

v. 1148. *deners.* An obvious allusion to the thirty pieces of silver agreed upon by Judas and the High Priests as the price for Jesus. Strictly speaking, shekels (Matthew 26:16) were not the same as denarii (1 shekel = 4 drachmas), but *deniers* was commonly used in this sense. *Conte del graal,* vv. 6269–6270: "*Car hui fu cil en crois pendus | Qui fu trente deniers vendus.*"

v. 1149. *devreit.* See OXFORD TEXT, ENGLISH TRANSLATION, v. 389.

v. 1151. *esleger.* Burger, "Les deux scènes du cor," p. 115: "un rappel évident de la scène de l'investiture de Roland" [i.e., v. 759].

v. 1157. *su = sum.* See OXFORD TEXT, ENGLISH TRANSLATION, v. 42.

v. 1158. *renges.* Almost certainly a scribal error for either *lengues* (= *langues*), the reading found in Châteauroux, Venice VII, Paris, and Lyon, or *frenges.* The word *renges* usually refers to the ring or straps used to hang a sword from a belt.

v. 1165. *alez.* Most editors emend this word, which was added by the revisor above the line, to *le.* However, see Moignet.

v. 1174. *Cil ki la sunt ne funt mie a blasmer.* The line is repeated almost verbatim in v. 1718. Bédier believed Oliver was alluding here to the rearguard, rather than to Charles and his men. See, however, Burger, "Les deux scènes du cor," pp. 120 and 121, n. 6; Jones, p. 88.

v. 1204. *Pleine sa hanste.* The meaning of this expression is much debated. Jenkins;

Foulet, *Glossaire*, p. 446; D. J. A. Ross, "Pleine sa hanste," *Medium Aevum* 20 (1951): 1–10; W. D. Elcock, "Pleine sa hanste," *French Studies* 7 (1953): 35–47; Julian Harris, "*Pleine sa hanste* in the *Chanson de Roland*," *French and Provençal Lexicography: Essays Presented to Honor Alexander Herman Schutz*, eds. Urban T. Holmes and Kenneth R. Scholberg (Columbus: Ohio State University Press, 1964), pp. 100–117; Noel L. Corbett, "Encore une fois *pleine sa hanste*," *Revue de linguistique romane* 33 (1969): 349–52; Dufournet, *Cours sur Roland*, pp. 39–42; Diana Teresa Mériz, "Encore une fois *pleine sa hanste*," *Romania* 94 (1973): 549–54; Charles François, " 'Pleine sa hanste': remises en question," *Marche romane* 25 (1975): 11–29.

v. 1207. *Ultre.* Ménard, *Le Rire*, pp. 124–25: "Il faut donc voir dans *outre* quelque chose qui signifie 'videz le champ', 'quittez ce bas monde', 'allez au diable'." Cf. Moignet: 'Arrière' (discussion, p. 104).

v. 1214. *er = ert.* See OXFORD TEXT, ENGLISH TRANSLATION, v. 452.

v. 1221. *E se s'escriet.* Some editors emend to *E si escriet*, others to *E si s'escriet*. The conjunction *se* 'if' (Lat. *si*) is at times written *si* in this manuscript, but the conjunction and adverb *si* 'and', 'then' (Lat. *sic*) is never spelled *se*. However, the latter form is not uncommon. Lucien Foulet, *Petite Syntaxe de l'ancien français*, 3d ed., 2e série: Manuels (Paris: Champion, 1930), par. 439; Ménard, *Syntaxe*, par. 311.

v. 1236. *estrage = estrange.* See OXFORD TEXT, ENGLISH TRANSLATION, v. 42.

v. 1237. *le = les.* See OXFORD TEXT, ENGLISH TRANSLATION, v. 44.

v. 1243. *arcvesques.* On the effacement of Anglo-Norman mute *e* in interconsonantal position, see Pope, *From Latin to Modern French*, par. 1134.

v. 1251. *arere.* Many editors emend to *a tere*, a reading found in all the other versions; cf. also v. 2885. The letter *r* is easily confused with *t* in this copy. Samaran, p. 34. See, however, Joseph Bédier, "De l'édition princeps de la *Chanson de Roland* aux éditions les plus récentes: Nouvelles remarques sur l'art d'établir les anciens textes," *Romania* 64 (1938): 218; Dufournet, *Cours sur Roland*, p. 37.

v. 1274. *Gente.* Jones, p. 63: 'violent'.

v. 1279. *qui qu'en peist u qui nun.* Whitehead: 'no matter whom it grieves'; Ménard, *Le Rire*, p. 111: 'Le pleure qui veut!'; Moignet: 'qu'on en soit fâché ou non' (in note, p. 110: "mot à mot 'à qui qu'il en pèse ou à qui non' "); Owen: 'whoever grieves or no'.

v. 1294. *entre les dous furceles.* See OXFORD TEXT, ENGLISH TRANSLATION, v. 2249.

v. 1297. *fiet = fiert.* See OXFORD TEXT, ENGLISH TRANSLATION, v. 316.

v. 1300. *les pans.* See OXFORD TEXT, ENGLISH TRANSLATION, v. 3141.

v. 1301. *trechant = trenchant.* See OXFORD TEXT, ENGLISH TRANSLATION, v. 42.

v. 1308. *.XII. pers.* See MANUSCRIPT, v. 990.

v. 1312. *isnels.* Jones, p. 28: 'courageous'.

v. 1327. *le cors.* Venice IV's *li cef* (= *le chef*) offers a more plausible reading (Segre; Dufournet, *Cours sur Roland*, p. 55, n. 1), but a word for 'coif' (v. 3436: la coife; cf. v. 1293: la ventaille) would be even more satisfying. Cf., however, v. 1372.

v. 1341. *su = sur.* See OXFORD TEXT, ENGLISH TRANSLATION, v. 47.

vv. 1388–1389. All editors agree that the scribe unintentionally conflated two verses here. For conjectures, see Segre. *Burdele* (Lat. *Burdigala*, MFr. *Bordeaux*) is found in vv. 1289 and 3684, but the form without an *e* is not uncommon. Bédier, *Commentaires*, p. 182.

v. 1405. *De ço qui calt.* See COMMENTARY, 20.

v. 1406. *servis = servise.* See OXFORD TEXT, ENGLISH TRANSLATION, v. 210.

v. 1409. *pendre.* Hanging seems to be in conflict with the quartering in store for Ganelon at the end of this poem. Bowra, *Heroic Poetry*, p. 323, suggests that the poet is setting a false trail in order to surprise us later. Actually, dismemberment is hinted at in the preceding verse. Dorfman, *Narreme*, p. 109. In Venice IV (v. 6000), the traitor is drawn and quartered, then hanged, thus reconciling both outcomes. The original may have read *perdre*. Cf. v. 937: *Li .XII. per tuit sunt jugez a perdre*. This would mean that the poet assonated oral *e* with nasal *e*, which he does not do elsewhere (Jenkins, pp. ci, civ). However, for similar instances of so-called false assonances, see Bédier, *Commentaires*, pp. 270–97.

v. 1417. *millers*. Mortier, Whitehead (p. 122), and Segre read *millere*. The last letter, which is either a long *s* or an elongated *e*, may have been added by the revisor (Whitehead, p. 122), although this is not mentioned by Samaran, p. 21. Cf. v. 1439.

v. 1420. *guarnemenz*. Various interpretations of this word are discussed by Segre, pp. 250–51.

v. 1426. *e menut e suvent*. See COMMENTARY, 26 (v. 2364).

vv. 1443–1444. Mortier ascribes this phrase to the poet, not Turpin.

v. 1457. *juree*. The verb *jurer* here evidently means 'to enter into a conspiracy' (cf. Lat. *conjurare*), as is clear from Paris (*Que Ganelons a vers noz porparlee*) and from the notion of concealment in the following verse.

vv. 1467 ff. On the order of Laisses 113–126, see COMMENTARY, 17.

v. 1512. *chef*. Segre reads the last letter of this word as a long *s*.

v. 1514. *jamais*. On the meaning here, see Foulet, *Glossaire*, p. 408.

v. 1516. *Encuntre mei fait asez a preiser*. Jenkins, note to v. 1559: "Several translators understand *encontre* as merely locative (Gautier: 'à mes côtés,' cf. v. 793), but the meaning is rather 'as compared with me,' as plainly in vv. 376, 926, 1496 [= 1657]. Roland keenly enjoys the feats of his brother-in-arms, but he is by no means ready to admit Oliver as a serious rival to himself. It is a bit of good-humored boasting. Or, have we here the *orgueil* of which Ganelon complained so bitterly (v. 389)?" Similar observation apropos of Roland's pride "[qui] conduit à Roncevaux" in Le Gentil, p. 123, without, however, conceding the possibility of a comradely exchange.

v. 1547. *paient*. On inorganic *t* in this copy, see Bédier, *Commentaires*, p. 261.

v. 1557. *azur*. Not the color of the clear sky, but the heraldic tincture, a bright blue. Brault, *Early Blazon*, pp. 113–14.

v. 1560. *tens*. On this and similar expressions, see Brault, "Le Thème de la Mort," p. 225, n. 11. The example in v. 2366 was accidentally omitted from this list.

v. 1591. *ki oït del cuntence*. The word *oit* was added above the line between *ki* and *del* by the revisor. The other copies provide various phrases containing the verb *curre* 'to run'. Bédier, *Commentaires*, p. 216: "On n'a rien proposé de satisfaisant pour l'interprétation de ce vers"; Whitehead: 'exerts himself in running, puts forth his full speed'; Owen: 'on to a fiery pace'; Moignet: 'qui entendit la dispute' (in note, p. 130: "Le texte est douteux et le sens obscur"). For conjectures, see Jenkins, note to v. 1634; Segre.

v. 1600. *voel* = *voelt*. See OXFORD TEXT, ENGLISH TRANSLATION, v. 452.

v. 1605. *le* = *les*. See OXFORD TEXT, ENGLISH TRANSLATION, v. 44.

v. 1615. Most editors agree that a verse, identifying the speakers (doubtless the pagans), is missing here. For discussion, see Bédier, *Commentaires*, p. 161; Segre.

v. 1619. *de* = *del*. See OXFORD TEXT, ENGLISH TRANSLATION, v. 23.

v. 1633. *Teches*. Editors usually omit the *t*, which the revisor added over the line between the *e* and the *c*. Cf., however, English words of Anglo-Norman provenance such as *vetch*.

v. 1652. *copiez*. The reading (*coplez* = *colpez*?) and meaning of this word are much debated. See Jenkins, note to vv. 1490 ff.; Foulet, *Glossaire*; Moignet, p. 122; Segre. The expression may have given rise to the peculiar depiction of the martlet in heraldry, which is traditionally shown without feet. Brault, *Early Blazon*, pp. 241–42.

v. 1653. *quisse*. Many editors read *quifse*, but the horizontal stroke of the *f* may be due to the bulge half way up the shaft of the following long *s*. Cf. Samaran, p. 32.

v. 1660. *l'escut a miracle*. Jenkins places a comma after *l'escut* to indicate that what follows refers to the blow, not the shield (note to v. 1499: "Turpin dealt a *superhuman* blow upon Abisme's shield"). Jenkins's interpretation was accepted by Whitehead, p. 153 ('with prodigious force') and Owen ('a wondrous blow'). Moignet reads *a miracle* as one word and translates 'de l'émir (?)'. That *a miracle* refers to Abisme's shield seems clear from the details that follow, notably the allusion in v. 1663 to its diabolical origin. For similar views, see Lejeune and Stiennon, 1:33, 39–40 (n. 17: 'à merveille'); Segre, note to v. [1660], pointing to OFr. *a miraville*. The shield is not marvelous in the usual sense, that is, it does not excite amazed admiration the way a miracle would. Rather, it is to be equated with *males arz* (v. 886), *artimal* (v. 1392), *sorz* and *falserie* (v. 3665), and produces a shudder of horror. Turoldus, like his contemporaries, viewed necromancy as *mors animae* (*Pseudo-Turpin*, ed. Meredith-Jones, p. 229). Cf. the use of *martirie* in a pejorative sense in vv. 591, 1166, and 1628. On the belief that the devil could work miracles, see Le Goff, *Civilisation*, p. 208.

v. 1663. *Val Metas.* Is there perhaps an inverted connection here with the expression *inter duas metas* 'between two boundary marks [of Nero's Circus]', the traditional scene of Saint Peter's crucifixion? On the latter, see Réau, III, 3:1078.

v. 1679. *dulor.* Moignet: 'souffrance'. See, however, Jones, p. 86.

v. 1686. *quatre turs.* Is Turoldus referring here to the whole battle or merely to the second phase? For bibliography and discussion, see Horrent, p. 227, n. 1; Aurelio Roncaglia, "Les quatre eschielles de Rollant," *Cultura Neolatina* 21 (1961): 191–205.

v. 1693. *que vos en haitet.* Jenkins: 'What do *you* think we had better do?' Whitehead: 'what cheer?, how do you feel about it?' Moignet (in note, p. 134: "*haitier* . . . équivaut ici à 'paraître bon'").

v. 1710. *hardement.* Burger, "Les deux scènes du cor," pp. 120–21: "Je comprends donc: 'Si vous cornez il n'y aura miette de hardiesse', c'est-à-dire que les derniers combattants perdront courage: en le voyant sonner avec ses bras ensanglantés, ils comprendront que Roland lui-même désespère de la victoire . . ."

v. 1711. *Ja.* Ernest Hoepffner, "Les rapports littéraires entre les premières chansons de geste," *Studi Medievali*, n.s., 4 (1931): 243, n. 3: 'Déjà' ("constatation, non exclamation"). For Bédier's translation ('Mais'), see COMMENTARY, 18, n. 18. Jenkins, p. 335: 'behold!'; Foulet, *Glossaire*, p. 408: "'Dès maintenant', peut avoir valeur augmentative, 'les choses étant ce qu'elles sont', 'tout bien considéré', 'un fait est acquis, c'est que'. On traduira suivant les cas par 'certes', 'ah', 'bien' . . . et 1711 'mais je vois que'." Segre, note to v. 1711, claims that the Old Norse translation (see COMMENTARY, 18, note 18) "conferma in tutto la lez. di O" (thus *Ja* 'Maintenant').

v. 1715. *Ne sereit vasselage.* Burger, "Les deux scènes du cor," p. 120: 'Ce ne serait pas d'un bon vassal'. In the discussion that followed Burger's paper, Le Gentil characterized this interpretation as "ingénieuse, mais discutable"; Burger replied: "Roland n'agirait pas en vassal s'il appelait Charlemagne, maintenant qu'il est trop tard, au risque de lui attirer le reproche d'avoir tardé" (p. 125). Dufournet, *Cours sur Roland*, p. 153, accepts Burger's view.

v. 1718. *Cil ki la sunt.* See OXFORD TEXT, ENGLISH TRANSLATION, v. 1174. Burger, "Les deux scènes du cor," p. 120: "Il s'agit donc d'un argument personnel d'Olivier et non de la reprise ironique d'un argument de Roland."

v. 1729. *faite u prise.* Bédier, *Commentaires*, p. 218: "comment une bataille *faite* peut-elle s'opposer à une bataille *prise*? . . . La leçon reste obscure. Comment interpréter le fait singulier que les syllabes *u prise* se répètent au début du vers suivant: U *pris u mort* . . . ?" Foulet, *Glossaire*, p. 450: "l'emploi du mot *prise* au v. 1729 reste obscur"; Moignet: 'faite ou remportée (?)' (in note, p. 136: "le texte n'est pas clair; *faite e prise* 'livrée et gagnée', serait meilleur." For conjectures, see Segre.

v. 1761. *ahans.* On the hagiographic background of this term, see Anna Granville Hatcher, "The Old French Poem St. Alexis: A Mathematical Demonstration,"

Traditio 8 (1952): 138, note; Burgess, *Vocabulaire pré-courtois*, pp. 71–72, n. 16, 141–42.

v. 1764. *De sun cervel le temple.* One thinks of the temporal artery rather than of the temporal bone here.

v. 1769. *sunast.* On this use of the subjunctive imperfect in a conditional sentence, see Jenkins, p. cxxxii.

v. 1773. *orgoill.* See OXFORD TEXT, ENGLISH TRANSLATION, v. 28.

v. 1790. *Baron i fait la peine.* Jenkins emends *peine* to read *peinte* and translates: '(Yes, and it is) because it is the blast of a hero (Roland)'. For other readings and interpretations of this word, see Segre.

v. 1792. *feindre.* Jenkins: 'to be undecided as' to, hesitate as to' (in note to v. 1792: "*s'en feindre* is to 'hang back' in time of battle, for discreditable reasons; to Naimon's mind, to act upon Ganelon's advice would be a disgrace"); Foulet, *Glossaire:* 'Hésiter à agir, se dérober'; Whitehead: 'act in a craven or half-hearted fashion'; Moignet: "*soi feindre*, c'est feindre de faire quelque chose et, en conséquence, ne pas faire quelque chose." The verb may be an allusion to Judas's leave-taking (John 13:21 ff.) after the devil has entered his body. See COMMENTARY, 8.

v. 1809. *flabur = flambur.* See OXFORD TEXT, ENGLISH TRANSLATION, v. 42.

v. 1822. *des mielz e des pejurs.* Moignet: 'des meilleurs et des pires'; Owen: 'both the best and worst'. Cf., however, Jones, p. 20: "*bon* usually means advantageous, useful, or fit for a given function."

v. 1848. *blecet.* Jenkins, note to v. 1848: 'distressed'; Foulet, *Glossaire:* "'Blesser', mais en un sens plus large qu'aujourd'hui: 'mettre à mal'"; Whitehead: 'in difficulties'. Cf., however, Harrison: 'injured'; Owen: 'With such a wound'.

v. 1862. *rubostl.* Jenkins, p. 365: 'cruel, harsh'; Foulet, *Glossaire:* "Ce mot, dont la forme est suspecte, doit sans doute être identifié à l'adjectif *rubeste, rubestre*, 'sauvage', 'âpre', 'funeste': *a tant rubostl exill* 'par une destruction si complète'"; Whitehead, p. 124: "the *l* most probably due to the *ll* of *exill* and replacing an original *e*; *ruboste* is a hapax, but may easily be a genuine variant of *rubeste* ('harsh')"; Moignet, and Dufournet, *Cours sur Roland*, p. 36, agree with Foulet.

v. 1867. *murra = murrai.* See OXFORD TEXT, ENGLISH TRANSLATION, v. 290.

v. 1887. *bataill = bataille.* See OXFORD TEXT, ENGLISH TRANSLATION, v. 210.

v. 1914. *Marganices.* Many editors emend to *l'Algalifes* on the basis of v. 681. See also vv. 1943 and 1954.

v. 1922. *matyrie = martyrie.* See OXFORD TEXT, ENGLISH TRANSLATION, v. 316.

v. 1932. *Quan = Quant.* See OXFORD TEXT, ENGLISH TRANSLATION, v. 452. Cf. v. 601.

v. 1937. *car jol vos recumenz.* Cf. vv. 1677, 1884. Foulet, *Glossaire:* 'recommencer le combat' ("le *vos* a le même sens que dans 'je *vous* lui ferai son affaire'"); Moignet: 'car je recommence à vous le dire'; Owen: 'once more I'll lead you to the fray'.

v. 1941. *orgoil.* 'Overconfidence' because of the pagans' Lucifer-like self-sufficiency.

v. 1948. *col = colp.* See OXFORD TEXT, ENGLISH TRANSLATION, v. 317.

v. 1963. *altrui.* Here, as in v. 380, the pronoun seems to mean simply 'another, someone else'; however, its use in v. 3959 suggests that *altrui* could refer to members of one's own family as well.

v. 1966. *sez.* On this term, which is derived from Lat. *satis*, see *Perlesvaus*, 2:337, note to line 8190.

v. 1979. *Teint fut e pers, desculuret e pale.* The epithets in this verse are all synonymous. Silvio Pellegrini, "Iterazioni sinonimiche nella *Canzone di Rolando*," *Studi mediolatini e volgari* 1 (1953): 160, 163. On the form *desculuret*, see OXFORD TEXT, ENGLISH TRANSLATION, v. 2218.

v. 2013. *al tere.* Most editors emend to *a la tere*, but the use of the enclitic *al* before a feminine noun is not unusual in Anglo-Norman; cf. vv. 3368, 3668.

v. 2030. *mor* = *mort* (or *morz*). See MANUSCRIPT, v. 1926; OXFORD TEXT, ENGLISH TRANSLATION, v. 452.

v. 2042. *sis unt paiens vencut*. Lejeune, "La composition," p. 258, proposes the emendation *si sunt paien vencut*, the word *si* meaning 'et pourtant'. This suggestion is accepted by Payen, *Le Motif du repentir*, p. 129, n. 68.

v. 2063. *recreant*. Foulet, *Glossaire*, p. 464, erroneously lists this word under the definition 's'avouer vaincu'. Cf. Jones, p. 54, 'coward'. For the use mentioned by Foulet, see v. 2088, a line said by Burgess, *Vocabulaire pré-courtois*, p. 107, to sum up chivalric virtue.

v. 2065. *le* = *les*. See OXFORD TEXT, ENGLISH TRANSLATION, v. 44.

v. 2097. *E*. This appears to be a graph for *En* (Moignet, p. 160; cf. OXFORD TEXT, ENGLISH TRANSLATION, v. 42), but the interpretation of this passage is much debated. See Segre.

v. 2099. *gentemet* = *gentement*. See OXFORD TEXT, ENGLISH TRANSLATION, v. 42.

v. 2110. *grasles* = *graisles*. See OXFORD TEXT, ENGLISH TRANSLATION, v. 290.

v. 2126. *Ne lur lerat*. The letters *ler* were added over the line by the revisor. The verse is not found in any other copy. According to Moignet, *ne* = *nel*, but other editors emend to *nes*. For these and other conjectures, see Segre.

v. 2131. *Ça vus traiez*. The adverb *ça* means 'here' in v. 374, but 'there' in v. 1784. Venice IV, v. 2274 (for numbering, see Segre, p. xxxix), substitutes the phrase "*Iosteç vos*" ('Come close to me'; cf. Oxford, v. 1976), suggesting that *ça* in the Bodleian copy means 'here'. The Norse version has an equivalent expression (Aebischer's translation: "Tenons-nous ici les deux ensemble") and ascribes the phrase to Turpin and Roland. However, Turoldus consistently uses the first-hemistich formula *Dit* or *Dist l'un a l'altre* when referring to Saracens (vv. 1910, 1942, and 2114; cf. v. 3798). The Emperor's imminent return is mentioned by Turpin in v. 2145, but everywhere else, Charles's coming inspires the Saracens with fear (vv. 2114, 2115, and 2149).

v. 2143. *Durendal*. Other versions of the poem also mention Almace, Turpin's sword, here, attenuating the seeming immodesty of Roland's claim.

v. 2145. *nus*. It is possible to read this word as *vus*.

v. 2147. *jurz ... ajurnez*. On this *figura etymologica*, see Zumthor, *Langue et techniques poétiques*, p. 113 (bibliography in n. 1).

v. 2157. *L'escut Rollant*. The scribe wrote *Le Roll'*, which the revisor corrected by inserting the word *lescut* over the line, inadvertently adding an extra article in the process.

v. 2159. *ad*. Most editors emend to *unt*, but the possibility that the poet wished to suggest that not a single spear touched Roland is not to be ruled out. Whitehead evidently intended to emend (p. 124, note), but he neglected to do so in his text. Cf. OXFORD TEXT, ENGLISH TRANSLATION, v. 2204.

v. 2183. *est vostre*. The original reading was almost certainly *nostre*, which, Segre points out, is supported by all other copies.

v. 2187. *Attun*. This name, which it is possible to read as *Atuin*, appears to be a variant of the oblique form of Otes, who is said to be Berengier's companion in v. 795.

v. 2205. *les ad*. Most editors emend to *l'ad*. See, however, Whitehead; Dufournet, *Cours sur Roland*, pp. 37–38. Cf. OXFORD TEXT, ENGLISH TRANSLATION, v. 2159.

vv. 2211, 2213. In these two verses the second hemistich is identical and a scribal error is suspected in v. 2213, which, moreover, does not appear in any other version. It is possible to read *veintre* as *veincre* in v. 2211, but not in v. 2213.

v. 2218. *desculurer*. All editors emend to *desculurez*, and it would appear that the scribe simply made a blunder, perhaps because his eye was drawn to the ending of the verses that precede and follow. A simple confusion of *z* with *r* is also possible. However, in a similar circumstance the scribe used the form *desculuret*, not *desculurez* (v. 1979: Teint fut e pers, desculuret e pale). Also, Venice IV reads *il est discolorer*, while Cambridge and Paris, the only other copies preserving this verse, provide *print a descoulourer* and *prinst a descoulorer*, respectively. Since the line may very well be corrupt, then, no emendation seems permissible.

v. 2249. *entre les dous furceles*. The locution also appears in v. 1294. Mario Roques, "*Entre les dous furceles (Roland, vv. 1294 et 2249)*," *Studies in French Language and Mediaeval Literature Presented to Professor Mildred K. Pope by Pupils, Colleagues, and Friends* (Manchester: University Press, 1939), pp. 321–28, suggests that the collarbone and the midriff are the two 'little forks'. The expression is curious, however, and the customary locution, *entre les dous mameles*, which is found in Venice IV and Cambridge, may simply have been misread by the Oxford copyist. On the confusion of *a* and *u*, see Samaran, p. 34, and MANUSCRIPT, vv. 1215 and 1452. Samaran also notes *ri* for *n* (cf. here *rc* for *m*). Crossed hands over the breast are a sign of humility (Katzenellenbogen, *Allegories*, p. 83) or repose (Erwin Panofsky, *Tomb Sculpture* [New York: Abrams, 1964], p. 56). Cf. Meredith-Jones, p. 319, note to p. 204, line ii.

v. 2260. *s'e* = *s'en*. See OXFORD TEXT, ENGLISH TRANSLATION, v. 42.

v. 2265. *Dun* = *Dunt*. See Moignet, p. 170; OXFORD TEXT, ENGLISH TRANSLATION, vv. 452, 979.

v. 2279. *mortel rage*. See OXFORD TEXT, ENGLISH TRANSLATION, v. 747.

v. 2283. *tireres*. Most editors emend to *tirer*. Jenkins: "possibly this reading hides the common OF expression *en cel termine*, 'at this juncture.' None of the other versions suggests a reading *tirer* in this verse: at this point they speak merely of a recovery from fainting." Cf., however, Moignet, p. 170: "*Tireres* du ms. peut être conservé: c'est une forme de cas sujet (avec faute d'emploi) de l'infinitif substantivé." In the other copies of the poem, the Saracen pulls Roland's beard. For bibliography and discussion, see Segre. Add Ian Short, "Roland's Final Combat," *Cultura Neolatina* 30 (1970): 135–55.

v. 2287. *unkes*. The meanings 'Pas un instant' and 'en aucune façon' are listed by Foulet, *Glossaire*, p. 494, but no reference to this verse is provided.

v. 2288. *ki gemmet fut a or*. Bédier: 'gemmé, paré d'or'. Cf. Henry, *Chrestomathie*, 2:18, note to v. 30: "plutôt 'garni de pierres précieuses serties dans l'or'."

v. 2300. *byse*. Venice IV substitutes *brune*, which fits the assonance better. See Segre.

v. 2304. *bone*. The meaning of this term is discussed by Jones, pp. 19–21.

vv. 2312, 2313. *sardonie*, *n'esgrunie*. Many editors emend *sardonie* to *Sardanie* (Sartaigne = Ceritania, Spain, or Sardeigne = Sardinia). Cf. CL *sardonyx* 'onyx' and Late Latin (*lapis*) *sardinis* 'sard, sardine (a kind of chalcedony)'. For these conjectures, see Jenkins; Segre. The words *sardonie* and *n'esgrunie* do not assonate properly. Bédier, *Commentaires*, p. 297. For conjectures, see Segre.

v. 2319. *agle* = *angle*. See OXFORD TEXT, ENGLISH TRANSLATION, v. 42. Samaran, p. 34, suggests the scribe inadvertently omitted the titulus and that the original reading was *angele*.

v. 2337. *Pere*. The manuscript reads *pre* with a horizontal stroke through the tail of the *p*, the abbreviation for *per*. See Whitehead, p. xv and n. 3. On this type of dittography, see Samaran, p. 33.

v. 2352. *avrai cunquises*. On this tense, see OXFORD TEXT, ENGLISH TRANSLATION, v. 446.

v. 2359. *ensumet*. Editors generally delete this word (Moignet, p. 176: "Après *olifan*, le ms. porte le mot *ensumet* qui n'offre aucun sens") and are thus able to correct a hypermetric line. However, *ensumet* may be a corruption of *ensement* (or *ensemet* = *ensement*; see OXFORD TEXT, ENGLISH TRANSLATION, v. 42) 'also', and the error may be elsewhere in this verse. In this copy *ensement* is always followed by *cume* (vv. 3173, 3223, 3249; see Foulet, *Glossaire*) and means 'just as, just like', but cf. such uses as

Vie de Saint Thomas Becket, v. 5580: *La cause saint' iglise e la sue ensement*. The only two other versions that preserve this line are Venice IV (Desor lui [se] mist sa spea et l'olifant) and Cambridge (De dessoubz lui tourna son olifan).

v. 2367. *Devers Espaigne*. Cf. vv. 2360 and 2376.

v. 2384. *Patene* = *Paterne*. On this form, see OXFORD TEXT, ENGLISH TRANSLATION, v. 316. This word, which recurs in v. 3100 (Paterne), and *resurrexis* (v. 2385) are listed as Latinisms by Zumthor, *Langue et techniques poétiques*, p. 76. According to Jenkins, the term is derived from Ecclesiastical Latin (*imago*) *paterna = Deus*. See INTRODUCTION, 12; Foulet, *Glossaire*; Bloch and Wartburg, *Dictionnaire*, s.v. Cf. MFr. *Véronique* (Ecclesiastical Latin *vera icona*). Réau, II, 2:465 (but see n. 1); Brieger, *English Art*, p. 137 and, especially, n. 1. I have not found the expression *imago paterna* in any Latin source. The feminine noun *paterna* 'picture of God the Father' is attested in Medieval Latin (Du Cange, 6:211, s.v.), but this could be an ellipsis of, say, *gloria paterna* (Blaise, par. 216). In v. 2384 *Paterne* is God the Father who forgives; in v. 3100 God the Father who protects.

v. 2393. *Cherubin*. Moignet, p. 178: "on s'attendrait plutôt au troisième archange, Raphaël." Cf., however, Jenkins: "there was a widespread belief, drawn from *Gen.* iii:24, that an angel named 'saint Cherubin,' held the flaming sword at the exit of Paradise." See also Bédier, *Commentaires*, p. 312, n. 1; Tuve, *Allegorical Imagery*, p. 155; COMMENTARY, 24 (v. 2262). According to *Tournoiement Antechrist* (*Li Tournoiemenz Antecrit von Huon de Mery*, ed. Georg Wimmer, Ausgaben und Abhandlungen aus dem Gebiete der romanischen Philologie 76 [Marburg: Friedrich, 1888]), v. 1332, Cherubim are *Plus vert que n'est erbe de pré*, but in the General Prologue to the *Canterbury Tales* (*The Works of Geoffrey Chaucer*, ed. Robinson), v. 624, the Summoner *hadde a fyr-reed cherubynnes face*. See also E. Kirschbaum, "L'angelo rosso e l'angelo turchino," *Rivista di archeologia cristiana* 17 (1940): 209–27. Réau, II, 1:41, notes that Cherubim are blue in Enguerrand Quarton's *Coronation of the Virgin* (1453).

v. 2394. *E seint Michel del Peril*. Editors often insert the words *de la mer* between *Michel* and *del*. This emendation is supported by Venice IV. For bibliography and discussion, see Jenkins; Lejeune, "Le Mont-Saint-Michel-au-Péril-de-la-Mer," pp. 417, 419, 430–31; Segre.

v. 2412. *tant me pois enrager*. *Poeir* + infinitive 'to have reason to'. See Jenkins, note to v. 2216, and *Glossary*, p. 355; Foulet, *Glossaire*, p. 448.

v. 2414. *iret*. On the meaning 'anger', not 'anguish', see Foulet, *Glossaire*, p. 407, s.v. iraistre (cf. also irance, ire, ireement, irur ["Le mot désigne tantôt 'colère' 1098, tantôt 'chagrin' 2877, et le plus souvent un sentiment complexe qui tient des deux"]); Jones, p. 46.

v. 2423. *ad fait que proz*. Moignet, p. 182, explains: 'a fait ce que fait un preux', but translates, p. 183: 'a agi en homme de sens'.

v. 2445. *turnez*. Moignet, p. 184: "Le sens est douteux; *turner* semble avoir le sens factitif de 'faire tourner'." For bibliography and discussion, see Jenkins; Segre; Dufournet, *Cours sur Roland*, p. 34.

v. 2473. *miez = mielz*. This is the only occurrence of this form (cf. *mielz, meilz, melz*) in this copy. On the effacement of preconsonantal *l*, see Pope, *From Latin to Modern French*, par. 387.

v. 2475. *Mare fustes, Rollant*. Jenkins provides the literal translation: 'Alas! Roland, that you are no more' and rejects the reading *Mar veistes, Rollant* found in all the other copies. Bédier, *Commentaires*, p. 174, accepts Jenkins's argument. For a contrary view, see Segre.

v. 2476. *paiens*. The manuscript reads *paiens*, but the *s* was added by the revisor. Lecoy, "Notules sur le texte du *Roland* d'Oxford," p. 795; Segre; Dufournet, *Cours sur Roland*, p. 33.

v. 2485. *le = les*. See OXFORD TEXT, ENGLISH TRANSLATION, v. 44.

v. 2491. *e = en*. See OXFORD TEXT, ENGLISH TRANSLATION, v. 42.

v. 2534. *tempez*. The normal OFr. masculine form is *tempier* (< VL *temperium*), found in Venice IV and Paris. Moignet, p. 190, states that the scribe derived a masculine noun from the feminine *tempeste* (< VL *tempesta*), attested in v. 689, but *tempez* may also represent *tempers* with effacement of preconsonantal *r*; see OXFORD TEXT, ENGLISH TRANSLATION, v. 47; on the interchange of the symbols *s* and *z* in Anglo-Norman, see Pope, *From Latin to Modern French*, par. 1231. Possible confusion of *z* and *r* is also not to be ruled out.

v. 2555. *vien = vient*. See OXFORD TEXT, ENGLISH TRANSLATION, v. 452.

v. 2556. *perrun*. On the meaning 'pillar', see references provided in COMMENTARY, 28, n. 11.

v. 2557. *s'i, brohun*. All editors and translators consider *s'i* to be the adverb *si*, "terme de liaison" (Foulet, *Glossaire*, p. 475), but the notion of Charles on a stone step, holding a bear with two chains is very curious. A much more satisfactory reading is provided if one considers *si* to be *s'i*, that is, the elided form of the reflexive pronoun *se* followed by the adverb *i* (= MFr. *y*): 'a bear was being restrained there by two chains'. This requires interpreting *un brohun* to be the subject, which poses no particular problem in this copy, where the oblique functions in this manner in one out of every four cases (Moignet, p. 284, referring to Brian Woledge, J. Beard, C. H. M. Horton, and Ian Short, "La déclinaison des substantifs dans la *Chanson de Roland* [Recherches mécanographiques]," *Romania* 88 [1967]: 145–74). On the animal in question (bear or dog), see Herman Braet, "Le *brohun* de la *Chanson de Roland*," *Zeitschrift für romanische Philologie* 89 (1973): 97–102.

v. 2585. *ses*. Whitehead, p. 126: "*ses ceptre* is generally emended to *sun sceptre*; *ceptre* is, however, a common spelling and the wrong case may be due to the original author."

v. 2586. *pendent*. It is difficult but not impossible to imagine a statue being tied by its hands, then tumbled over (v. 2587). For conjectures, see Segre.

v. 2594. *peinz e escrites*. Foulet, *Glossaire*, p. 383: "faut-il voir dans *escrites* un synonyme de *peinz* ou s'agit-il d'inscriptions explicatives des peintures?" On p. 355 Foulet notes that *culur* in the Oxford copy always refers to the face, except in this passage; Segre observes that, in the Flemish version, Marsile's face is referred to.

v. 2608. *doel*. Jones, pp. 83–84: "The word *doel* is often used in the *SR* to denote the dismay or chagrin felt by the victim of an insult or injury.... Although *doel* is sometimes consociated with pity or affection, it is more often consociated with anger and shame."

v. 2616. *survesquiet*. Jenkins, citing Settegast: "Does it mean 'He lived to a greater age than either Vergil or Homer' (so Bédier) or, 'He lived as long as Vergil and Homer, and survived them'?"

v. 2653. *U = Un*. See OXFORD TEXT, ENGLISH TRANSLATION, v. 42. For *faldestoed*, see OXFORD TEXT, ENGLISH TRANSLATION, v. 115.

v. 2672. *messages*. The term is used in the meaning 'message' as well as 'messenger' in Old French.

v. 2676. *o*. Jenkins: "*o*, or *oi* 'chance', 'occasion'; cf. vv. 3004, 3025. The word appears to be Lat. *ubi*." Jules Cornu, "Trois passages de la *Chanson de Roland* corrigés à tort," *Romania* 9 (1880): 118.

v. 2677. *pleiet*. Jenkins: "The custom of presenting folded the object which constituted the gage, is often attested." Because of the similarity of *pleier* 'to fold' and *plegier* 'to pledge'?

v. 2687. *alte = altre*. On the effacement of postconsonantal *r*, see Bédier, *Commentaires*, p. 260.

v. 2691. *u li burgeis estunt*. Moignet: 'où se tiennent les bourgeois'; Owen: 'where all the townsfolk are', but cf. Segre: "Abbiamo, in O solo ... un valore particolare di *ester*, 'dimorare'."

v. 2704. *perrun*. Dismounting at a horse-block is an epic cliché. Horrent, *Pèlerinage*, p. 55.

v. 2708. *altisme*. On this Latinism, see Zumthor, *Langue et techniques poétiques*, p. 76.

v. 2710. *li*. See COMMENTARY, 32.

v. 2738. *voel* = *voelt*. See OXFORD TEXT, ENGLISH TRANSLATION, v. 452.

v. 2753. *Pui* = *Puis*. See OXFORD TEXT, ENGLISH TRANSLATION, v. 44.

v. 2762. *li*. See COMMENTARY, 32.

v. 2767. *esfreedement*. For the conjectured reading [*tuit*] *esfreed*, see Segre; Dufournet, *Cours sur Roland*, p. 34. The letters *dement* are said by Lecoy, "Notules sur le texte du *Roland* d'Oxford," p. 796, and Dufournet to be by the revisor. The writing is spaced somewhat differently, but I share Segre's view that the entire word is by the original scribe.

v. 2795. *perdit*. All editors emend to *perdiet* in order to avoid a false assonance. However, the argument presented by Bédier, *Commentaires*, p. 294, in defense of *faillir* (v. 801) in an *-e* / *-ie* laisse has won general acceptance and applies here as well.

v. 2815. *de tutes mes oz*. After these words the revisor wrote *launade* (the *n* is above the line between the *u* and the *a*) over an erasure. For conjectures, see Jenkins; Segre.

v. 2816. *est munté*. The revisor added *est* over the word *brun*, and *munté* at the end of the line. Editors agree that the first-hemistich word order found in v. 660 (cf. also vv. 92, 1142, 2708, 2811, 2851, 3003, 3091, and 3869) should be followed here.

v. 2832. *Teres tutes ici*. The revisor erased several letters at the end of this line, added what appears to be *uos redemas* over this, then erased that, too, and wrote *rengnes*. *uos rendemas*, none of which makes any sense. For conjectures, see Whitehead, p. 126; Segre.

v. 2844. *Frant*. The *r* appears over the *a* and the word has been interpreted as *ferant*. Bédier: 'ils pressent leur fuite'; Moignet: 'ils s'enfuient à force d'éperons'.

v. 2846. *eperere* = *emperere*. Cf. MANUSCRIPT, v. 16, and see OXFORD TEXT, ENGLISH TRANSLATION, v. 42. All editors assume that the titulus was inadvertently omitted by the scribe (Samaran, p. 34), which is also possible.

v. 2847. *Sein* = *Seint*. See OXFORD TEXT, ENGLISH TRANSLATION, v. 452.

v. 2849. *descent* = *desceint*. This interpretation, first put forth by Bédier, is accepted by Moignet, p. 208. For other views, see Jenkins; Segre.

v. 2857. *a* = *as*, *Seignus* = *Seignurs*. See OXFORD TEXT, ENGLISH TRANSLATION, vv. 44 and 316.

v. 2875. *en treis perruns*. See COMMENTARY, 24 and 34, note 11.

v. 2879. *Entre ses mains ansdous*. The revisor erased the words that follow and substituted *le priest suus*, a phrase whose meaning is unclear. For conjectures, see Segre.

v. 2894. *vei* = *veit*. See OXFORD TEXT, ENGLISH TRANSLATION, v. 452; Moignet, p. 281.

v. 2900. *Cum en Espaigne venis mal, seignur*. The line is hypometric, the phrasing singular, and no proposal to date is entirely satisfactory. Dufournet, *Cours sur Roland*, p. 38. H. R. Lang, "*Seignor* as a Vocative Singular," *Romanic Review* 3 (1912): 309–10, suggested adding a comma after *mal*, as I have done here (see also Segre), but Foulet, *Glossaire*, p. 472, points out: "partout ailleurs [that is, in this copy] *seignur* a le sens de 'suzerain'. Il n'est jamais employé comme vocatif: c'est *sire* qui a cet emploi." Many editors (e.g., Jenkins, Bédier, Whitehead, Moignet) emend to *venis a mal seignur*, the reading found in Venice IV. Thus Bédier: 'Quel mauvais seigneur tu suivis en Espagne'; Moignet: 'Comme tu es venu en Espagne avec un mauvais seigneur'; Harrison: 'How bad a lord you followed into Spain'; Owen: 'How wrong your lord was to bring you to Spain'. Jenkins explains: "As overlord to Roland, Charles looks upon himself as a failure." See also Vance, *Reading the Song of Roland*, p. 69. For other conjectures, see Eugene Vinaver, "Note sur le vers 2900 de la *Chanson de Roland*," *Mélanges Rita Lejeune*, 2:929–34; Segre.

v. 2910. *Loün*. Cf. v. 2917: *Eis*. This allusion to two different capitals has been much discussed. To the references provided by Menéndez Pidal, pp. 331–33, add Jenkins, note to v. 2910; Horrent, p. 305; Aebischer, "Halt sunt li pui," pp. 18–19; Eugene Vinaver, *A la recherche d'une poétique médiévale* (Paris: Nizet, 1970), p. 205; Dufournet, *Cours sur Roland*, p. 168.

v. 2958. *timonie*. It is also possible to read this word as *timoine*. Whitehead, p. 127.

v. 2971. *Otes*. The first letter can also be read as *a*.

v. 2972. *guiez*. On the erasure that follows this word, the revisor wrote *tres ben*, which results in a false assonance. Most editors emend to *al chemin* on the basis of Venice IV.

v. 2973. *galazin*. From Galata or Galaza? For discussion, see Jenkins.

v. 2978. *nen est fins que t'en alges*. On the interpretation of this phrase, see Harris, "*Nen est fins que t'en alges* (*Roland* 2978) and its Context." Cf. Whitehead, p. 147, citing Bédier: 'there is no question of your going'; Moignet: 'tu n'en verras pas la fin en t'en allant'.

v. 2990. *muet*. The scribe originally wrote a word beginning with the letters *est* (Samaran, p. 49) or *esc* (Whitehead, p. 127; Segre), then erased it and substituted *muet*. Samaran, p. 22, unaccountably lists the erasure, but not the new word as the work of the revisor. The correction may have been made by the first copyist. Many editors believe the original word was *escunset*, a reading supported by Venice IV (no asconde), but, as Segre concedes, the space after *esc* / *est* and the barely visible final letters (*et*[?]) do not fit this conjecture. Paris, the only other copy of the poem that retains this verse, coincides with the correction in the Oxford manuscript (ne mua).

v. 3001. *atalentet* = *atalentent*. See OXFORD TEXT, ENGLISH TRANSLATION, v. 42.

v. 3003. *escience*. The word is sometimes read as *science* and has puzzled scholars. For a decisive confrontation with a passage in *Hugues Capet*, see Segre.

v. 3010. *demet* = *demente*. See OXFORD TEXT, ENGLISH TRANSLATION, v. 42. The opposition *fol* / *demente* in this verse appears to be a pun.

v. 3049. *poisset*. The original scribe wrote *poisset*, which the revisor made into a plural by the addition of a titulus over the *e*. Lecoy, "Notules sur le texte du *Roland* d'Oxford," p. 769. The collective noun *gent* can be singular or plural in Old French (Foulet, *Glossaire*), but the singular is used in a similar phrase in v. 1555 (cf. also v. 1993). Dufournet, *Cours sur Roland*, p. 34. Note, finally, that *poisset* could represent *poissent* in this copy. See OXFORD TEXT, ENGLISH TRANSLATION, v. 42.

vv. 3073, 3075. *Entre*. On the meaning of this preposition, see Foulet, *Glossaire*. Its occurrence in the Baligant episode is noted by Horrent, p. 254.

v. 3090. *cunoisances*. Distinctive but, presumably, not hereditary devices. Jenkins; Brault, *Early Blazon*, pp. 147–48.

v. 3095. *out pris*. On the past perfect historic, see Foulet, *Petite Syntaxe*, par. 327–28; Ménard, *Syntaxe*, par. 148.

v. 3097. *se*. Moignet, p. 222, interprets this as *s'e* = *s'en*. For other conjectures, see Segre.

v. 3098. *su* = *sun*, *soleill levant*. For *su*, see OXFORD TEXT, ENGLISH TRANSLATION, v. 42. The customary translation of *soleill levant* 'rising sun' implies early morning, which, considering what has already occurred on Day 7, requires quite a stretch of the imagination. However, it may be that *levant* is to be taken more as a geographical point than as an indication of time. *Le Levant* is still used today to designate countries bordering on the eastern Mediterranean, and facing the Orient for prayer is an epic cliché. Altona, *Gebete und Anrufungen*, p. 37; Sister Marianna Gildea, *Religious Thought and Feeling*, p. 167, n. 64.

v. 3109. *pois = poisse*. The form which is the subjunctive present of *poeir*, lends itself to confusion with the indicative present in this copy. Editors generally emend to correct the hypometric verse.

vv. 3110 ff. Jenkins, Whitehead, and Segre distinguish a new laisse starting with this verse, which begins with a large initial. See, however, the "Notes critiques" in Bédier's edition: "Il y a, par erreur, une grande initiale à *Cum*" (p. 352). Moignet does not start a new laisse here.

v. 3128. *en la marche*. Concerning Bédier's omission of this expression in his translation, Lejeune, "La signification du nom 'marche'," p. 273, notes: "Du point de vue de la critique textuelle, il n'y a aucune raison pour supprimer les détails 'vers Espagne' et 'la marche': ces leçons sont assurées par la tradition manuscrite."

v. 3129. *emplein*. The word is a hapax, but it is generally assumed to mean 'plain', that is, an expanse of flat, open land. Jenkins, *Glossary*, p. 315, suggests 'filling; a rise (of ground)', but Venice IV (pra), Châteauroux and Venice VII (plein), and Paris (champ) support the traditional view. See OXFORD TEXT, ENGLISH TRANSLATION, v. 3294.

v. 3135. *Or oi grant vasselage*. Considering the close parallel between vv. 2978–2981 and 2984–2986, on the one hand, and vv. 3132–3136, on the other, *vasselage* here evidently alludes to v. 2981. Foulet, *Glossaire*, referring to Paris and Cambridge: "Le v. 3135 . . . ne signifie pas 'Bonne nouvelle pour des vaillants!', mais: 'J'apprends des nouvelles qui témoignent que les Français sont des vaillants!'"; Whitehead: 'I hear tell of great valour'; Moignet: 'Voici que j'entends l'annonce d'une belle vaillance'; Owen: 'Of true valour you tell'; Dufournet, *Cours sur Roland*, p. 154: "Nous comprenons: 'J'entends parler de gens qui sont de bons vassaux (et, partant, qui sont courageux)'." On the phrasing, cf. v. 2714.

v. 3136. *sacet = sacent*. Jenkins: "the overstroke for *n* forgotten." See, however, OXFORD TEXT, ENGLISH TRANSLATION, v. 42.

v. 3141. *pan*. One of "the two sections of the skirt of the *broigne*, or *osberc* (slashed to facilitate walking and riding)," according to Jenkins, *Glossary*, p. 352. At least some byrnies were so made and looked like culottes, that is, the modern woman's garment giving the appearance of a skirt, but actually divided like knee-length drawers. Knudson, "La brogne," p. 1629, doubts that the hauberk ever had short pants, rejecting what he terms the inconclusive evidence of the Bayeux Tapestry. See, however, the illustration (fig. 4) of the byrnie in my article "Le Coffret de Vannes et la légende de Tristan au XIIe siècle," *Mélanges Rita Lejeune*, 1:652–68. At any rate, nothing proves that each leg was referred to as a *pan*. See OXFORD TEXT, ENGLISH TRANSLATION, v. 3426 (cf. also v. 1300).

v. 3146. All editors agree that a verse stating that 'He called it Precieuse' was inadvertently omitted here by the scribe. For the name, see vv. 3298, 3471, 3564. The various readings found in other copies of the poem are discussed by Jenkins and Segre.

v. 3151. *roet*. On this design, see Brault, *Early Blazon*, p. 283, s.v. tout roué.

v. 3158. *es*. Most editors emend to *les* in order to restore symmetry in this verse. In phrases of this type the epithet *graisle(s)* is generally followed by the noun it modifies, preceded by *par le(s)* or the definite article alone. Colby, *Twelfth-Century French Literature*, pp. 60–61 and passim. However, the contraction *es* (= *en les*), synonymous with *par les*, cannot be ruled out here. See Jenkins.

v. 3176. *Malpramis*. Most editors agree that the correct form of this name is *Malprimes*, as found in other copies of the poem. For discussion, see Segre. Posttonic *e* was sometimes raised to *i* in Anglo-Norman, thus *-es = -is*. Pope, *From Latin to Modern French*, par. 1127 and 1140.

v. 3181. *gestes*. Only Jenkins translates this word as 'families'. Interestingly enough, Venice IV offers the variant: *E plusor gent* (Châteauroux and Venice VII read as in the Oxford version).

v. 3185. *Li altrer.* For discussion of the variant reading (Ier) in Venice IV, see Segre.

v. 3189. *guant.* This and other similar expressions are discussed by A. Robert Harden, "The Depreciatory Comparison: A Literary Device of the Medieval French Epic," *Mediaeval Studies in Honor of Urban Tigner Holmes, Jr.,* eds. John Mahoney and John Esten Keller, University of North Carolina Studies in the Romance Languages and Literatures 56 (Chapel Hill: University of North Carolina Press, 1965), pp. 63–78; Ménard, *Le Rire,* pp. 111–14.

v. 3192. *escheles.* After this word there is an erasure over which the revisor wrote *en uunt.* For discussion and conjectures, see Segre.

v. 3199. *orgoillusement.* Jones, p. 68: "The adverb . . . is distinctly complimentary . . . since the pagan Malpramis [read Baligant] is speaking very favorably of the Franks."

v. 3204. *Torleu.* To the speculations concerning this name (e.g., Jenkins, referring to Suchier), add the Canadian-French expletive *Torgueu* (< *Corps Dieu*). *Glossaire du Parler Français au Canada* (Quebec City: L'Action Sociale, 1930), p. 669.

v. 3212. *A itel ore.* Jenkins: at such an (unlucky) hour, that'; Moignet, p. 228: "Il faut probablement sous-entendre un *que* à fonction d'introducteur de consécutive entre *ore* et *unches.*"

v. 3239. *sun = sunt, traver = travers.* See OXFORD TEXT, ENGLISH TRANSLATION, vv. 452 and 44, respectively.

v. 3246. *la Desert.* Jenkins: "There seems to be no way to keep the feminine article here." Consequently, editors emend to either *al* or *le.* Châteauroux and Venice VII provide no support, for they read: *des desers.* For discussion, see Segre. However, the scribe may have been influenced by such designations as *Babiloine la deserte* (cited by Jenkins in this connection). For other examples of that title, see Flutre, *Table des noms propres,* p. 230; West, *Index,* p. 49.

v. 3257. *de.* There is an erasure after this word.

v. 3269. *Des = Dis.* On this unusual form, see Bédier, *Commentaires,* pp. 255–56. Cf. OXFORD TEXT, ENGLISH TRANSLATION, v. 3529.

v. 3272. *afflictiun.* Jenkins: "The word, in OF and OPr. sometimes means 'genuflexion,' but also 'recitation of the penitential psalms in an uncomfortable posture'." Foulet, *Glossaire:* 'prosternation'. The present translation follows Whitehead, Moignet, and Owen.

v. 3273. *bassent = baissent.* See OXFORD TEXT, ENGLISH TRANSLATION, v. 290.

v. 3275. *Fanceis = Franceis.* See OXFORD TEXT, ENGLISH TRANSLATION, v. 2687 (cf. also v. 3358).

v. 3278. *seit.* After this word, the original scribe wrote *uuc . . . et.* The letter after the *c* was erased and, in its place, the revisor substituted a *g.* For conjectures, see Jenkins; Segre.

v. 3286. *esembl'ot = ensembl'ot.* See OXFORD TEXT, ENGLISH TRANSLATION, v. 42.

v. 3294. *en mi la pleine tere.* Dufournet, *Cours sur Roland,* p. 31, criticizes Moignet for neglecting to translate the word *pleine:* "il signifie *plate*; il s'agit donc d'une plaine." See also Jenkins, *Glossary:* 'smooth, flat'; Harrison: 'on the plain'. The battle unquestionably takes place on a plain (v. 3305: *plaigne*), and this sense is supported by Venice IV: *par une plane vie* (Paris: *parmi une bruiere* 'on a heath'). See OXFORD TEXT, ENGLISH TRANSLATION, v. 3129. However, *pleine* in v. 3294 can also mean 'open, unbroken'. Jenkins, note to v. 3294, refers to: "This open field of battle"; Bédier: 'par la terre découverte'; Owen: 'in open land'. The latter interpretation fits the context better, for in this verse Turoldus stresses the unencumbered view.

v. 3295. *averse.* The use of this expression is termed "surprising" by Jenkins. Skidmore, *Moral Traits of Christians and Saracens,* p. 31, refers to Turoldus's "naïveté" in this respect. However, Foulet, *Glossaire,* observes: "le mot finit par devenir une espèce de nom propre." On Lat. *adversarius* 'devil', see INTRODUCTION, note 563.

v. 3302. *ki trestut les esclairet*. Jenkins, *Glossary:* 'to encourage'; Foulet, *Glossaire*, citing Roques: 'donner du coeur à'; Moignet: 'qui les remplit tous d'ardeur'; Whitehead: 'cheer, brighten'.

v. 3331. *par*. The tail of the *p* is crossed with a horizontal bar, thus constituting the abbreviation for *par*, evidently a dittography. Cf. Samaran, p. 33. Jenkins concedes a possible connection with *parat* (< Lat. *paravit*), but in his *Glossary* he lists the word as an intensifier. Segre agrees with the latter view.

v. 3342. *li ad*. The words are joined together by another letter, producing what looks like *liaad*. However, the first *a* is light and was probably partially rubbed out by the scribe.

v. 3358. *Fanceis* = *Franceis*. See OXFORD TEXT, ENGLISH TRANSLATION, v. 2687 (cf. also v. 3275).

v. 3367. *gent*. After this word the scribe wrote *iesnie*, which is almost certainly a misreading of an original *paienime* (cf. v. 1921) or *paienie*. Venice IV reads *paganie*, Châteauroux and Venice VII, *paienie*.

v. 3368. *al plus verai juïse*. Whitehead, p. 151: 'to execute His righteous judgement (*or* where he will give true judgement?)'; Moignet, p. 238: "'pour prononcer le jugement le plus juste', à savoir que Charles a pour lui le droit."

v. 3372. *trecevant*. A hapax, which many editors emend to *tresturnant*. However, Jenkins points out that *trechever* (*tres* + *achever*) cannot be ruled out and suggests that the word means 'to put an end to, despatch'. Cf. Whitehead: 'bring completely to an end, destroy'.

v. 3384. *trestutes*. The manuscript reads *trestes*. The revisor noted the error and added *tu* over the line. His intention, however, was doubtless to emend the word to read *trestutes*, not *tresttutes*.

v. 3390. Editors generally agree that a line, completing the sentence beginning in the preceding verse, is missing here. Bédier, *Commentaires*, pp. 194, 200–201, argues that the phrase beginning with *ki* is similar to those found in vv. 368 and 3131, and constitutes a complete sentence. However, the fact that all other copies of the poem contain the missing line cannot be dismissed so easily. See Whitehead, p. 128; Segre.

v. 3409. *que gueredun vos en dei*. See OXFORD TEXT, ENGLISH TRANSLATION, v. 3812.

v. 3426. *les dous pans*. The word *dous* is suspect here; it is only found in the Oxford copy. See OXFORD TEXT, ENGLISH TRANSLATION, v. 3141, and Segre.

v. 3436. *la coife*. See OXFORD TEXT, ENGLISH TRANSLATION, v. 1327.

v. 3445. *de ferir mult le hastet*. Bédier, *Commentaires*, pp. 236–37, suggests that *le* refers to *Carles de France* in v. 3443 and translates as 'presse son adversaire de frapper vite', an interpretation accepted by many subsequent editors. However, it seems more likely that the striking is to be done by the Saracen. Cf. v. 3456. Jenkins: 'urges him (dares him?) to strike (back)'; Whitehead: 'hastens to strike him (?)'; Harrison: 'hurriedly . . . closes in'.

v. 3446. *mar le baillastes*. Jenkins: 'your victory will bring you no good fortune'. However, in his note to the preceding verse, Jenkins suggests that the verb means 'to take prisoner'; see also his *Glossary*, p. 293. Foulet, *Glossaire:* 'mettre la main sur'; Whitehead: 'touch, lay hands on'; Moignet: 'c'est pour ton malheur que tu t'en es pris à lui' (in note, p. 244: 'vous l'attaquâtes'). Venice IV substitutes: *mal li tocé*, a reading supported by Venice VII and Cambridge.

v. 3460. *par amur e par feid*. Whitehead: 'in love and loyalty'; Moignet: 'avec amour et fidélité'. Jones, p. 44, note 17a: "The term *par amur e par feid* seems to have legal as well as emotive meaning even in v. 3460. Along with the other barons, Naimes has just renewed his oath of loyalty to Charlemagne (3416), and the latter has just fulfilled his obligation by saving his vassal in battle."

v. 3494. All editors agree that a line, naming Charles, was inadvertently omitted here by the scribe. For conjectures based on the corresponding verse in other versions of the poem, see Segre.

v. 3497. *este* = *estes*. See OXFORD TEXT, ENGLISH TRANSLATION, v. 44.

v. 3503. *Blanc*. Most editors emend to *Blanche*. See, however, Jenkins; Moignet. The scribe may have momentarily confused this epithet, which possessed a distinctive feminine form, with words such as *grant*, derived from Latin two-termination adjectives, which had none. Cf. OXFORD TEXT, ENGLISH TRANSLATION, v. 3659.

v. 3510. *ai*. The revisor erased the following word, joined the letters *oc* to *ai*, then added *euud* over the line. For conjectures, see Segre.

v. 3512. *Avrum*. There is a faint zigzag, the customary abbreviation for *er* (Samaran, p. 33), over the first *u* of *Aurum*. For conjectures, see Jenkins; Segre.

v. 3529. *ses* = *sis* = *si les*. The word may also be an error for *les*. Whitehead, p. 128; Moignet, p. 248. The form *ses* is said by Segre to be unique, but see OXFORD TEXT, ENGLISH TRANSLATION, v. 3269. There is a horizontal stroke through the tail of the *p* of *rumpent* in this verse, which suggests the reading *rumperent*. However, this interpretation is rejected by all editors. The bar constitutes a dittography (for similar errors, see Samaran, p. 33), unless this is an instance of tampering by the revisor.

v. 3558. *demandereiz*. On this construction, see Foulet, *Petite Syntaxe*, par. 496.

v. 3564. *amiraz* = *amiralz*. Preconsonantal *l* does not normally disappear or vocalize in this copy. Cf. OXFORD TEXT, ENGLISH TRANSLATION, v. 2473.

vv. 3573–3574. The scribe may have inadvertently transposed the final word in these two verses. See Segre.

v. 3591. *esciente* = *escientre*. See OXFORD TEXT, ENGLISH TRANSLATION, v. 2687.

v. 3598. *pui* = *puis*. See OXFORD TEXT, ENGLISH TRANSLATION, v. 44.

v. 3603. *Fier* = *Fiert*. See OXFORD TEXT, ENGLISH TRANSLATION, v. 452.

v. 3628. *Si esclargiez voz talenz e voz coers*. For bibliography and discussion, see Burgess, "*Talent* in Early Old French," pp. 451–52.

v. 3644. *vers sa pareit se turnet*. Jenkins notes that the hero in *Tristan de Thomas*, v. 3031, and Hezekiah in 2 Kings 20:2, assume similar postures. However, Jones, pp. 182–83, points out: "the Hebrew king turned to the wall to pray to God, whereas the maimed and defeated king of Saragossa turned to the wall to hide his shame and sorrow." Tristan's dying attitude approaches Marsile's despair. In 1 Kings 21:4–5, Ahab lays down on his bed and gloomily turns his face away. Cf. *Piramus et Tisbé*, vv. 335–336. To the modern example in Camus's *La Peste*, cited by Jones, add those in Balzac's *Eugénie Grandet* and Flaubert's *Madame Bovary*. In the latter work, however, the heroine faces the wall in modesty. The best explanation of the Saracen king's behavior is that, like the fleeing Cain, he seeks to avoid being watched by God's hostile eye. On the theme of *derkou theama*, see Frye, *Anatomy of Criticism*, p. 238. Marsile's look contrasts with Roland's hopeful gazes toward the mountains and heaven.

v. 3646. *doel, pecchet*. The term *doel* is generally assumed to mean 'sorrow', but as Jones, pp. 46, 83, 84, 86, 87, 113, 178–80, has made clear, Turoldus associates it with words signifying anger, dismay, or shame caused by a sense of failure or frustration. In the present instance the French locution *la rage au coeur*, a synonym for sin (Payen, *Le Motif du repentir*, p. 213), comes closest to expressing Marsile's state. The glossaries in Jenkins, Bédier (i.e., Foulet), and Whitehead (see also Moignet and Owen) agree that *pecchet* here means 'calamity' rather than 'sin'. However, Bédier's translation has 'péché' and Harrison 'sin'. Jones, p. 31, allows that Marsile "could have been burdened by sin as an unshriven heathen or crushed by calamity as a defeated ruler." Viewed from a medieval perspective, the Saracen king's earlier conduct is patently sinful and, if further proof is required, one need only consider the conscious act of surrendering one's soul to devils in the very next verse. For a similar interpretation, see Payen, pp. 158–59. Cf. also the example in the *Chevalerie Ogier* cited by Payen, pp. 214–15, in another connection. In Conrad Brechmunda (Bramimonde) speaks of purging (v. 8599: "Macht ich dich geraine") and redeeming her husband (v. 8603: "Nune mac ich niemen wider gewinne"), two concepts related to sin.

v. 3648. *alquant*. The revisor erased the word that follows and substituted *cunfundue*, which all editors reject. Emendation to *turnet* (or *tornez*) *en fuie*, a reading based on Venice IV (torni en fuge), is a distinct possibility. See Jenkins; Whitehead; Segre.

v. 3651. *que . . . mais defendue*. The copyist appears to have written *quele* (= *qu'ele*) *mais defendue*. Samaran, p. 50. The last two letters of *quele* were subsequently erased, perhaps by the same scribe, with the intention of inserting the verb in the space. Noticing the blank, the revisor added *elle nest* (= *n'est*) above the line. It is also possible that the revisor erased the *le*. At any rate, the other copies (Venice IV, Paris, and Cambridge) all omit the pronoun and put the verb in the future. This suggests the reading *n'ert*, rather than *n'est*.

v. 3653. *Par poëstet*. The present interpretation is provided by Jenkins; Foulet, *Glossaire*; and Whitehead. Bédier suggests 'par droit de conquête', a translation also favored by Jones, p. 15. Cf. Moignet: 'par la loi du plus fort'.

v. 3659. *Clers*. This adjective should be feminine. Cf. OXFORD TEXT, ENGLISH TRANSLATION, v. 3503.

v. 3668. *entesqu'al* = *entresqu'al*. Cf. OXFORD TEXT, ENGLISH TRANSLATION, v. 2687.

v. 3684. *la citet de . . .* The line is incomplete in the manuscript. For conjectures, see Segre.

v. 3694. *a Deu e a ses nuns*. On this expression, which alludes to the traditional 72 (or 100) names of God, see the bibliography and discussion in Frappier, *Chansons de geste*, 2:138 and n. 2.

v. 3698. *halçur*. This Latinism is cited by Zumthor, *Langue et techniques poétiques*, p. 76.

v. 3714. *esforcet*. Jenkins, *Glossary*: 'magnified; advantageous, superior'; Foulet, *Glossaire*: 'Accroitre, augmenter de valeur'; Jones, p. 43: 'even better'; Moignet: 'encore plus prestigieux'. I do not believe, however, that the term necessarily connotes superiority. OFr. *esforcier* indicates the application of force and suggests power and strength.

v. 3715. *mielz ne sai a parler*. Jenkins: 'I cannot do better than that'. Cf. Bédier: 'je ne sais pas mieux te dire'; Moignet: 'je ne saurais dire mieux'; Owen: 'better I cannot say'.

v. 3717. *estrange*. Jenkins, *Glossary*: 'repugnant'; Nichols, "The Interaction of Life and Literature," p. 70: 'foreign'. See INTRODUCTION, 17.

v. 3733. *Mult grant honur i ad li reis dunee*. Bédier: 'Le roi l'a hautement honorée'. Foulet, *Glossaire*; Whitehead, *Glossary*; Moignet; Owen support this interpretation. However, Jenkins explains: "'great endowment' in lands, for the construction and upkeep of the church and of the tomb." Jones, p. 48: "Bédier understands this to mean that he honored Alda greatly, but it is more likely that he donated extensive lands to the convent. Whereas Conrad makes no mention of any donation, Stricker (11,285) says that Charlemagne gave the convent an estate (*ein guot*)." Harrison: 'the king provided her a great endowment'. In the *Pseudo-Turpin*, p. 215, Charles grants all the land for six miles around Blaye as a fief to the church of Saint-Romain 'in honor of Roland'. The Latin chronicler says that the Emperor is following the example of Judas Maccabaeus, apparently a reference to the donation of 2,000 drachmae in order to have an atonement sacrifice offered for the slain (2 Maccabees 12:43).

v. 3747. *noveles*. Jenkins: "These are evidently Charles' speech in accusation vv. 3750–56, and Ganelon's two speeches in denial; or, in general, 'the speeches on both sides'." Bédier omits this word from his translation, suggesting that it is synonymous with *le plait* 'le plaid'. Foulet, *Glossaire*: 'Nouvelles'; Whitehead: 'debate (?)'; Moignet: 'l'affaire'; Harrison: 'rebuttals'; Owen; 'the trial'.

v. 3786. *En vos.* In the space after *vos*, on what appears to be an erasure, the word *ami* or possibly *ams* (Samaran, p. 50) was written by the revisor (Samaran, p. 22), or perhaps by the original scribe (Whitehead, p. 129). For conjectures, see Segre.

v. 3792. *a ses piez.* Jenkins: "a juristic formula *adsto tuis pedibus, eo pedibus ejus* = 'I accept with thanks'."

v. 3796. *curteis.* Jenkins: "One may hesitate between *corteis* = 'skilled in law,' as *Thèbes*, v. 7860, and *corteis* = 'compassionate'." Frappier, "Vues sur les conceptions courtoises dans les littératures d'oc et d'oïl au XIIᵉ siècle," p. 137: "dans l'épisode du plaid de Ganelon, Turold attribue à bon escient l'épithète de *courtois* aux barons d'Auvergne—leur pays natal appartient, notons-le, au domaine d'oc—apparemment plus soucieux que les autres d'une politesse recherchée." I believe that this term, which has the general meaning 'worthy', is specialized here in the sense 'useful in council'. See OXFORD TEXT, ENGLISH TRANSLATION, vv. 176 (proz), 576 (curteis). A similar interpretation is given by Glyn S. Burgess, "Remarques sur deux vers de la *Chanson de Roland* (v. 3796-7)," *Société Rencesvals. VIᵉ Congrès International*, pp. 63-78. Burgess, p. 74, translates the two verses in question as follows: 'Ceux d'Auvergne y sont les conseillers les plus sages (ou mieux: 'De ceux d'Auvergne y sont les conseillers les plus sages'). A cause de l'intervention de Pinabel, ils (les juges) se montrent plus enclins à la paix'.

v. 3804. *ki.* After this word the scribe wrote *aa*, which editors emend to *ja*, *la* or *or*.

v. 3812. *Ja por murir n'en ert veüd gerun.* This verse and the one that follows closely parallel vv. 3802-3803, but *murir* here unquestionably refers to Ganelon's death. Jenkins emends *gerun* to *getons* and translates: 'Never, at any possible cost, will any scion of his (Roland's) be seen'. Joseph Bédier, "Remarques sur vingt passages difficiles de la *Chanson de Roland*," *Mélanges d'histoire du moyen âge offerts à M. Ferdinand Lot par ses amis et ses élèves* (Paris: Champïon, 1925), pp. 38-40 (summary in Dufournet, *Cours sur Roland*, p. 44), identifies *gerun* as a part of a man's bliaut, roughly synonymous with *pan*, which could be held in the hand when pledging. *Gerun* thus came to mean 'accord'. He paraphrases vv. 3212-3213 as follows: 'Quand même Ganelon ou tels et tels des contestants seraient livrés à la mort, on ne verra point le giron se tendre, on ne verra point l'accord s'établir entre les parties, et ce n'est pas de l'argent qui nous le rendra (qui nous rendra celui qu'il n'est pas besoin de nommer, Roland)'. However, in his *Commentaires*, p. 240 (see also *Romania* 64 [1938]: 176), Bédier retracted this labored explanation. Whitehead emends the verse to read *Ja por murir n'en ert veüd cist barun* (a hypermetric line), and he observes: "the unintelligible *gerun* probably arises from the conflation of the *ge-* of *gentilz*, with the last syllable of a word ending in *-run*, almost certainly *barun*" (p. 129). Segre believes that *gerun*, an insignificant portion of clothing (or, for that matter, *gerun* 'moustache', that is, an insignificant part of the body) amounts to saying 'nothing at all'. He translates the second hemistich as 'non ne (di Rolando) rivedremo neanche l'ombra'. Other earlier proposals listed by Segre include: *Morz est Rollanz, n'en ert veüd gerun; Ja por murir n'en ert venud gran prod*; and *Ja por murir Rollant ne reverum.* No one to date seems to have thought of emending *gerun* to *gueredun*, pronounced as a two-syllable word (cf. v. 3409: "Ben le conuis que gueredun vos en dei"); editors since Theodor Müller, seeking to restore the correct meter, have usually omitted the *en*, not found in Paris [Jenkins, however, drops the *que*]). On the effacement of interconsonantal *e* in Anglo-Norman, see Bédier, *Commentaires*, p. 265; Pope, *From Latin to Modern French*, par. 1134. The term *guerredon, gardon* was widely used in Old French in various meanings, notably 'amount paid for services, reward, wage', Tobler and Lommatzsch, 4:748-52. If one accepts this emendation, the line may be translated: 'Even though he were to die, that wouldn't be an adequate compensation (or, that wouldn't make amends)'. Cf. this passage in *Eracle* (Henry, *Chrestomathie*, p. 134, vv. 88–90:

> Li dui cr</br>ient por lor desserte
> Que gerredons lor soit rendus,
> Qu'ele soit arse et il pendus.

Note, finally, the following example from Gautier de Coincy cited by Greimas, *Dictionnaire*, p. 325: *Avoir porrons e recovrer / Le guerredon et le loyer*; cf. *aveir . . . recuverum* (v. 3813), and *gerun / gueredun* (v. 3812).

v. 3818. *chevalers*. The line is hypometric and the assonance is false. Cf. v. 3821. Everything seems to indicate that the name *Tierris* belongs at the end of this verse.

v. 3821. *bruns*. The line is hypometric and the assonance is false. Cf. v. 3818. Editors generally add *li vis* or emend to *brun le vis*.

v. 3832. *metre*. The scribe conflated this verse and the next. For conjectures relative to the second hemistich of v. 3832, see Segre.

v. 3848. *recrrai*. This verb occurs in a different tense in v. 3852. Editors generally emend to *recrerai*; cf., however, Whitehead, p. 129: "probably a mistake for *rec'rrai* = *recrerrai*." The effacement of unstressed interconsonantal *e* is a well-known Anglo-Norman feature. Bédier, *Commentaires*, pp. 253, 265. On the meaning, see Jenkins; Bédier, *Commentaires*, p. 320; Jones, p. 56 and n. 50.

v. 3860. *acuminiez*. The middle part of this word is partially effaced. Some editors read *acumuniez* or *acumunjez*.

v. 3871. *pitiet*. CL *pietas* 'piety' took on, in Ecclesiastical Latin, the added meaning of pity, that is, 'compassion for another's suffering or misfortune'. Bloch and Wartburg, *Dictionnaire*, s.v. pitié. The word *pitet, pitiet* occurs eleven times in the *Song of Roland* with three different meanings: (1) grief, sorrow (vv. 1749, 2206, 2417, 2419, 2873, 3120, 3725); (2) anguish, distress (vv. 825, 2547); and (3) nostalgia, yearning (v. 822). On the latter two senses, see INTRODUCTION, 16, A. *Pitet* is only used to express emotions felt by the Franks, especially Charlemagne (vv. 825, 2547, 2873, 3725), and, with one exception—the Emperor's dream, v. 2547—is always accompanied by weeping. Here, in v. 3871, *pitiet* translates the Franks' anguish for Thierry and their grief over Roland's death, emotions clearly perceived as related since one word conveys both feelings.

v. 3920. The second hemistich of this verse is identical with that in the preceding line and, therefore, highly suspect. For conjectures, see Segre.

v. 3927. *fait = frait*. See OXFORD TEXT, ENGLISH TRANSLATION, v. 2687.

v. 3936. *quarante*. Many editors emend to *quatre* to avoid a false assonance and to relate this line to vv. 3937–3938, where four barons are specified. See, however, Whitehead, p. 129; Segre.

v. 3943. This line is hypometric. For conjectures, see Segre.

v. 3956. *el*. Many editors emend *el* to *plus* in order to avoid a false assonance. Cf. v. 2812. However, *el* appears in similar locutions in vv. 1185 and 2961.

v. 3967. *acoeillent*. Jenkins, *Glossary*, p. 285: 'to receive, take charge of'; Whitehead, p. 130: 'take hold of (?)'. Cf., however, Bédier: 'poussent'; Foulet, *Glossaire*: 'pousser vers'; Moignet: 'poussent devant eux'; Harrison: 'urge them on'; Owen: 'goad and urge them on ahead'; and see *FEW*, 1:15; 24:78–81.

v. 3968. *ewe*. Léon Gautier's translation 'jument' was initially accepted by Bédier, but it was later eliminated by him in favor of 'cours d'eau'. Foulet, *Glossaire*, p. 388: "La traduction que j'ai donnée des vers 3967–8 est erronée." Jones, p. 18 and n. 33, persists in this interpretation, but it is universally rejected today.

v. 3973. *fel recreant*. Bédier: 'un félon prouvé'. Foulet, *Glossaire*: 'lâche'. However, Jones, p. 53, suggests that the original meaning of Lat. *recredere* 'to change religion' is involved here: "Ganelon dies a shameful death as fits a *recreant* (3973), because he has apostatized by aiding the pagans." Cf. v. 393.

v. 3979. *essamples*. Bédier: 'paraboles'. Cf. Foulet, *Glossaire:* "Récit qui met en scène des personnages empruntés à l'histoire ou à la vie contemporaine, en vue de tirer des faits un enseignement moral." See also Frappier, *Chansons de geste*, 2:65, n. 1.

v. 3983. *cruiz e linees dames*. The meaning of the words *cruiz* and *linees* is not clear. For conjectures, see Jenkins; Segre.

v. 3984. *les c*. . . . The word after *les*, which begins with *c* or *ci*, was lost when the corner of the folio was torn away. For conjectures, see Segre (add Moignet: 'piscines [?]').

v. 3986. *truvee*. Many editors emend to *truvet*, but Keller, "La conversion de Bramimonde," p. 18, n. 61, citing Pope, *From Latin to Modern French*, par. 1235, points out that *truvee* is a genuine Anglo-Norman masculine form.

v. 4002. *Ci falt la geste que Turoldus declinet*. The meaning of several words in this explicit has been much debated. For bibliography and discussion, see Jenkins; Horrent, pp. 326–30; Riquer, *Chansons de geste*, pp. 31–33; Dufournet, *Cours sur Roland*, pp. 11–17. Add Curtius, *Littérature européenne*, p. 111; B. LeBlond, "Ci falt la geste que Turoldus declinet," *Annales de Normandie* 7 (1957): 159–63; Zumthor, *Langue et techniques poétiques*, p. 76; and Aebischer, *Préhistoire*, pp. 222–28. Bibliographical references for the name Turoldus are provided in INTRODUCTION, note 18.